What was the truth about Diana's rumored pregnancy?

How did William and Harry cope with their shock and grief?

What was the Queen's curious behavior when notified of Diana's death?

THE UNTOLD STORY . . .

. . . ABOUT PRINCE CHARLES:

"He was a very gentle man who did not conceal his pain. It was something none of us had expected."
—Thierry Meresse, communications director of Pitié-Salpêtrière, the hospital where Diana died

. . . ABOUT DODI:

"Dodi was always generous picking up the tab, but when it came to real money, the reins were pulled by his father. He was still a little boy."—Claudine Christian, actress and longtime friend

. . . ABOUT DIANA'S FEELINGS FOR CHARLES:

"Her love for him never really died. Diana seemed to have only good memories of their years together."—Natalie Symonds, friend of Diana

. . . ABOUT CHARLES'S REACTION
TO DIANA'S DEATH:

"He uttered a cry of pain that was spontaneous and came from the heart, before breaking into uncontrollable sobs."—a British official, eyewitness to the event

THE DAY DIANA DIED

"Andersen's book makes some fresh contributions. . . . But the book's greatest strength lies in the success of the conceit that the title implies. Diana's last day builds to a climax whose outcome we already know. Andersen recounts the story in such crisp detail and from so many perspectives that Aug. 30, 1997, becomes grist for a narrative thriller. Andersen's insights can be as sharp as his details."—*Newsweek*

"Filled with details surrounding Diana's death."
—*Chicago Sun-Times*

ALSO BY CHRISTOPHER ANDERSEN

Jackie After Jack: Portrait of the Lady

An Affair to Remember: The Remarkable Love Story of
Katharine Hepburn and Spencer Tracy

Jack and Jackie: Portrait of an American Marriage

Young Kate: The Remarkable Hepburns and the
Shaping of an American Legend

Citizen Jane

The Best of Everything
(*with John Marion*)

The Serpent's Tooth

The Book of People

Father

Susan Hayward

The Name Game

THE
DAY DIANA DIED

CHRISTOPHER ANDERSEN

A Dell Book

Published by
Dell Publishing
a division of
Random House, Inc.
1540 Broadway
New York, New York 10036

Grateful acknowledgment is made to the following for permission to use the
photographs in this book:
All Action: 42, 50, 51
Alpha: 52, 54, 64
Archive Photos: 2, 3, 5, 11, 19, 23, 28, 33, 35, 37, 39, 41, 43, 46, 55, 57, 59, 65
Associated Press: 4, 13, 20, 21, 30, 31, 34, 36, 40, 45, 47, 48, 49, 56, 58, 60, 61, 63
Corbis: 6, 12, 14
Globe Photos: 1, 8, 9, 26, 27, 29, 44, 62
LGI Photo: 17
Retna: 15, 16, 24, 25, 53
SYGMA: 7, 10, 32

Copyright © 1998, 1999 by Christopher Andersen

Dell books may be purchased for business or promotional use or for special sales.
information please write to: Special Markets Department, Random House,
Inc., 1540 Broadway, New York, NY 10036.

Dell® is a registered trademark of Random House, Inc., and the colophon is a
trademark of Random House, Inc.

ISBN: 0-440-23533-2

Reprinted by arrangement with William Morrow and Company, Inc.

Printed in the United States of America

Published simultaneously in Canada

August 1999

10 9 8 7 6 5 4 3 2 1

WCD

For my incandescent Kelly

When I was born I was unwanted.
When I married Charles I was
  unwanted.
When I joined the Royal Family I was
  unwanted.
I want to be wanted.

> —*Diana,*
> *Princess of Wales*

She had a way of going straight to the heart.

—*Vivienne Parry,*
Diana's friend

All people want to be touched.

—*Diana*

THE
DAY DIANA
DIED

PREFACE

Where were you the day Diana died? Like Pearl Harbor and the assassination of John F. Kennedy, the tragic death of the Princess of Wales on August 31, 1997 is one of those defining moments in history—an event that touched each of us so profoundly we will never forget the moment we heard the news. Indeed, nothing quite like it had happened or was likely to happen ever again—an unprecedented outpouring of grief on a truly global scale, cutting across all boundaries of race, religion, age, gender, and nationality.

Linked by the same omnipresent media that would be accused of hounding her to death, people around the world shared in the heartaching sense that they had lost a friend. The countless millions of Americans who dragged themselves out of bed at 5 A.M. to share the joy of Diana's July 29, 1981 storybook wedding to Prince Charles on television now rose somberly at the same early morning hour to mourn with the rest of humanity at the sight of her flag-draped casket in

Westminster Abbey. No single image was more poignant than the bouquet of white rosebuds on the coffin. With the bouquet was Harry's handwritten note that read, simply, MUMMY.

"It is with great sadness I sit here in front of my computer," wrote one of the countless thousands who posted messages on Internet Web pages and bulletin boards. "I cannot be at the embassy to sign the condolence book . . . I cannot be at the service to say goodbye to a wonderful human being. For Diana was more than a royal . . . she was real."

Surreal was the word that perhaps best described Diana's shockingly sudden, inexplicably senseless death at age thirty-six. Over a period of seventeen years, we had watched her evolve from "Shy Di," the fresh-scrubbed, self-effacing English schoolgirl with bowed head and bashful smile, into an impossibly beautiful, defiantly self-assured woman-with-a-mission. She was also unquestionably the most glamorous creature on the planet—like Jacqueline Kennedy Onassis before her, an avatar of style, fashion, and grace.

Yet it was her gift for feeling pain—her own and that of others—that made her both a threat to the British Royal Family and irresistible to the rest of humankind. When she went public with the sordid details of her disastrous marriage, her bulimia, her depression, and her suicide attempts, the public sympathtized. When her own illed-fated extramarital affairs became grist for the tabloid mill, Diana was forgiven. More and more, the image of Diana the troubled, globe-trotting princess was tempered by her public acts of kindness.

Beyond the grueling royal rounds of ribbon-cuttings, charity galas, and groundbreaking ceremonies, Diana was the first member of the Royal Family to actually make a human connection with the suffering. "She had a huge capacity for unhappiness, which is why she responded so well to the suffering face of humanity," said her best friend, Rosa Monckton. "She understood real unhappiness . . . and had a unique ability to spot the broken-hearted."

Diana embraced AIDS patients when others kept their distance, consoled battered wives, shook the hands of lepers, cuddled crack babies, whispered soothing words to those in the final stages of cancer, and gave voice to those horribly maimed by land mines. She was a devout believer in hugs and the healing power of touch. "When I cup my hands around the face of someone suffering," she confided to a friend, "they are comforting me as much as I am comforting them." Whatever the cause, whatever the affliction, Diana felt they had one thing in common. "The biggest disease this world suffers from," she said, "is the disease of people feeling unloved."

Abandoned by her mother, rejected by her husband, scorned by the Royal Family, betrayed by lovers, and hunted by the paparazzi, Diana knew this feeling better than anyone. She also vowed to herself that her own sons, William and Harry, would grow up in the kind of loving environment that neither of their parents had known as children.

Diana was, in every sense of the word, larger than life—a force of nature that, as the British Royal Family discovered much to its chagrin, could be neither dismissed nor ignored. She was outspoken, rebellious, mischievous, approachable, and touchingly vulnerable. She took her children to McDonald's and to Disney World, and broke with royal tradition by unabashedly enjoying herself.

There were also times when Diana could be distant, moody, petulant, and manipulative. She portrayed herself as a victim of fame and yet reveled in her own unparalleled celebrity, secretly nurturing her own media contacts even as she condemned the press for harassing her.

Her insecurities were legion, but they mirrored our own. An unhappy childhood, a broken marriage, eating disorders, depression, the joys and terrors of parenthood—these were facets of a life with which we could easily identify. We looked at her and, instead of being blinded by the glare, saw ourselves more clearly.

Diana was, in a word, *human*—and the world embraced her for all the contradictions that made her, on one level, just like the rest of us. That is precisely why her stunningly brutal death, so unthinkable yet somehow so inevitable, made so many millions of people the world over feel they had lost a family member. And why none of us will ever forget where we were and who we were with *The Day Diana Died*.

The question you ask yourself afterwards is, did she know she was so loved?

> —*Béatrice Humbert,*
> chief nurse at Pitié-
> Salpêtrière Hospital,
> Paris

We walked silently among the ocean of floral tributes. I could almost hear her voice in my ear: "Rosa, no, not all this! For me?" She never knew how much she was loved.

> —*Rosa Monckton,*
> Diana's closest friend

If anything ever happens to me, do you think they'll think of me as another Jackie Kennedy?

> —*Diana,* to royal
> milliner Philip
> Somerville

1

She looked down at the most famous face in the world. "It's not her," Béatrice Humbert thought to herself. "It isn't possible. I'm dreaming." For a moment Humbert, chief nurse at Paris's Pitié-Salpêtrière Hospital, felt her knees begin to buckle and the room begin to swim as she desperately fought the overpowering urge to faint. Clad in her white hospital coat, the trim, businesslike Humbert looked every inch the seasoned professional that she was. And in a career that spanned three decades, Humbert had seen the mangled corpses of hundreds of accident victims. Yet nothing had prepared her for this. The nurse was gazing, she had to keep telling herself, at the lifeless body of the Princess of Wales.

From the moment she saw Diana lying there, beneath a white cotton sheet that had been pulled up to her bare shoulders, it struck Humbert how sad it was

3

that the Princess looked "so all alone." Three hours earlier her body had been brought up from the basement operating room to the blue-walled second-floor room just above the main entrance to Pitié-Salpêtrière's eight-story teal-green glass and cement Gaston Cordier Pavilion. Although this was the most modern section of the hospital, parts of which date back to the seventeenth century, Gaston Cordier had just undergone several months of extensive renovations. The blue-walled room above the entrance, chosen because hospital officials were told blue was Diana's favorite color, had been painted only three days before; the bracing smell still lingered in the air. There had been no need to inconvenience any other patients to make room for Diana; the wing had not been scheduled to reopen to patients until the following day, September 1.

Humbert was soon joined by Jeanne Lecorcher, Pitié-Salpêtrière's chief emergency nurse, and an ashen-faced Sir Michael Jay, Britain's ambassador to France. Moments later Sylvia Jay walked in and stood at the foot of the bed, choking back tears. Humbert was somewhat surprised to notice that the ambassador's wife, who blew her nose into an Irish lace handkerchief, was already dressed from head to toe in black.

Thierry Meresse had been there when they first wheeled Diana, still clinging to life, into the operating room at 2:05 A.M. "At first I didn't dare look," said the hospital's thirty-six-year-old communications director. "I had a certain vision of what she should look like that I wanted to preserve in my mind. And I thought, this beautiful face is going to be horribly disfigured by such an awful accident." Hours later, when he finally did summon the courage to look at Diana, he was astounded to discover that "she looked entirely peaceful. Her face hadn't been marked at all, really. Just a little bruising, that's all."

At Pitié-Salpêtrière, disbelief gradually began to yield to an overwhelming, soul-crushing sadness. "The way you see her on television," Humbert said, "with those big blue eyes and that marvelous smile, and then the big blue eyes were no longer there, nor was the marvelous smile. There was the closed, pallid face of a cadaver, that's all. It wasn't an expression of peace, or the absence of peace. It was as though, stupidly, I was waiting for a smile. And then I thought, we'll never see this smile again . . ."

Father Yves Clochard-Bossuet, who had worked for Air France until he joined the priesthood just five years earlier, had been trying to come to terms with that realization for hours. Short and balding at age forty-six, Pitié-Salpêtrière's resident priest had been fast asleep in his apartment when he was jolted awake by a phone call at 3 A.M. "The emergency unit of the hospital told me someone very important needed the

Last Rites," he later recalled. "When they said it was Princess Diana, I thought someone was playing a joke. I thought they were drunk." He slammed down the receiver and tried to get back to sleep. But, he said, "Something kept me awake."

When Father Clochard-Bossuet called back, hospital officials confirmed that Diana had been in a car crash with her Egyptian-born boyfriend, Dodi Fayed, Dodi's bodyguard Trevor Rees-Jones, and the car's driver, acting Ritz Hotel security chief Henri Paul. Dodi Fayed and Henri Paul, Clochard-Bossuet was told, had died on the scene. Rees-Jones had suffered multiple fractures and half of his face had been literally ripped away, but he was likely to survive. Diana was not.

The priest leapt out of bed and quickly dressed. Even as he fumbled with his clerical collar, Mohamed Al Fayed's helicopter was touching down at Paris's Le Bourget Airport. Dodi's controversial father, owner of Harrods department store in London as well as Paris's Ritz Hotel, had been at his baronial estate in Oxted, Surrey, when Ritz president Frank Klein called over two hours earlier with news of "a terrible accident." Dodi, Klein said, trying to find some way to soften the blow, had "passed away."

"An accident? Do you really think it was an accident?" Mohamed Al Fayed asked Klein. Within minutes, Dodi's father was aboard his Sikorsky S-76 heading for Paris. At Le Bourget, he was met by Alexander "Kes" Wingfield, one of his son's bodyguards, and by Dodi's regular chauffeur, Philippe Dourneau. Unaware that Dodi and Henri Paul had been taken directly from the site of the accident to the Paris morgue, Mohamed Al Fayed ordered Dourneau to take him to Pitié-Salpêtrière, where Diana was still in surgery.

It seemed oddly fitting that the life of the Princess of Wales, whose compassionate nature led her to reach out to the disinherited, should have ended there. Founded in 1656 by Louis XIV to care for the poor and the insane, Pitié-Salpêtrière (literally "Pity-Saltpeter") took its name from its charitable mission and from the saltpeter once used in arms production on the site. Much of the original seventeenth-century structure still stands—including the hospital's landmark Chapel of St. Louis with its distinctive octagon-shaped dome—in stark contrast to the modern Gaston Cordier wing where Diana was taken.

Mohamed Al Fayed reached the hospital at 3:50, and was met by Ambassador Jay and French Interior Minister Jean-Pierre Chevènement. "Mr. Al Fayed got there so quickly," Thierry Meresse said, "that we naturally assumed that he must have been in Paris when the accident occurred." Ten minutes later, at 4 A.M. Paris time, Diana was pronounced dead. "I could not believe it," Dodi's father said. "The situation was too desperate to take in."

Yet Al Fayed wasted no time waiting to pay his respects to Diana. Already all but convinced that Dodi and Diana had been assassinated, presumably by enemies of the Al Fayed family within the British Establishment, Mohamed moved swiftly to protect his interests. Employees of Al Fayed's far-flung empire, many of whom already suspected that their phone calls were bugged and their actions monitored, were now instructed under pain of immediate dismissal not to speak to *anyone* regarding Dodi and the Princess. In a move that angered hospital officials, Al Fayed also ordered that everything belonging to the Princess and Dodi be packed up immediately and shipped back to London along with their luggage. It was only then that he asked to be driven to the morgue to see the body of his son. Diana's body was still on the operating table when Al Fayed left the hospital.

Father Clochard-Bossuet, who at first had dismissed reports of an accident involving Diana as a tasteless practical joke, now crossed paths with Mohamed Al Fayed just as Al Fayed was heading out the door. From the moment the cleric arrived at Pitié-Salpêtrière, he later recalled, "I saw it had to be true. There were so many people—police, the British ambassador, doctors, and outside, journalists were already congregating. I was shocked. It took a long time for me to absorb what was happening." Many of the high-ranking French officials milling in the halls wore jeans, short-sleeved shirts, and sneakers. Most were unshaven. Like Chevènement, they were winding down from the weekend when they were told the shocking news.

At 4:20, Ambassador Jay approached Clochard-Bossuet. His voice trembling, Sir Michael told the priest that the Princess of Wales had succumbed to her injuries. Would he, Sir Michael asked, read her the Last Rites?

The priest stepped into the room where Diana's body had been taken and turned to close the door behind him. The room was dark, illuminated by only a small wall lamp. Clochard-Bossuet's heart pounded furiously as he moved closer to the single bed in the center of the room. Diana's long, nude body was covered only by a thin white sheet. "She looked extremely young," someone who saw her at about this time later said. "Her eyes were open and so vivid . . . Her skin was so smooth. She looked like the most exquisite china doll. I felt very much in awe."

The decision to have Last Rites administered by the only cleric available—a Roman Catholic priest—seemed almost certain to raise eyebrows back in England. Not only was Diana a Protestant, but her son William would as king someday be the titular head of the Anglican Church. "I was very aware of the Princess's position in the Anglican Church and, although I was never frightened by my task, I was very discreet," he said. The ritual, also known as Extreme Unction, was nondenominational and could be administered to any Christian.

Reacting as so many others would that day, Father Clochard–Bossuet felt he might collapse at any moment. Struggling to remain steady on his feet, he reached over and gently closed Diana's eyes. Then he used his thumb to anoint Diana's forehead with holy oil. For the first time, he noticed one of the injuries she had sustained in the crash—a quarter-inch-long nick just below the hairline. Then he reached under the sheet to find her hand. Gently lifting it out, he turned her palm up and dabbed the center of it with oil. Then he walked to the opposite side of the bed and did the same to the palm of her other hand, all the while reciting the words of the holy sacrament: "Through this holy anointing and his most loving mercy, may the Lord assist you, by the Grace of the Holy Spirit so that, when you have been freed from your sins, he may save you and in his goodness raise you up."

The ritual completed, Father Clochard–Bossuet pulled a chair close to the bed. He would stay alone with Diana for the next several hours, praying for her soul as the world outside was only beginning to waken to the terrible news. "I could not believe I was at her bedside, in front of her," he later said. "It was difficult to comprehend the enormity of the situation. All I could think of was the sadness of this young woman dying when she had everything to live for. I prayed for her sons, William and Harry."

Fully four hours later, at 8:30 A.M., Father Clochard-Bossuet's solitary vigil ended when Bernadette Chirac stepped into the room. The wife of French President Jacques Chirac, dispatched from the Elysée Palace as Chirac's personal emissary, had worked with Diana on several humanitarian causes. Like so many others at or near the centers of power, she considered Diana her friend. Now Madame Chirac and the priest bowed their heads by Diana's bedside and prayed, trying not to be undone by the muffled sobs of hospital personnel standing in the corridor.

Forty-five minutes later, they were joined by Lionel Jospin. The French Prime Minister had been presiding over a Socialist Party conference in the seaside town of La Rochelle, and immediately commandeered a military aircraft for the flight to Paris aboard a military plane as soon as he was informed of the accident. A Protestant, Prime Minister Jospin did not join in the prayers. "The Prime Minister was very sad, but he said nothing," nurse Jeanne Lecorcher recalled. "He just paid his last respects in silence."

Emotionally drained and physically spent, Father

Clochard–Bossuet was relieved when the Reverend Martin Draper from the St. George's Anglican Church in Paris arrived to take his place.

It would be the last time the airline-worker-turned-priest gave anyone the Last Rites at Pitié-Salpêtrière. So profoundly changed by the experience, he resigned to become minister at a nearby children's hospital on the banks of the Seine. "I often think back to that night in August," he later mused, "and wonder if it can be true."

As they stood by Diana's body shortly before 10 that Sunday morning, nurses Humbert and Lecorcher also feared their grasp on reality was tenuous at best. Yet there was no time for introspection. Ambassador Jay informed them that Prince Charles would be arriving that afternoon at 5 to escort the body of his ex-wife back to London.

The nurses sprang into action. Humbert's first thought was that they were going to have to cool the room to keep the body from decomposing. "I knew it was going to be hot during the day," said Humbert, who asked that an air conditioning unit be installed in the room. "But that's a natural professional reflex, to immediately think of preserving the body. And I thought of all the people who would be coming, that it would create a lot of movement, and a lot of heat. The first thing was to chill this room."

Even the installation of an air conditioner presented special problems. To prevent the throng of reporters as well as run-of-the-mill curiosity seekers from learning which room Diana was in, sheets had been placed over all the second-floor windows of the immense hospital complex. There was ample reason for such caution: Several enterprising tabloid journalists had rented rooms across the street from the hospital.

Rather than mount the air conditioner in a window and risk opening a breach—"We can't leave an opening because someone might stick a camera through it," Humbert told the technicians—the unit was hooked up to a sink in the room, using the running water as the cooling element. "It worked," Humbert recalled. While the heat in the hospital corridors was scarcely bearable, the room where the body of Diana lay remained a cool 60 degrees F. "It was," the nurse added without irony, "the most agreeable place in the building."

Sadly, only a single bouquet arrived for Diana all morning—two dozen red roses from former French President Valéry Giscard d'Estaing and his wife, Anne-Aymone, another friend of Diana's. That afternoon, more flowers would arrive—this time an arrangement of lilies Prince Charles had asked the hospital to make up "because they are her favorite." In striking contrast to the ocean of floral tributes that would engulf central London, these were the only flower arrangements in Diana's otherwise spartan hospital room that day.

There would be an autopsy, but it would take place in England, not in France. Until that time, the body would not be embalmed. Meanwhile, every effort would be made to make Princess Diana presentable to the scores of dignitaries who would undoubtedly come to pay their respects throughout the day. "The body is very important, whether it's Princess Diana or someone else," Humbert explained. "You have to think of the family, their pain. To come to contemplate a body whose hair has not been arranged, that hasn't been washed . . ."

Members of the hospital's amphitheater staff—the nurses and orderlies who prepared cadavers for anatomy courses and dissection—arrived to carefully wash Diana's body and shampoo her hair. Diana's face and her famous blond coif were, understandably, of particular concern. A female cosmetician and a male hairstylist dispatched from a Paris funeral home arrived carrying a large color photo of Diana that had run in a recent issue of *Paris Match*.

"They tried to fix her the same way, with a curl in front," Humbert recalled, "and to make up her face to look exactly like she looked in the picture. They never stopped sending for me throughout the day, to ask if this was the way it should be, or that . . . It was very touching, and very hard to take. It was all rough. Very rough."

While the couple from the funeral home applied lipstick and styled and restyled her hair to match the photo in *Paris Match,* Humbert faced an alarming fact: They had nothing to dress her in. The white pants and black short-sleeved top she had been wearing that night had been cut off her by emergency medical personnel at the scene of the crash. All that remained of her personal effects—Diana's black jacket, her black size 9 Versace high-heeled shoes, her purse, her Jaeger-leCoultre gold watch with white stones, her bracelet with six rows of pearls and a dragon-shaped clasp, a black size 30 Ralph Lauren woman's belt, a single gold earring—were placed in a plastic bag and stored in the basement.

"She was completely nude under the sheet," recalled Humbert, who asked British Consul General Keith Moss to call the Ritz and have them supply a dress. They were shocked to discover that all the Princess's possessions had been packed up and, on Mohamed Al Fayed's specific instructions, shipped back to London. "Everything!" Humbert declared. "That very morning!"

While British Embassy officials scoured Paris for a suitable dress, the nurses were suddenly faced with yet another emergency. Most of the Royal Family—specifically the Queen, Prince Philip, Charles, and Diana's two sons—had been enjoying their summer holiday at Balmoral Castle in Scotland at the time of the accident. The Queen, who remained behind with Prince William and Prince Harry while Charles flew to Paris, had phoned the British Embassy in Paris—not with questions about Diana's medical care or how much she might have suffered, but with concerns of quite a different sort.

"The Queen! The Queen!" Consul General Moss blurted to Humbert as he rushed into the room where Diana still lay naked under a sheet. If there were any royal jewels among Diana's effects, Her Majesty wanted them returned to the Royal Family *immediately*. "Madame," said Moss, "the Queen is worried about the jewelry. We must find the jewelry, quickly! *The Queen wants to know, 'Where are the jewels?'* "

"But there wasn't any jewelry," replied Humbert, somewhat stunned at the apparent callousness of the question. "No wedding band, of course, no rings, no necklace."

Before boarding the plane for Paris, Prince Charles had also called ahead with a question about Diana's jewelry. Knowing that she would have wanted to look her best for those coming to pay their respects at the hospital, Charles called the hospital and personally requested that her gold earrings be put on. "Diana always likes to wear her earrings in public," Charles said, still speaking of his ex-wife in the present tense.

"There will be so many people there, looking at her. I'm sure she'll want the earrings . . ." But after scouring the premises, hospital officials failed to find the missing earring.

It would be seven weeks before the gold earring, which had been ripped from Diana's ear by the force of the crash and embedded deep in the dashboard, was recovered from the crumpled interior of the Mercedes by crash investigators. Still, Humbert later said she was impressed by the Prince's interest in preserving Diana's dignity, even in death. "That he cared to think of such details," Humbert later said, "oh la la, that surprised me."

Meantime, the hunt for a suitable dress continued for nearly two hours. Finally Ambassador Jay's wife, Sylvia, who was roughly Diana's size, offered one of her own. Shortly after noon, two men arrived at the hospital with a suitcase. One was a former bodyguard of Diana. The other was the man who had arguably been closest to Diana—her trusted butler, confidant, and protector, Paul Burrell. He had expected to be in Paris, but never under these circumstances; the evening before, Diana had phoned Burrell in high spirits, saying how eager she was to see her sons for the first time in five weeks. Would her old friend fly to Paris and accompany her on the flight home to London? she had asked.

Humbert stopped the two Britons, neither of

whom spoke French, at the door. "They wanted to see her," she recalled, "and they said that they had the dress in the bag." Before they could enter the room, Humbert insisted that they open the suitcase. "It was a black dress with a V-necked shawl collar that fastened in the front, in a light wool material that was a bit thicker than wool crepe." The dress, which came down just below the knee, had long sleeves and was belted at the waist. The suitcase also contained a pair of Sylvia Jay's black patent leather pumps.

While Burrell waited in the hallway, Humbert and Lecorcher took the suitcase into the room, placed it on a chair, opened it, and removed the dress. Humbert, who with the others had marveled at the extent to which Diana's face had remained unmarred, steeled herself as Lecorcher pulled back the sheet. In an instant, the brutal nature of her injuries became horrifyingly apparent. A scar crisscrossed with sutures ran from her sternum almost to her navel—the graphic, Frankenstein-like result of the surgeons' frantic attempts to repair her heart. Diana's hands and feet were bruised, as was her right side—the only external evidence that her ribs had been crushed. Similarly, her right forearm, which had been badly fractured, was also black and blue. As they maneuvered Diana's body so they could slip the dress over it, the nurses discovered more injuries, including a two-inch-long cut on the right buttock and a nasty three-inch gash on the right thigh.

All of Diana's injuries were duly noted on her chart, although no one reading it would have had the slightest inkling as to the identity of the patient. On her chart, Diana was not listed by name. "We used the saint's name of the day, St. Patricia," Humbert explained. "She was listed on her chart simply as Patricia." Appropriately St. Patricia, patron saint of Naples, was born into a noble family in Constantinople, fled to Italy to escape a royal marriage, distributed her wealth to the poor, and died young.

Diana had once told Burrell that she wanted to be buried in a casket with a window in it so that her face could be clearly seen. Now just such a gray metal casket—the strangest either of the nurses had ever seen—was rolled into the room. Humbert and Lecorcher, aided by the undertaker and two British Embassy staffers, then lifted Diana's body ("one takes the arms, the other the legs," Humbert explained) and placed her inside. They then carefully arranged her arms and feet. For the dignitaries who would arrive that afternoon, the coffin lid was left open. Just ten weeks earlier, an auction of seventy-nine gowns belonging to Diana at Christie's in New York had raised over $3 million for AIDS research—an idea that originally had been proposed by her increasingly publicity-savvy son William. Now the most fashionable woman in history lay in her coffin wearing a borrowed dress.

Diana often described the burly, soft-spoken Burrell as "my rock—the only man I can trust." As soon as he saw her, Diana's rock dissolved. "He broke down, just came undone," Béatrice Humbert remembered, contradicting later reports in the *Sunday Times* of London and elsewhere that Diana's butler had never lost his composure. Burrell "wept, with great sobs." He placed his hand on hers, which the two nurses had lovingly folded across her chest. ("He had to touch her because he just could not believe she was dead," Lecorcher said.) Then he "sat down at the Princess's feet, and he cried and cried."

Burrell reached into the suitcase that had contained the dress and pulled out a rosary. "These were a gift to the Princess from Mother Teresa," he said, handing Lecorcher the beads. Burrell then asked if the rosary could be placed in Diana's hands. Lecorcher gently opened Diana's fingers and placed the rosary inside. Then Burrell produced a framed photograph of William and Harry that Diana always traveled with, and a snapshot of her adored late father, Earl Spencer. These were also placed in Diana's hands.

Burrell began to stagger, as if he were about to faint. "We were afraid he was going to pass out," Humbert said. "We made him sit down, we tried to reassure him." But Burrell was beyond consolation.

"He didn't want to leave her body. We had to tell him, 'Paul, it's time to leave now . . .' "

Burrell was not the only devastated mourner Humbert tried to comfort that day; she had been assigned the thankless task of escorting all visitors to Diana's bedside. The reaction of France's Health Minister Bernard Kouchner was typical. Monsieur Kouchner was, Humbert said, "overwhelmed" when he saw her.

"It's impossible, it's impossible, it's impossible," Kouchner kept saying. "This beautiful lady. It's impossible." Humbert would become emotional when she remembered this. "It is dreadful, every time I think of these people. It was very hard for me."

At 2 P.M. about thirty people—including Dr. Bruno Riou, who headed the emergency medical team that tried to save Diana, Chief of Police Philippe Massoni, the heads of protocol from the Elysée Palace and the British Embassy, as well as several security chiefs and press attachés—met to decide how the afternoon was to proceed. The most pressing question: How would the coffin carrying the body of the Princess of Wales leave the hospital? At first, it was assumed that the casket would leave via the hospital's rooftop helipad. From there, it would be taken to Villacoublay, a military airfield southwest of Paris, and placed on a British military aircraft for the journey home.

But Charles himself, in constant touch from Scotland via phone, insisted Diana leave by the main entrance. By then a crowd of thousands had gathered in front of the hospital. "People want to see her and they should," said Charles, much to the relief of police officials, who feared any attempts to spirit her body away in secret might spark a riot. "There is no reason to sneak out. We have to leave normally."

To Meresse, the hospital's communications director, the atmosphere was decidedly Shakespearean. "It reminded me of *Hamlet,*" he said. "Inside the castle everything is conspiratorial, very quiet, very hushed. Outside there is this gathering mob."

There was, it turned out, legitimate cause for concern. Early news dispatches had already laid the blame for the crash on the notorious Parisian paparazzi. Outside, the angry mob shouted "Bastards! Assassins! Murderers!" at the pool of six reporters and six photographers allowed inside. "I did not want an ugly scene to greet Prince Charles when he arrived," said Meresse, who had spent the morning sprinting between the emergency wing and his press office down the street. "It would not have looked good for the hospital. It would not have looked good for France."

Tossing off his jacket, Meresse climbed over the police barriers and waded into the anxious crowd. "I picked out the ones that seemed to be ringleaders," he said, "and told them that Prince Charles was about to arrive and I didn't want to hear a word, not a murmur, nothing. To my total astonishment, they agreed. No one wanted to do anything that might upset the family."

By 4:30 P.M., in strict accordance with protocol, a red carpet had been rolled from the curb to Pitié-Salpêtrière's main entrance, flanked by officers of the French President's colorfully garbed Republican Guard. The rest of the hospital was not so pristine. In the wake of a wave of bombings by Algerian terrorists, trash receptacles throughout the hospital had been sealed. To make matters worse, the maintenance staff had not yet arrived to clean up the mess that had accumulated over the weekend. As a result, the hallways and stair landings were strewn with discarded plastic coffee cups, candy wrappers, and cigarette butts. Members of the nursing staff were dragooned into picking up brooms and hastily tidying up before the arrival of His Royal Highness.

The British Royal Squadron BAe 146 carrying Charles and Diana's sisters, Lady Sarah McCorquodale and Lady Jane Fellowes, touched down at Villacoublay at 5 P.M. Thirty minutes later, their silver Jaguar limousine pulled up in front of the entrance to the hospital's Gaston Cordier wing. Meresse's admonition to the crowd had worked. "All you could hear was the whisper of the luxury car's tires," he said. "A vibrating silence." The trio emerged from the car,

Charles wearing a double-breasted dark blue suit, Lady Jane in a tan coat draped with a floral print scarf, and Lady Sarah dressed all in black, her glasses hanging from a chain around her neck. French President Chirac bent down and took Charles's hand as he offered words of condolence. The Prince, smiling bravely, thanked the French President and Madame Chirac in his perfect French, then placed his right hand into his jacket pocket as he was led inside.

Chirac accompanied them to the second floor, but stopped short of accompanying them to Diana's body. Instead, Chief Massoni, the British protocol chief, and Béatrice Humbert escorted Charles and his former sisters-in-law down the hall. As they reached the two uniformed police officers guarding the room, Humbert recalled, "The British protocol chief turned to me and said, *'Madame, ici s'arrête mon rôle, c'est à vous d'introduire son Altesse royale'*—'Madame, my role ends here. It is up to you to introduce His Royal Highness.' "

Humbert was stunned; she had been told that Charles and Diana's sisters would enter the room alone. What shall I say to him? she thought to herself. What will happen?

She forged ahead. "Your Highness," she said in French, "if you will, please follow me." They went to the door, and Charles entered first. Lady Jane and Lady Sarah followed. "Prince Charles stopped, frozen before the casket," Humbert said. "Lady Jane burst into sobs."

Even after hours of watching grief-stricken dignitaries pay their respects, Humbert was astonished by Charles's reaction. As he looked for the first time at Diana's lifeless body lying in her coffin, a breeze from the air conditioner lifting a lock of her hair, Charles's head snapped back as if hit by some unseen force. "The Prince of Wales recoiled," she said. "He drew back his head in one involuntary motion, as though he had actually been stricken. As though he simply couldn't take it in. He couldn't believe it. You could feel his immense sorrow."

Two chairs had been set up on either side of the coffin. Charles pulled one of them over from the other side, and beckoned Diana's sisters to sit down on either side of him. All three bowed their heads in silent prayer. Lady Jane—"utterly devastated," Humbert observed—was crying loudly now. Charles put his arm around her and whispered something in her ear.

"I was all alone with them," said Humbert, who waited, wondering what to do next. Charles, his pale blue eyes brimming with tears, turned to her.

"Madame, could we have an Anglican priest?" he asked.

Within minutes, Reverend Draper and Father Clochard Bossuet joined them and, Humbert said,

"Together, we all prayed." In English, Reverend Draper led them in reciting the Lord's Prayer.

"I knew the Princess of Wales through the prism of the media and found her very sympathetic," said Meresse, who observed Charles from the sidelines. "She liked to, as we say in French, 'kick the anthill'— stir up trouble with the Establishment—and we loved that about her. She was much more sympathetic than the Prince. But he surprised me. I think he surprised us all. He was so totally broken up by what he saw, it was very moving. At one point he came very close to fainting, but managed to steady himself at the last minute. Charles was clearly devastated by the sight of Diana's body."

The hospital staff was no less impressed by the way Charles treated Diana's sisters. "He was very extremely kind, very caring toward them," Meresse recalled. "He was a very gentle man who did not conceal his pain. It was something none of us had expected."

Then Charles asked to be alone with Diana. When he emerged five minutes later to rejoin President Chirac and the rest of the official party in the hallway, it was clear to everyone that he had been crying. "There was great anguish, great melancholy in Charles's face," Meresse said. "His face was transformed by despair."

Charles pulled himself together enough to individually thank Humbert, Lecorcher, Meresse, and other hospital staffers for all they had done. Introduced to two of the surgeons who had tried, in French medical terms, to "reanimate" Diana, Charles groped for the right words but failed to find them. "Congratulations!" he blurted in French as he firmly shook Dr. Riou's hand. Then, regaining his command of the language, Charles thanked the bespectacled Riou and leading French cardiovascular surgeon Dr. Alain Pavie, who by chance had been on duty that night, for their heroic efforts. In the hours since they had finally been forced to acknowledge defeat, both Riou and the balding, gaunt Pavie had shaved and changed out of their blood-spattered green surgical gowns into crisp white hospital coats.

While the casket was being readied for departure, Charles launched into a series of questions. What were the circumstances surrounding Diana's arrival at the hospital? he asked. How she was treated? What had been the role of each person in trying to save the Princess's life? "He was very, very anxious about everything," Humbert said. "He stayed for half an hour and he talked and he talked. He wanted to talk. He needed to talk."

Lecorcher, meanwhile, went into a lounge area that had been set up in the room adjoining Diana's and shared a cup of tea with Lady Jane and Lady Sarah. Again, both of Diana's sisters broke down.

"Tell me," Lady Jane pleaded, "did she suffer?"

"No," Lecorcher replied, "it all happened so fast, she must not have suffered."

"Did anyone pray for her?"

The nurse reassured Lady Jane that the hospital priest had prayed for Diana and for her children. "She seemed," Lecorcher said, "very comforted by that."

It was 6 P.M.—the appointed time at which, according to the schedule worked out during the hospital staff's afternoon strategy session, Diana's body was to begin her journey home. The casket was carried down the main staircase by four pallbearers hired by the funeral home. The Princess's face would have been clearly visible through the small glass window had the casket not been draped with the lion-festooned gold, purple, red, and white royal standard that had accompanied the Prince of Wales's party on the plane. In front of the coffin was the Reverend Draper, wearing a white cassock over his black clerical garb, a Bible clasped in his hands. Directly behind Diana was Charles, followed by Lady Sarah and Lady Jane, then the French President and Mrs. Chirac. Each face in the funeral party was etched with shock and grief.

A dozen members of the Republican Guard stood rigidly at attention, the late afternoon sun glinting off the gold shields on their red-plumed hats. As a lone bagpiper played, more than two hundred hospital staffers and patients, some trailing intravenous lines, emerged from the Gaston Cordier wing to pay their respects. Charles and Diana's two sisters stopped beneath the canopied entrance and, with their arms hanging straight at their sides, stood motionless as the pallbearers lifted up the coffin and slid it into the black and silver hearse.

Seemingly oblivious to the eerily silent crowd of well-wishers pressing against the police barricades, Charles once again thanked President Chirac and numbly climbed into the back of Ambassador Jay's green Jaguar while his former sisters-in-law were escorted to the silver and gray limousine. No sooner did Lady Jane and Lady Sarah settle into their car than a staffer from the British Embassy bolted toward it grasping a plastic garbage bag in his left hand. It contained the clothes Diana had been wearing when she was brought into the emergency room. He threw open the trunk lid and gently placed the bag inside. As the staffer closed the trunk, the driver glanced in the rearview mirror and saw that the young man was crying unashamedly.

As the cortege began to pull away from the grounds of Pitié-Salpêtrière, the crowd that had been so reverently silent burst into spontaneous, if muted, applause. "Diana we love you!" someone shouted as the applause grew louder. And then another, "WE LOVE YOU! WE'LL NEVER FORGET YOU, DIANA!"

Thirty minutes later, the procession rolled onto the tarmac at Villacoublay airfield. A Royal Air Force honor guard slowly removed the flag-draped coffin from the hearse and carried it aboard the military transport as Charles, the Spencer sisters, and several British dignitaries stood respectfully on the side-lines. She was bound, finally, for England. The world had no way of knowing that in her hands was the rosary from Mother Teresa and pictures of her boys—or that, on her final journey home, the people's princess wore a borrowed dress.

From the day I entered this family, nothing—*nothing*—could ever be done naturally.

—*Diana*

She wanted the royal family to be human. There was no kindness there, and she was a kind person.

—*Lady Elsa Bowker,* a longtime friend

Her dark side was that of a wounded, trapped animal, and her bright side was that of a luminous being.

—*Rosa Monckton*

2

"Just tell me, is it bliss?" Like everyone else on the planet, Rosa Monckton had seen the photographs of her best friend cavorting with her new lover as they cruised the Mediterranean aboard his sleek, white-hulled 195-foot yacht, *Jonikal*. She called Diana's cell phone that afternoon of August 27, 1997, desperately wanting a straight answer.

Diana's reply left no room for misinterpretation. "Yes, bliss. Bye-bye."

Only ten days earlier Diana had been with Monckton, the president of Tiffany's in London, exploring the Greek isles aboard a small motor cruiser, the *Della Grazzia,* with a crew of three (compared to *Jonikal's* sixteen-man crew). The captain kept one step ahead of the pursuing paparazzi by phoning friends around the Greek islands to find where photographers were lying in wait, and then heading in the opposite direction. For five days, they managed to elude the press in this manner, allowing Diana to unwind in the comparatively cozy vessel she called "our cottage."

Diana had come to Monckton's emotional rescue when she had miscarried after six months. "She instinctively found the words to ease the pain," Monckton recalled, "and at the same time knew that I should name my daughter, and bury her . . . I will never, ever forget her face, her touch, her warmth and compassion on the day that we buried Natalya." When Monckton's daughter Domenica was born with Down's syndrome, Diana rushed to her bedside with a list of organizations and other Down's syndrome parents. "And if you don't mind," Diana added, "I'd love it if you'd ask me to be Domenica's godmother."

Understandably, then, Monckton was fiercely protective of the famously fragile Diana. She had cause to be. From the beginning, Diana had felt unloved and unwanted. After the births of Lady Jane, Lady Sarah, and a badly deformed son who lived only ten hours, the Spencer family was so determined that the baby born on July 1, 1961, be a boy that they did not bother to select any girls' names. It was a week before they settled on Diana Frances. Another three years would pass before Diana's brother, Charles, arrived, providing the Spencers with the male heir they so craved.

Like her future husband, Diana grew up in a co-

coon of wealth and privilege—all stemming from a fortune built on sheep trading during the fifteenth century. Since then, the Spencers had always occupied a place at Court. Diana's paternal grandmother, Countess Spencer—Diana later came to believe the Countess was her protector in the spirit world—had served as a lady-in-waiting to the Queen Mother. Diana's father was equerry to both George VI and Queen Elizabeth II.

None of this mattered to the six-year-old girl whose world was irreparably shattered when her mother walked out on the family, leaving Diana and Charles to be raised by a succession of nannies (Sarah, then twelve, and ten-year-old Jane were already away at boarding school). A bitter custody battle ensued, but in the end Diana's father, whose title and position gave him a distinct legal advantage, prevailed in the courts. The furious arguments, her mother's car door slamming shut before she drove off down the gravel drive, little Charles crying for his mother—these were the sounds and images of an unhappy childhood that would be burned into Diana's memory forever. She sought solace in the menagerie of stuffed animals she kept on her bed, but this was not enough. Many nights, Diana would later recall of this period, she sobbed for hours into her pillow so that no one else would hear.

Diana's treatment at the hands of the nannies hired

by her father often verged on the Dickensian. One banged brother Charles's and Diana's heads together when they misbehaved, another routinely struck Diana on the head with a wooden spoon. Brother and sister fought back, and in so doing forged a special bond that would last into adulthood. "Diana was an excellent little mother to her brother Charles," said Evelyn Phillips, headmistress at the Silfield School, the primary school they both attended as youngsters. "She always looked after him."

Together, Diana and Charles often visited their brother John's grave at Althorp and speculated about what might have happened had he lived. Diana was convinced that, with the birth of a boy, they would have been satisfied and she would never have been born. "From the very beginning," one family friend said, "she wondered if she even had the right to exist at all."

"Her own childhood was hell," said Diana's friend Peter Janson. "Her parents hated, despised each other. She grew up under that." A month after her divorce from Diana's father was finalized, Diana's mother married wealthy wallpaper manufacturer Peter Shand Kydd. The children took an instant liking to the affable, unaffected Shand Kydd. The same could not be said for the woman Earl Spencer chose to replace their mother. From the moment the flamboyantly ambitious Raine, Countess of Dartmouth and daughter of romance novelist Barbara Cartland, swept into their father's life trailing clouds of heavy perfume, Diana and Charles declared their unalloyed contempt for her. Although Diana would become friends with her only after Earl Spencer's death, Raine never stepped out of her assigned role as Wicked Stepmother as far as the rest of the Spencer children were concerned.

Diana attended a boarding school, West Heath in Kent, where she was an enthusiastic athlete but a less-than-mediocre student. And like so many other British schoolgirls, she had a crush on the Prince of Wales. "Diana *adored* him," said her piano teacher, Penny Walker. "She had pictures of him everywhere."

At sixteen, she enrolled in the Institut Alpin Videmanette, an expensive Swiss finishing school, to brush up on her typing, sewing, cooking—and especially her skiing. Shortly after she returned from Switzerland, she met Prince Charles for the first time when he was invited for a shoot at Althorp, the Spencers' spectacular five-hundred-year-old estate in Northamptonshire. They were standing in a freshly plowed field at the time.

It was eldest sister Sarah, however, who first caught the Prince's eye. Although Diana had absolutely no interest in Prince Andrew, her sisters always joked that she would someday marry him. Within the family, Diana was known as "Duch," for Duchess—the title bestowed on Diana's friend Sarah Ferguson when Fergie wed Andrew and became the Duchess of York.

It would be three years before Charles began seriously courting Diana, his interest piqued by a comment she made at a barbecue in the summer of 1980. Several months earlier, Charles's great-uncle and mentor, Lord Mountbatten, had been assassinated by IRA terrorists. Diana told Charles that she was impressed by how "desperately sad" he had looked at Mountbatten's funeral, and how, Charles later recalled, she "sensed my loneliness."

By this time, Diana was sharing an apartment with three other young women and teaching three days a week at the Young England Kindergarten School in central London. Handling young children came naturally to Diana, who even as a child showed an inordinate concern for the welfare of those younger than herself. "If another child was hurt playing, or was crying because he was being teased," Evelyn Phillips said, "Diana was the first one there with a hug and kind words. She'd been hurt so often she couldn't stand to see someone else in pain."

Alexander Steavonson, then four, was having a peeing contest with another boy when "Miss Diana" opened the door. "So we turned around—in panic— and caught her across the shins." Diana scolded them for being "naughty," but once they were out of ear-shot she dissolved in laughter.

The other two days were spent taking care of an American family's baby boy—a job she got through Knightsbridge Nannies, one of the two employment agencies where she signed on. (The other, Solve Your Problems, sent Diana out on the occasional cleaning job.) Mary Robertson had no idea that the nanny for her son Patrick was seeing the Prince of Wales until a mob of photographers appeared outside her house. "Gee, he's thirty-two. I'm only nineteen," Diana told her. "I never thought he'd ever look twice at me."

But the shy nursery school teacher did meet all the criteria for a royal bride. "First on the list was virginity," insisted Harold Brooks-Baker, managing director of *Burke's Peerage,* the chronicler of British bloodlines. "Second was the ability to do the job. Third, she must be seen to have the potential to bear heirs to the throne."

Yet Charles continued to stall, and Diana, now hounded by the press at every turn, grew more and more despondent. "She came through the door one day and burst out weeping," a friend recalled.

"He won't ask me," Diana wailed. "I don't understand. Why won't he ask me?"

But even after he proposed, Charles appeared less than wholly committed to the idea of matrimony. When a television interviewer asked if they were in love, Diana instantly replied, "Of course." After an awkward pause, Charles added, "Whatever 'in love' is."

Constantly hounded by the press during their engagement, she was soon dubbed "Shy Di" for her bashful, downcast look. Even more than being called shy, she hated the name Di. When someone in a crowd of admirers called out "Di!" she replied with obvious annoyance, "Please don't call me that—I've never been called Di. I really don't like it."

The July 29, 1981, royal wedding itself—unquestionably the marriage ceremony of the century—was a spectacle witnessed live by a worldwide television audience of 750 million. There was cause for celebration again one year later; on June 21, 1982, William Arthur Philip Louis Windsor, future heir to the throne, was born in a $175-per-day, twelve-foot-by-twelve-foot room at St. Mary's Hospital in London. His brother, Henry Charles Albert David Windsor (just plain Harry to family and friends) was born in the same room two years later.

While the world delighted in William's antics (among other things, he tried to flush his father's shoe down the toilet), his iron-willed mum proved herself a match for her mother-in-law, the Queen. When Diana went on her first major overseas trip to Australia in 1983, for example, she overrode Elizabeth's objections and brought little "Wills" along.

Diana, as it turned out, would take a firm hand in planning all her official trips abroad. During the couple's headline-making royal visit—Diana's first—to the United States in 1985, it was the Princess who made sure Clint Eastwood, John Travolta, Neil Diamond, Tom Selleck, and Mikhail Baryshnikov were invited to the White House dinner held in the Prince and Princess of Wales's honor. It was this evening that yielded the famous photograph of Diana beaming as she swept across the dance floor with Travolta.

Behind the glittering facade, however, the storybook marriage was in trouble from the start. Two days before the wedding, Diana had discovered a bracelet Charles had had made for Camilla Parker-Bowles, his longtime mistress. The bracelet bore the intertwined initials G and F—for "Gladys" and "Fred," the pet names Charles and Camilla had for each other. (Camilla, who is sixteen months older than Charles, numbers among her ancestors the celebrated Alice Keppel, mistress of Edward VII. On meeting Charles for the first time in 1972, she quipped, "My great-grandmother and your great-great-grandfather were lovers. So how about it?")

"I can't marry him, I can't do this," Diana told her sisters at the time. "Well, bad luck, Duch," they quipped. "Your face is on the tea towels so you're too late to chicken out."

During the engagement, Charles's fiancée received

words of encouragement from an unexpected source. When she showed up at a charity event in a black gown, her future husband carped that "only mourners wear black." Princess Grace of Monaco overheard the comment and ushered her into the ladies' room. Grace locked the door behind them and then listened patiently as Diana shared her doubts about becoming the Princess of Wales. "Don't worry," Princess Grace said with a laugh, "it will get a lot worse." (A year later, the woman who had preceded Diana in the role of fairy tale princess was killed in a car crash. To compound the irony, Diana insisted on representing the Royal Family at Princess Grace's funeral—her first official solo trip abroad.)

Despite the reassurances from her sisters and Princess Grace, on the eve of her nuptials Diana still "felt I was a lamb to the slaughter." With all the world's eyes on her as she walked down the aisle at St. Paul's, the bride's eyes were trained on her rival Camilla—"pale gray, veiled pillbox hat, saw it all, her son Tom standing on a chair . . ."

Diana was "madly, desperately" in love with her husband. But unlike other royals' wives who had borne their husbands' infidelities with a stiff upper lip, Diana refused to accept Charles's continuing affair with Camilla, whom she called "The Rottweiler."

From the beginning, Diana later said, "there were three of us in this marriage, so it was a bit crowded."

Yet she was determined to overcome the obstacles. "I think, like any marriage, especially when you've had divorced parents like myself, you'd want to try even harder to make it work, and you don't want to fall back into a pattern that you've seen happening in your own family," she later explained. "I desperately wanted it to work. I desperately loved my husband, and I wanted to share everything together. I thought that we were a very good team . . . Here was a fairy story that everyone wanted to work. And it was isolating, but it was also a situation where you couldn't indulge in feeling sorry for yourself. You had to either sink or swim, and you had to learn that very fast. I swam."

For a full decade, it took all the emotional strength Diana could muster just to keep afloat. "She was naturally shy," said Lady Elsa Bowker, one of her closest confidantes. "So when she had to go out and visit people or make a speech, she fell apart. She cried for *one hour* before every function. But she did what she had to do—and no one ever knew."

To the outside world, she was the planet's most admired, imitated, photographed, written-about, and talked-about woman—the most dazzling jewel in the Windsor crown. Yet her profound unhappiness over Charles's love for Camilla was compounded by the sense that she was a prisoner of Britain's entrenched Establishment. Her every action was controlled by the

Queen's advisors—Buckingham Palace's famous "men in gray"—and her every move monitored. "Everyone said I was the Marilyn Monroe of the 1980s and I was adoring every minute of it," Diana later mused. "Actually, I've never said, 'Hooray, how wonderful!' Never."

If it was praise she desired for breathing new life into the monarchy ("All I want is one 'Well done,' that's all"), none was forthcoming. Those who ran "The Firm," as the Royal Family called itself, were in the habit of offering "constructive criticism," not words of encouragement. After a time, Diana later explained, "you see yourself as a good product that sits on a shelf and sells well. People make a lot of money out of you . . ."

Paradoxically, Diana's unparalleled popularity with the British people was just another problem in her already foundering marriage. During royal outings, Charles would be all but ignored in the stampede to see Diana. "It was a blow to his male ego," she said. "He became very jealous, and took it out on me."

The bulimia had begun scarcely a week after her engagement to Charles was announced, triggered when he put his hand around her waist and said, "Oh, a bit chubby here, aren't we?" At its height during her marriage, Diana was making herself vomit five, six times a day until her waist had shrunk from twenty-nine inches to twenty-two inches. As pressures mounted, she was caught in a downward spiral of self-abuse and suicidal depression. A string of psychiatrists were called in to treat her, each with a new set of medications that only seemed to make matters worse. Valium, administered in increasing doses, seemed to be a particular favorite.

"They've destroyed me," she sobbed to Lady Elsa Bowker. "I am destroyed inside." Another friend, Lord Palumbo, was also privy to the doubt-riddled Diana the public never saw. "There would be crying, sobbing, wailing for two or three hours until the black mood had run its course. Then she would step out of the darkness into the light as if there had been no darkness at all."

Bowker was deeply concerned. "One day," Lady Elsa said, "I thought she was going to kill herself." In a grotesque bid for attention Diana, then three months pregnant with William, attempted suicide on New Year's Day, 1982, at Sandringham, the 20,000-acre royal estate. After a bitter argument with Charles about Camilla, Diana threw herself down a staircase. While Diana remembered the Queen as "absolutely horrified," and "physically shaking" at the sight of her daughter-in-law sprawled at the bottom of the stairs, a fed-up Charles accused her of "crying wolf" and went ahead with his plans to go riding. Although her abdomen was severely bruised, tests revealed that there had been no harm to the fetus.

In an orgy of self-mutilation, at various times Diana slashed her wrist with a razor, stabbed herself in the chest with a pocketknife, cut herself with the jagged edge of a lemon peeler, and hurled herself against a glass display case, shattering it. Nothing worked. Increasingly, she was convinced that the "men in gray" might even be considering a move to institutionalize her. "I was 'unstable,' a problem," she said. " 'What do we do with her?' "

"There was a huge amount of antagonism at Buckingham Palace," agreed her friend Vivienne Parry. "A whispering campaign that this woman was a cracked vessel, that she was potty—a danger to the family."

But Diana refused to give in, and those who knew her appreciated her defiant streak. At a dinner party, a guest told Diana that she understood the Princess didn't like dogs. "Oh, no," Diana said. "It's not dogs I don't like; it's corgis. They get the blame for all the farts." The Queen is a fanatical breeder of corgis.

On a Virgin Atlantic plane flying over Windsor Castle before landing at Heathrow, Diana dressed up as a Virgin stewardess. She seized the intercom and said, "If you look out the window to your right now you'll see Granny's place."

Her wry humor notwithstanding, Diana told friends she was "falling apart at the seams." To help her cope with the pressure, Diana turned to the first in a long line of spiritual advisors. Not that she was eager to share her beliefs. "I'd never discuss it with anyone," she said. "They would think I was a nut."

In 1986 Fergie introduced Diana to astrologer Penny Thornton. The following year she began seeing another stargazer, Betty Palko, whom she frequently consulted until 1992. Palko cautioned Diana about "deceit and treachery," and pointedly told her what she already knew all too well—that Charles was unfaithful.

When a party was thrown in 1988 to celebrate the fortieth birthday of Annabel Elliot, Camilla's sister, Diana initially had no intention of going. But she changed her mind when "a voice inside me said 'Go for the hell of it.' " That same voice prompted Diana to confront her husband's mistress.

"Camilla," she told the startled Parker-Bowles, "I would just like you to know that I know exactly what is going on between you and Charles. I wasn't born yesterday. I'm sorry I'm in the way, I obviously am in the way and it must be hell for both of you but I do know what is going on. Don't treat me like an idiot." Charles and Diana fought in the car on the way home, and that night she "cried like I have never cried before. I cried and cried and cried . . ."

Nothing changed. The Queen made it abundantly clear that divorce was out of the question. Since Charles obviously had no intention of ending his affair with Camilla, Diana would simply have to accept the status quo.

Predictably, the gulf between the Prince and the Princess of Wales grew ever wider. When eight-year-old William suffered a depressed skull fracture after being accidentally struck with a golf club at school, his distraught mother sat in the hospital for hours while he underwent surgery. Charles, satisfied that everything was under control, instead went ahead with plans to attend a performance of *Tosca* at Covent Garden. Charles blamed Diana for making too much of their son's injury when, the next day, he was roundly condemned for leaving the hospital.

On March 29, 1992, while the Waleses were on a skiing holiday in Austria, Diana's father died suddenly. Charles, well aware of the public relations ramifications, insisted on returning with his wife to London—strictly for the sake of appearance. When Diana refused to go along with the ruse, Charles called his mother. The Queen ordered them both to return to London together. Once there, Charles, who had not spoken a word of comfort to his grieving wife, left for his country estate at Highgrove.

Increasingly, Diana turned to her once-estranged mother for support. Frances Shand Kydd knew all too well how difficult her son-in-law the Prince could be. At Harry's christening in 1984, he complained that his wife had not only given birth to another boy, but one with "rusty" hair. Diana and her siblings all had naturally reddish hair. "You should just be happy," scolded Diana's mum, "that your son is healthy." From that point on, Charles cut off Mrs. Shand Kydd completely.

Diana's relationship with her mother deepened after Peter Shand Kydd left Frances for another woman in 1988. From then on, they met secretly and often— at Kensington Palace, at Highgrove, or occasionally at one of Diana's favorite restaurants, San Lorenzo in Knightsbridge. "She would call me," Mrs. Shand Kydd said, "from wherever she happened to be in the world, and at all times of the day and night."

By late 1991, Diana had already set in motion a plan to get her side of the story across. "I was at the end of my tether, I was desperate," she later explained of her decision to tell all to journalist Andrew Morton. Before proceeding, she had asked her friend Dr. James Colthurst to arrange a meeting with astrologer Felix Lyle. According to Lyle, the charts did not rule out cooperating with Morton. But if she did, said the stars, confusion would reign and Diana would embark on a "long and painful journey."

"In the end," Lyle recalled, "we agreed that she had a tremendous grievance. She was fighting for her independence and, despite my warning, she felt that this might be the only opportunity she would get to express how difficult it had been for her."

For the next several weeks, Dr. Colthurst brought Morton's written questions to Diana at her Kensington Palace apartments. Sitting alone in her private sitting room, she then poured out her heart into a tape recorder. Colthurst then secretly delivered the tapes to Morton.

Not only did the publication of *Diana: Her True Story* in June 1992 cause an international furor, it uncorked a series of scandals that would further shake the monarchy to its foundations. That August, transcripts of an illegally taped telephone conversation between Diana and her friend James Gilbey were printed in the British tabloids. Gilbey, who called her "Darling" and "Squidgy," listened patiently as she discussed her problems with Charles and the rest of the royals ("after all I've done for this fucking family"), her anxiety over becoming pregnant, and even her affection for another man, her riding instructor James Hewitt. Its comic aspects notwithstanding, "Squidgygate," which revealed Diana to be almost pathetically needy, dealt a serious blow to Diana's already flagging self-esteem.

(The following January, Charles found himself in the same boat when a similar transcript of one of his phone conversations with Camilla was published in the tabloid press. During the passionate exchange, the Prince of Wales expressed the bizarre wish to be turned into one of Camilla's tampons.)

On December 3, 1992, Diana visited William and Harry at Ludgrove, the elite boarding school they both attended in Berkshire, to break the news that their parents were about to separate. Now ten, William was well aware of the role Camilla played in the breakup. "I put it to William," she recalled, "particularly, that if you find someone you love in life, you must hang on to it and look after it and if you were lucky enough to find someone who loved you, then one must protect it. William asked me what had been going on and could I answer his questions, which I did. He said, 'Was that the reason why your marriage had broken up?' and I said, 'Well, there were three of us in this marriage, and the pressure of the media was another factor, so the two together were very difficult, that although I still loved Papa, I couldn't live under the same roof as him, and likewise with him . . .' I put it gently, without resentment or any anger."

It was a tearful moment, but now Diana could breathe a sigh of relief. "From day one I always knew I'd never be the next queen," she said. "No one ever said that to me. I just knew it . . . I just had to get out."

On December 9, 1992, Prime Minister John Major stood up in Parliament to formally announce the separation of the Prince and Princess of Wales. That same year, the marriage of Prince Andrew and Sarah

Ferguson came to a nasty end, and Windsor Castle nearly burned to the ground. For the Royal Family it had been, as the Queen herself would put it, an *annus horribilis*. Alas, it would not be the last.

After the separation, Diana threw herself into the causes that most appealed to her. In an obvious reference to her own *persona non grata* status among the royals, Diana later observed, "I was very confused by which area I should go into. Then I found myself being more and more involved with people who were rejected by society . . . and I found an affinity there."

Indeed. "Her overall effect on charity," said Stephen Lee, director of Britain's Institute of Charity Fund-raising Managers, "is probably more significant than any other person's in the twentieth century." In truth, the Royal Family was known for its philanthropic efforts before Diana's arrival on the scene. The Queen is patroness of no fewer than 221 charities, Prince Charles the patron of 161. But it was Diana's personal touch—her "special genius for compassion," as Rosa Monckton called it—that transcended what had been little more than *noblesse oblige*.

Without her husband or the full backing of Buckingham Palace, Diana still dazzled at a seemingly endless number of openings, galas, and celebrity fund-raisers—standing in receiving lines, making small talk, and raising millions in the process. "Diana used her power just like a magic wand, waving it in all kinds of places where there was hurt," said Debbie Tate, who runs a group of homes in Washington, D.C., for abused and abandoned children. "And everywhere she used it, there were changes—almost like a fairy tale."

Increasingly, she opted for the kind of one-on-one contact for which her friend Rosa Monckton said she had a "special genius." She extended an ungloved hand to shake hands with AIDS patients, perched on the hospital beds of children undergoing chemotherapy for cancer, and sat cross-legged on the floor to chat with battered women.

It was her conviction that she had been emotionally if not physically battered that led Diana to address a conference on women and mental health on June 1, 1993. She discussed her fears for women "trapped in the private hell of mental turmoil" and of mothers thrust into "deeper and darker depression" by feelings of powerlessness. When another speaker, Dr. Miriam Stoppard, said living with a man was a health hazard that should carry a government health warning, Diana nodded in agreement. "We all know about that," she whispered to her private secretary, Patrick Jephson. "She's not far wrong."

That same day, Diana sat down with her solicitor in Kensington Palace and signed a will stating flatly that, should she die, Charles would not have the sole final word in their children's upbringing. "I express the wish," the will read, "that should I predecease my husband, he will consult with my mother with the regard to the upbringing, education, and welfare of our children."

In a swipe at the Royal Family, Diana insisted that, in the event that both she and Charles died, their sons would be raised by her family, not his. "Should any child of mine be under age at the date of the death of the survivor of myself and my husband I APPOINT my mother and my brother EARL SPENCER to be the guardians . . ." The bulk of the estate, the document stipulated, would be divided equally between William and Harry but held in trust until they turned twenty-five. Signed "Diana" in the Princess's distinctively bold hand, the will was witnessed by Jephson and her trusted butler Paul Burrell. Its contents, which revealed the depth of Diana's distrust toward the Royal Family, would remain secret for the next five years.

For the most part, Diana kept her lingering feelings of bitterness to herself and she plunged headlong into her various causes. In addition to her grueling schedule of daily public appearances, there were also countless unpublicized acts of kindness. Diana routinely visited seriously ill children in hospitals, then dropped in unannounced on their parents to see how they were coping. In scores of cases, she established friendships that lasted months, even years. "I pay attention to people, and I remember them," she said. "Every meeting, every visit, is special."

This gift for compassion did not come without a price. After hours spent holding the hand of a dying child, or listening to horrifying stories of domestic abuse, Diana would call up a friend like Rosa Monckton and, said Monckton, "simply cry, totally drained and exhausted."

By this time, Diana was, with the exception of Mother Teresa, arguably the world's best-known humanitarian. Certainly she shared Mother Teresa's guiding philosophy. On the desk in Diana's Kensington Palace study was a statute of Christ draped with rosaries given to her by the Nobel Peace Prize winner and Pope John Paul II. On the desk was a note—something Mother Teresa told Diana that she jotted down in her own bold hand. "You can't comfort the afflicted," the note read, "without afflicting the comfortable."

Yet, according to Rosa Monckton, Diana "saw a complete distinction between her personal life and her public duty. She was no saint, and was as frail and vulnerable as the rest of us—in fact, rather more so."

That was never more evident than in her quest for "spiritual guidance"—particularly in the wake of her decision to stop seeing psychotherapist Susie Orbach after two years. Stephen Twigg, who first showed up at Kensington Palace in 1988 to treat the Princess's anxiety with deep massage therapy, became a trusted advisor. So did Debbie Frank, who replaced Betty Palko as Diana's permanent astrologer in 1992. Two years later, she also began seeing psychic Rita Rogers, whose work with parents trying to contact their dead children struck a chord with Diana. "She came to my little house," Rogers said, "and looked at the pictures of dead children on my walls and with tears streaming down her cheeks said, 'Rita, you do good work.' "

Diana was a devout believer in the healing power of touch. For three years, spiritual healer Simmone Simmons visited her at Kensington Palace once a week. (During her first house call, Simmons claimed to detect a "vast whirlwind of energy" on the left side of Diana's bed—the side she tended to sleep on.)

The Princess actually embraced a wide range of New Age therapies, from acupuncture (performed on Prince William as well as the Princess by Irish nurse Oonagh Toffolo) to hypnotherapy, homeopathy, and even aromatherapy. She practiced t'ai chi, and hired an expert in the Chinese science of feng shui to rearrange her furniture as a means of promoting harmony in her environment.

Diana also adhered to the notion that crystals possess magical powers; a white crystal (supposedly conferring upon the wearer stability and a clear mind) frequently dangled from her neck. Twice monthly she went to Ursula Gatley for colonic irrigation. Gatley soon became another close confidante.

If her spiritual search betrayed a certain inner restlessness, so too did her sometimes frantic search for love. In August 1994—just two months after Charles admitted to a national television audience that he had committed adultery—it was reported that Diana had made scores of harassing phone calls to millionaire art dealer Oliver Hoare, the married father of three children. That October, *Princess in Love* hit the bookshelves. In it, James Hewitt recounted in lurid detail his six-year affair with Di that had begun in 1986—including the dates, times, places, and circumstances of their trysts. Diana would later concede that she had been "madly in love" with Hewitt, and the book's publication constituted a devastating betrayal.

Concerned about the impact on William and Harry, Diana later said she "ran to them as fast as I could." Before she could say anything, twelve-year-old William produced a box of chocolates. "Mummy," he said, "I think you've been hurt. These will make you smile again."

After Hewitt, Diana became involved with the ruggedly handsome Will Carling, former captain of England's rugby team. "When Diana fancied him," said her hairdresser, Natalie Symonds, "she started studying the sports pages of the newspapers." Symonds and her partner, Tess Rock, became two of the Princess's closest friends. "To us," Symonds said, "she wasn't the Princess of Wales. She was just . . . Diana."

At one point, Diana pointed to a photo of Carling and asked Tess Rock, "Don't you think he's good-looking?"

"Not particularly," Rock replied. "He looks just like my brother."

Diana threw back her head and laughed. "I'd love to meet your brother!" she said.

Carling's wife, Julia, a British television personality, found none of this amusing. She fought back, publicly branding Diana a homewrecker. But the rugby star continued to see the Princess. Eventually, Julia Carling blamed Diana for the breakup of her marriage.

Just two weeks after the publication of Hewitt's scandalous confessional, Charles detonated a literary bombshell of his own. In *The Prince of Wales: A Biography,* Charles revealed to author Jonathan Dimbleby that he had been bullied by his abusive father, virtually ignored by his mother, and persecuted by a wife he portrayed as both spoiled and mentally unstable. Moreover, he made it clear that he had never loved Diana, and married her only after Prince Philip ordered him to do so.

"He did love me," Diana protested to her astrologer Debbie Frank, "and I loved him." As hurt as she was, what concerned Diana most was the impact that statement would have on their children. "Imagine being told that your parents never loved each other," she said. "How do you think poor Wills and Harry must feel?"

Camilla was among those who had urged Charles to tell his side of the story in a book, but the self-pitying tone angered the British public. "How awful incompatibility is," Charles moaned, "and how dreadfully destructive it can be for the players in this extraordinary drama. It has all the ingredients of a Greek tragedy . . . I never thought it would end up like this. How could I have got it all so wrong?"

The first excerpts from *The Prince of Wales*, published on the eve of the Queen's state visit to Moscow, enraged both Elizabeth and Philip. Nor were William, then twelve, and ten-year-old Harry spared. At Ludgrove, students are not permitted access to newspapers, magazines, or television. No matter. "William and Harry," said a former faculty member at Ludgrove, "know everything that's going on. The other boys can't resist teasing them about it, and it's impossible to keep them from smuggling the tabloids into the school."

As she had with each new headline-making revelation, Diana rushed to Ludgrove to reassure her sons. Satisfied that they were bearing up well, she then fled to Washington for some "quiet time" with her close friend Lucia Flecha de Lima, wife of Brazil's ambassador to the United States, Paulo Tarso Flecha de Lima.

No sooner did she return from Russia than the Queen moved to quash rumors that a divorce was imminent. "As was stated quite clearly when their separation was announced," a Palace spokesman insisted, "the Prince and Princess have no plans to divorce. That remains the position."

In truth, their respective camps were in the middle of intense negotiations that would drag on for months. Diana was insisting that Charles be the one to instigate divorce proceedings. "I'm not going anywhere," she said, smiling, "until he tells me to."

While polls indicated that the public at large remained in Diana's corner, it was equally true that she was increasingly being portrayed as what one senior member of the royal household called a "loose cannon." Once again, a voice told Diana to strike back. Over the years, she had politely turned down repeated personal requests for interviews by Oprah Winfrey, Barbara Walters, Diane Sawyer, and others. Now she agreed to do for BBC television correspondent Martin Bashir what she had done for Andrew Morton. Using compact cameras that had been smuggled into Kensington Palace, Bashir secretly taped a wide-ranging interview with Diana. Broadcast on the

BBC program *Panorama* in November 1995, the interview was nothing if not explosive.

"Friends on my husband's side," she said, gazing up from heavily mascaraed lashes, "were indicating that I was again unstable, sick, and should be put in a home of sort . . . I was almost an embarrassment." She went on to talk with unsettling candor about, among other things, her marriage, her husband's mistress, her own affair with James Hewitt ("Yes, I adored him"), her children, and what role she hoped to play. Above all, Diana said, she wanted "the man in the street" to know she would "always be there for him," and that she wished to reign not as Queen of England but as "the queen of people's hearts." Her concluding remarks would later seem sadly ironic. "There is a future ahead," Diana said. "A future for my husband, a future for myself, and a future for the monarchy."

These few conciliatory words did little to soften what was for all intents and purposes a sneak attack on the Royal Family. Certainly the Queen, who watched the broadcast in her private quarters at Buckingham Palace, was unprepared for Diana's broadside. She summoned the Archbishop of Canterbury, Prime Minister John Major, and senior members of the royal household staff and informed them that there was no longer a place for Diana in "The Firm." It was time to cut her noisome daughter-in-law loose. The

Queen wrote letters to both Charles and Diana insisting that a quick divorce was "highly desirable."

Charles had moved into quarters at St. James's Palace just down the Mall from Buckingham Palace, and it was there that Diana and he met to iron out the details of the divorce. Rather than wait for the Queen to make the formal announcement, Diana issued her own statement: "The Princess of Wales has agreed to Prince Charles's request for a divorce. The Princess will continue to be involved in all decisions relating to the children and will remain at Kensington Palace, with offices in St. James's Palace. The Princess of Wales will retain the title and be known as Diana, Princess of Wales."

Not so fast, the Palace replied. The Queen responded with a statement of her own, stating flatly that none of these issues had been resolved. It would take four more months of intense negotiations, in fact, before a final agreement was reached. On August 28, 1996, the divorce was finalized. Diana would be allowed to remain in her five-bedroom, four-reception-room apartment at Kensington Palace, and would receive a lump sum cash settlement of $22.5 million as well as $600,000 a year to maintain her offices. (Diana needed the cash. In her peak spending years, the Princess of Wales's expenses ran to $1.5 million annually.) Diana would also retain all her titles: Princess of Wales, Duchess of Cornwall, Duchess of Rothesay, Countess of Chester, Countess of Carrick, and Baroness Renfrew.

But the Queen pointedly stripped Diana of her royal status. Henceforth, she would no longer be addressed as "Her Royal Highness." That meant that her name was stricken from all official documents relating to the Royal Family and that, when the clergy was asked to pray for members of the Royal Family, they would no longer include Diana in their prayers. Only those inside the Palace knew of Elizabeth's other command regarding the Princess of Wales—that Diana's name was never again to be spoken in the presence of the Queen.

Diana had wanted to fight to retain her royal designation, but changed her mind after asking William what he thought. "I don't mind what you're called," he said. "You're Mummy."

She hid her pain from the public, but Diana deeply regretted that she had lost her chance to be Queen. "Yes, yes," she admitted to *New Yorker* editor in chief Tina Brown. "We would have been the best team in the world. I could shake hands till the cows come home. And Charles could make serious speeches. But it was not to be . . ."

Yet for now, she behaved as if the loss of her royal status mattered not at all. Instead, Diana seized the opportunity to carve out a new life for herself. As a member of the Royal Family, she had always felt that the Scotland Yard detectives assigned to guard her were an unwarranted intrusion on her privacy. She also suspected, with good reason, that they were spying on her. Now she notified Scotland Yard that she no longer desired the kind of round-the-clock protection provided Charles and their children.

Divorce also freed Diana to concentrate on those issues dearest to her. Toward that end, she slashed the number of charities she actively supported from more than one hundred to just five—the National AIDS Trust, a charity for the homeless called Centrepoint, the Leprosy Mission, the Royal Marsden Cancer Hospital, and the Great Ormond Street Children's Hospital. She also remained as patroness of the English National Ballet.

She lent her name to other causes, as well. One of her most daunting tasks was to focus public attention on the human suffering wrought by land mines. Her visits to Angola, where she was photographed walking through a minefield, and to Bosnia in the summer of 1997 unquestionably laid the groundwork for the anti-land mine treaty signed by more than 120 nations in Ottawa.

Lady Elsa Bowker was "astonished" at photographs of Diana walking through minefields. "Aren't you frightened?" she asked.

"I'm never frightened when I'm doing good," Diana replied without hesitation. "I'm never frightened."

The course of Diana's private life seemed less certain. "Imagine," said her friend Lord Palumbo, "incredible adulation during the day, then dinner on a tray in front of the television in Kensington Palace—alone." Despite persistent reports that Diana was desperate for male companionship, by the summer of 1997 she was juggling several serious "admirers." According to hairdressers Symonds and Rock, at this time she had "at least nine men" in her life. Among them: Placido Domingo, Luciano Pavarotti, George Michael, rocker Bryan Adams, Asian electronics tycoon Gulu Lalvani, and British businessman Christopher Whalley.

"We always used to laugh when we saw newspaper reports about her being lonely and isolated," Symonds said. "Men were constantly phoning her." So many, in fact, that in order to keep their identities a secret she devised a special code to identify them based on greyhound racing. They were all "traps" numbered one through nine, and, Symonds said, "each man's number went up or down depending on his popularity with her."

If Diana was in the middle of a meeting, her butler, Paul Burrell, would interrupt and say, "Trap Four is on the phone." That way, explained Symonds, "Diana kept their relationship with her a secret."

Accordingly, Symonds continued, "Luciano Pavarotti could be Trap Two one week and Trap Seven a month later. Placido Domingo dropped down the list when he began to come on a bit too strong. Diana said, 'He fancies his chances with me—Ha!' But she absolutely adored George Michael and thought he was incredibly handsome." Diana was "thrilled" when Michael gave her a gold watch, said Rock, but wondered aloud about the rock star's intentions.

Diana also nursed a schoolgirl crush on Tom Cruise, who had invited the Princess and William to watch him film *Mission: Impossible* at Pinewood Studios. Diana joked that she wouldn't mind if Cruise's willowy wife, Nicole Kidman, were out of the way. "Nicole kept giving me dagger eyes, as if to say, 'Keep your hands off my handsome husband!' " Diana laughed. She also told her hairdressers that she "adored" President Bill Clinton. "I love his Southern drawl," she told them. "It sounds incredibly sexy." But she also told Rock and Symonds that when she first met the President and the First Lady, she was surprised at how he deferred to Hillary. "She certainly is the one who wears the pants in that family," Diana told them.

Diana had apparently set her sights on another royal, King Constantine's eldest son, Prince Pavlos. The Princess of Wales was, according to Symonds, "devastated" when Prince Pavlos married the American heiress Marie-Chantal Miller. Diana "really fancied him for herself."

By Christmas 1996, the coveted Trap One designation was bestowed on Pakistani heart surgeon Hasnat Khan. Diana met the thirty-nine-year-old "Natty" Khan when he performed a triple bypass on the husband of her acupuncturist. "I couldn't help blushing and fluttering my eyelashes at him," Diana told Natalie Symonds. "He is such a brilliant surgeon, so dedicated to his work. He's saved so many lives . . . He's got no money. I'll have to keep him, but I've got a thing about doctors."

Soon Diana became obsessed with Khan, spending two or three hours a day with him at the Royal Brompton Hospital, where he worked. "She read medical reports on surgery and studied books on the Muslim religion in a bid to impress him," Symonds recalled. At Diana's request, Khan arranged for her to observe several heart operations. "They make me feel like throwing up sometimes," she told Symonds, "but I force myself to watch because I want to learn as much as possible about heart surgery."

Symonds visited Diana at her Kensington Palace apartments and found her watching a video of a black-and-white Pakistani film. "Aren't they a good-looking race?" she sighed. "The men are so handsome." Diana began burning scented joss sticks in the palace, and added Pakistani-made silk dresses to her wardrobe. She also made two trips to Pakistan to learn more about Khan's homeland.

On the first visit to Lahore, Diana was taken to Shaukat Khanum Memorial, a cancer hospital, where both the staff and patients could scarcely contain their excitement when she stepped through the door. Diana found herself the guest of honor at a children's party, serenaded by forty giggling patients in brightly colored costumes.

Suddenly, a little boy with "a serious face, sad eyes, and a wasted body" caught her eye. Reliving the moment, Diana said, "I no longer see anyone but him, I can't say why. I know he is going to die."

Diana asked the boy's mother if she could take him in her arms. "And we laugh politely as they hand the child to me," Diana continued. "But suddenly he says, with this anxious little voice, 'Please don't make fun of me.'

"My God!" Diana recalled. "How could we? He won't allow me to hold him. But his mother explains that we were just talking. But the child cannot see, no longer sees. Yes, he is blind. A tumor is devouring his brain. I hug him against me . . ."

The little boy died a few hours later. "I shall never forget him," she said quietly.

The Queen had been visiting sick children in hospitals long before Diana was born, but even during those visits her singular lack of compassion could be jarring. One witness to such a visit by the Queen recalled the moment when "her guide has something special to show her. She turns and there, indeed, is an angelic child, poignantly bandaged, its eyes shining with excitement at her arrival. And the Queen's face, from smiling, suddenly goes dead. She stares fiercely, almost unseeing, at the child, then turns abruptly to walk on down the ward . . ." It hardly mattered whether the Queen was afraid of unleashing her tears or simply resented having her emotions manipulated. The fact was that, where Diana responded with hugs and tears, the Queen expressed a shockingly callous disregard even for the feelings of a small child.

The Princess's second visit to Lahore was for a different, and very specific, purpose. When she returned in May 1997, it was to visit with Hasnat Khan's family. "I met his parents and they love me," she told her hairstylists. "There is absolutely no problem about me not being Muslim. So we can definitely get married now!" So, she went on, "spread it around—we're going to get married."

"She became so devoted to Hasnat," Symonds recalled, "that she said she at last began to understand the undying love Prince Charles shared with Camilla Parker-Bowles. She was wildly in love, totally obsessed by Dr. Khan."

Unfortunately, the media-shy Pakistani heart surgeon was not so eager to wed. "Alas, Dr. Khan was in no great rush," Symonds said, "to put on a morning suit. He was devoted to his career, and not willing to live in Diana's shadow." He angrily accused Diana of leaking stories about their romance to the press. After confronting her, Khan stormed out of Kensington Palace yelling, "Don't talk to me for at least a week. I don't want to talk to you. Let's cool it for a while." Several hours later, he phoned to apologize.

"What does it mean when a man behaves like that?" Diana asked Symonds.

"Perhaps he is just insecure."

"Yes, and I'm insecure so we have lots in common. But I don't think I'll ever understand men."

Just to make sure that she wasn't being taken for granted, Diana went out on the town with yet another Pakistani—fifty-eight-year-old businessman Gulu Lalvani. According to Symonds, Khan "went potty" when he read about Diana's nights on the town with Lalvani. He did the same when she had a few well-publicized lunch dates with a handsome young property developer she met at her health club, Christopher Whalley. "I think Diana did it," Symonds said, "just to wind Dr. Khan up and make him jealous."

Her tangled love life notwithstanding, Diana continued her crusade against land mines and her fundraising efforts. On a trip to the U.S. in June 1997

Diana, among other things, went to Katharine Graham's eightieth birthday party in Washington, breakfasted with Hillary Clinton at the White House, appeared at a benefit for the Red Cross, visited Mother Teresa at an AIDS hospice in the Bronx, and attended a preview party for an auction of her gowns at Christie's.

She also found time for lunch at New York's Four Seasons on East Fifty-second Street with her old friend Anna Wintour, editor of *Vogue,* and Tina Brown of *The New Yorker.* The Princess, Brown later recalled, wore "a mint-green Chanel suit with no blouse and a stunning tan." As she made her way through the crowd, Brown said, Diana had "the startling phosphorescence of a cartoon creation—too blond, too tall, too painfully recognizable . . . like a strange overbred plant, a far-fetched experimental rose."

Talk soon turned to her sons. "All my hopes are on William now," Diana said. "I don't want to push him." As he approached his fifteenth birthday, William now ranked as one of his mother's most trusted advisors. It was the Prince's idea to raise money for charity by selling off items from her wardrobe. On June 25, bidders spent $3.26 million on seventy-nine of Diana's gowns—including the midnight-blue velvet dress she wore the night she danced with John Travolta at the White House. It went for $222,500.

★   ★   ★

On July 1, 1997, Diana was guest of honor at a gala dinner-dance celebrating the centennial of London's Tate Gallery. It also happened to be Diana's thirty-sixth birthday. The following week she was invited to bring William and Harry along on a visit to Chequers, the Prime Minister's official country residence. She explained to the newly elected Labour Prime Minister Tony Blair that she saw a role for herself as Britain's roving ambassador for good, and Blair agreed. In fact, Blair and President Bill Clinton had actually talked over what role Diana might play on the international stage.

"I think at last I will have someone who will know how to use me," she confided to a friend. "He's told me he wants me to go on some missions. I'd really like to go to China. I'm very good at sorting people's heads out." She also allowed that she found the new P.M. "quite sexy."

No sooner had the Princess arrived home than she was confronted by Khan; again he reduced her to tears by accusing her of leaking details of their affair to Fleet Street. And again Khan apologized, this time with a dozen red roses. But Diana was no longer in a forgiving mood. On July 11, the day the flowers arrived, Diana left London with William and Harry for St.-Tropez—and her first holiday with the family of Mohamed Al Fayed.

I just want to see if there's a light at the end of the tunnel.

—Diana, to astrologer
Penny Thornton

She was ruled by her heart, and not her head.

—Roberto Devorik,
designer and friend

3

S he can't be serious," said the Queen, looking up from the memo at her pursed-lipped private secretary, Sir Robert Fellowes. *"Al Fayed?"*

"I'm afraid so, ma'am," replied Diana's brother-in-law.

"And she's taken William and Harry with her?"

"Indeed."

Diana had already left for Mohamed Al Fayed's palatial St.-Tropez estate—despite the fact that, under the terms of her divorce settlement, she was not permitted to take William or Harry out of the country without the Queen's written permission. Her Majesty, however, was hardly in a position to object. In just one week, Charles planned to throw a fiftieth birthday party for the wildly unpopular Camilla—the closest thing the Prince of Wales could make to a public declaration of love—and Buckingham Palace was bracing for the backlash. Diana alone saw the humor in the situation. "Wouldn't it be funny," she told a friend, "if I jumped out of the cake?"

But *Mohamed Al Fayed?* There were few more controversial figures in all the United Kingdom. Born in Alexandria, Egypt, Al Fayed started out selling Singer sewing machines, and in 1952 caught the eye of Saudi entrepreneur Adnan Khashoggi. Al Fayed went into business with Khashoggi exporting Egyptian furniture to Saudi Arabia. He soon married Khashoggi's sister Samira, and in 1956 Samira gave birth to their only child together, Emad. He was quickly nicknamed "Dodi."

By the time Dodi was two, the partnership between Al Fayed and Khashoggi had unraveled, along with his parents' marriage. Al Fayed moved on to greener pastures, befriending the Emir of Dubai and charging hefty commissions to broker deals for British development firms seeking to do business in the oil-rich Persian Gulf—an arrangement that earned Al Fayed more than $140 million in fees.

Dodi's father moved to London in 1965, and embarked on a thirty-three-year quest for respectability. In 1979, he purchased Paris's fabled Ritz Hotel and would ultimately spend $150 million restoring it to its original grandeur. He also refurbished another Paris landmark, the Duke and Duchess of Windsor's villa in the Bois de Boulogne. In gratitude, the French bestowed several honors on Al Fayed, including the Legion of Honor.

No such praise was forthcoming from the British, however—despite the fact that, above all else, he wished to become a British subject. It was apparently not enough that the four children produced by his second marriage were all British citizens, or that he employed thousands of people and paid millions each year in taxes.

Determined to show the powers-that-be that he was every inch an Englishman, Al Fayed acquired an impressive string of British icons: Harrods department store (purchased in 1985 for $689 million); *Punch,* the world's oldest satirical magazine; Balnagown Castle, set in the middle of 40,000 acres in the Scottish Highlands; the Fulham Football Club; and several apartment buildings on London's Park Lane—not to mention a personal fleet of no fewer than sixty-four Rolls-Royces. Moreover, Mohamed and his younger brother Ali bought Turnbull & Asser, the renowned shirtmaker that numbers Princes Philip, Charles, Andrew, Edward, William, and Harry among its clients.

Equally lacking in subtlety was his attempt to curry favor with the monarch. By virtue of his sponsorship of the Royal Windsor Horse Show, Al Fayed earned a place alongside the Queen in the royal box. But when a 1990 government report concluded that the money to purchase Harrods had actually been put up by the richest man in the world, Al Fayed's friend the Sultan of Brunei, the Egyptian's application for British citizenship was put on hold—indefinitely.

By 1995, he had had enough. Convinced that he was being denied citizenship because of his ethnic background, Al Fayed lashed out, publicly admitting that he had bribed Conservative members of Parliament with cash and free stays at the Ritz. "I could hire these Conservative MPs," he told *The Mirror,* "like hiring taxis." The resulting scandal helped to bring down the government of John Major. It also ensured, much to Al Fayed's dismay, that the public would continue to view him as little more than a vulgar *arriviste.*

One of the aristocrats Al Fayed had numbered among his true friends was Diana's father. The Egyptian billionaire had watched Diana grow up, and on his deathbed Earl Spencer presumably told Al Fayed to watch out for his children. To further cement his relationship with Diana's family, he put her stepmother, Raine, on the board of Harrods International. Not long after, in September 1996, Al Fayed made the same offer to Diana, who politely declined. Under the terms of her divorce, she explained, she was not permitted to engage in any commercial enterprise.

Nonetheless, in the Princess of Wales, Al Fayed saw a unique opportunity to exact revenge on the grandest scale imaginable. What better way to even the score than by linking the Al Fayed and Windsor dynasties through marriage?

Over the years, whenever they bumped into each other at Harrods or some fund-raising gala, Al Fayed had made a practice of inviting Diana to spend the holidays with him—depending on the season—at his castle in Scotland, his chalet in Gstaad, or at Barrow Green Court, his country estate in Surrey. But never before had the circumstances seemed so right.

Al Fayed paid close attention to Diana's romance with Dr. Hasnat Khan and her outings with Gulu Lalvani, which proved that she was not averse to becoming involved with Middle Eastern men. He knew that she was on the rebound from Khan, and therefore emotionally vulnerable.

He got a chance to remind Diana about his standing invitation on June 3, 1997. That evening, the notorious Egyptian tycoon and the rebel Princess were seated together at dinner following a benefit performance of *Swan Lake*.

For the first time, she did not decline his offer out of hand. Oddly, Diana's astrologers had been predicting for years that she would marry a foreigner, or at the very least someone of "foreign blood." The charts also pointed time and again to France as the place where she would find a new home—with a new love.

When she finally did accept Mohamed Al Fayed's

invitation to spend a few days unwinding with William and Harry at the Al Fayeds' sun-splashed St.-Tropez villa, Dodi Fayed's name (he dropped the Arabic "Al") was not mentioned. On the afternoon of Friday, July 11, Diana and her sons boarded Harrods' Executive Gulfstream IV jet bound for Nice with Mohamed Al Fayed, his Finnish-born wife, Heini, and their four children, aged ten to sixteen. (Diana did not exactly share Al Fayed's esthetic sense. Later, while riding aboard the Gulfstream IV jet with Rosa Monckton, the Princess leaned back in the pink plush seats and pointed down to the green carpeting festooned with pharaohs' heads. "Look at all this, Rosa," she said, laughing, "isn't it awful?")

Once the Al Fayeds and their guests arrived, they were driven to the harbor at St.-Laurent-du-Var and boarded Al Fayed's newly-purchased 195-foot yacht, the *Jonikal,* for the five-hour trip to St.-Tropez. With its saunas, spas, fully equipped gym, and helipad, the *Jonikal* impressed even the woman who had spent part of her honeymoon sailing aboard the royal yacht *Britannia.*

The *Jonikal*'s sixteen crew members were accustomed to serving Al Fayed's wealthy and powerful friends, but nothing prepared them for the moment when the Princess and her two sons unexpectedly materialized in their midst. "We weren't told in advance," said the yacht's chief stewardess, New Zealander Debbie Gribble. "We knew nothing about it until they all walked up the gangplank. Diana and her sons were the last people we expected to see." The Princess, wearing a beige pants suit, "seemed quite shy and a bit reserved at first," Gribble recalled. "So she just said 'Hello' as she boarded the boat."

Conversely, her host could barely contain himself. Al Fayed was "in his element," Gribble said. "You could tell he was thrilled to bits at the idea of having the Princess on his yacht."

Gribble was immediately struck by Diana's disarmingly easygoing manner. She refused to let anyone help her unpack, and was proud of the fact that all she brought with her was a single suitcase. "You see," she said, smiling, "I'm better than the men."

Of course, Diana had made a conscious effort to forgo formality early on. "I ordered dozens and dozens of suede gloves for her because the Royal Family always wore gloves," said her friend Anna Harvey, deputy editor of British *Vogue*. "Heaven knows where they all went, because she never wore any of them. She wanted flesh-to-flesh contact."

The London *Daily Mail*'s Richard Kay, a confidant of Diana's, remembered how, after having lunch at the home of a mutual friend, Diana "helped clear the table." Then she "stacked the dishwasher, soaked the pans and wiped the table with a damp cloth."

That first evening in St.-Tropez they arrived at

Castel Ste. Helene, Al Fayed's sprawling, $17 million compound overlooking the Mediterranean, and dropped anchor alongside his two-masted schooner *Sakhara*. Carved into the side of a cliff, the tile-roofed villa that had once belonged to Suez Canal builder Ferdinand de Lesseps boasted two swimming pools, terraced gardens, waterfalls, and a private beach.

Diana and the boys quickly settled into their quarters in the luxuriously appointed thirteen-room guest house quaintly referred to as the "Fisherman's Cottage." Never far away were two members of the "Royal Protection Squad," Scotland Yard detectives assigned to guard the princes. They seemed superfluous to Diana; the security-obsessed Al Fayed maintained a virtual private standing army of more than fifty armed guards, at least a half-dozen of whom watched over them at any given time.

Each morning Diana and her sons trekked down to Al Fayed's private beach to splash in the surf, sail, snorkel, and Jet-Ski. Afternoons they dined aboard the *Jonikal,* where two cooks—one French, the other Italian—vied to impress Diana and her princes. Lunch always began with Dom Pérignon—William was allowed a glass, but Harry stuck to Coke—and was followed by caviar and fresh lobsters served beneath a white canvas awning on the upper deck. Mummy invariably picked at a salad, but Wills and Harry, who were accustomed to the limited cuisine served up at their respective boarding schools, dug in. "William couldn't believe it when a whole fish was sent back to the kitchen untouched," Diana told Gribble. "I don't think he's ever seen so much food."

It was, of course, only a matter of hours before the press was alerted to their presence in St.-Tropez. Soon boatloads of camera-snapping paparazzi were bobbing within one hundred yards of Al Fayed's private beach. Wills and Harry complained, and their mother showed her displeasure by draping a pink towel over her head as she sunbathed aboard the *Sakhara*. Not surprisingly, the British tabloids wasted no time condemning Diana for exposing her sons to the likes of Al Fayed.

Diana was nothing if not adept at handling the press, and the next morning she sought to defuse the situation by making herself accessible to photographers. While Wills and Harry Jet-Skied, Diana walked onto the pier wearing a one-piece animal-print bathing suit and struck several poses that were just this side of cheesecake. Then she jumped into a speedboat with one of Al Fayed's men and, to everyone's astonishment, zoomed out to a boat full of British photographers.

"How long do you plan to keep this up?" she wanted to know, pleading with them not to spoil her children's holiday. "We've been watched every minute we've been here. There's an obsessive interest in me and the children." William, she went on, was "freaked out" by the constant hounding—to the point where he feared for his family's safety. "My sons are always urging me to live abroad to be less in the public eye, and maybe that's what I should do," she threatened, "go and live abroad." Then, as she sped away, she added cryptically, "You're going to get a big surprise with the next thing I do."

Diana's irritation with the press in St.-Tropez was decidedly short-lived. As stories began appearing in the British tabloids about Charles's upcoming fiftieth birthday party at Highgrove for Camilla, the Princess of Wales made herself increasingly available. She was well aware of Camilla's current disparaging nickname for her—"Barbie"—and, while Diana harbored a grudging respect for her rival, she had no intention of relinquishing center stage to Charles's mistress. There developed an unspoken understanding between Diana and the paparazzi: They would not harass her if she simply gave them what they wanted.

So she did. At precisely 11 each morning, Diana, Wills, and Harry arrived at the beach and cavorted willingly in full view of photographers. At one point, she even grabbed a rope and swung off the *Jonikal* and into the water like Huck Finn. The resulting shots of Diana swimming, diving, boating, and just seeming to have a glorious time in general were splashed on front pages around the world. So grateful were the French photographers that they sent her a bouquet of one hundred red roses.

Diana got the results she wanted, as well. Charles's party for Camilla—the Prince's much-heralded public declaration of love for the woman who broke up his marriage—was all but totally eclipsed by Diana's romp on the Riviera.

In the scramble to photograph Diana, no one noticed that someone new had joined the cast of characters in St.-Tropez. Dodi Fayed had planned to spend a romantic summer interlude on the Riviera with his fiancée, former Calvin Klein model Kelly Fisher, before their scheduled wedding on August 9. But before they left for the Côte d'Azur, they decided to linger behind at Dodi's apartment and watch the annual Bastille Day parade from his terrace.

Later that day, thirty-one-year-old Fisher, a native of Kentucky, was packing for their trip, when Mohamed Al Fayed called his son on an urgent matter. The senior Fayed wanted Dodi to drop whatever he was doing and fly immediately to Nice. From there Dodi, a dabbler in film (he co-produced or co-financed *Chariots of Fire, Hook, F/X,* and *The Scarlet Letter*), was to proceed to Cannes, where everyone would watch Cannes's spectacular Bastille Day fireworks display from aboard the *Jonikal.* Everyone, that is, but Fisher. At all costs, Al Fayed ordered his son, Kelly Fisher was to remain behind—and in the dark.

"I am sorry, but there is a business emergency and my father wants me to fly to London immediately," Dodi told Fisher. She felt she had little reason to doubt him. Dodi and Fisher had been a couple for more than a year, and they planned to move into the $10 million Malibu beach house that had once been the home of Julie Andrews.

But while Kelly waited impatiently by the phone, Dodi was hurtling toward his date with destiny aboard the *Jonikal*. It would not be the first time Diana and Dodi had met. They were initially introduced to each other in 1986, when Dodi's polo team beat Charles's team in a match at Windsor Great Park. Their paths would cross over the years—at the 1992 London premiere of *Hook,* for example—but they never exchanged more than a few words.

Yet this time, Al Fayed made certain that his son and the Princess of Wales were left alone together to talk. They would soon discover they had several things in common: They were both abandoned by their mothers at an early age, and they still bore the emotional scars from their parents' bitter divorces. Growing up in worlds of luxury and privilege, both Dodi and Diana were described by those who knew them best as fragile, needy, and often painfully shy. And when his mother succumbed to a massive heart attack in 1986, Dodi felt the loss as keenly as Diana had when her father died.

From childhood, Dodi, who was raised a Muslim, had moved effortlessly among French, Greek, Egyptian, British, and American friends. He attended St. Marc's school in Alexandria, and Le Rosey, the exclusive Swiss boarding school. His teenage years were spent bouncing from homes in France, Alexandria, London, and Dubai, but nothing was denied him. At fifteen, he was given his own chauffeur-driven Rolls-Royce—and his own apartment in Mayfair.

After a six-month stint at the Royal Military Academy at Sandhurst, Dodi passed up a commission in the United Arab Emirates Air Force to become an attaché at the UAE embassy in London. But it was a career in the movies that Dodi really wanted. With his father's backing, he set up a film company in London in 1979. Three years later, he collected the Academy Award for Best Picture as executive producer of *Chariots of Fire*. Dodi was in the audience at the Oscar ceremonies but was too timid to join the film's producer, David Puttnam, onstage.

For all his supposed shyness, Dodi cut a wide swath through Hollywood. At various times, he was linked romantically with Brooke Shields, Tawny Kitaen, Tina Sinatra, Joanne Whalley, Cathy Lee Crosby, Valerie Perrine, Mimi Rogers, Koo Stark, Patsy Kensit, and Winona Ryder.

While he was accused by one acquaintance of pursuing only "trophy women," most of Dodi's lovers praised him for his warmth, his generosity, and—a quality seldom found among single men in Hollywood—his willingness to listen. They also felt protected in his company, although at times Dodi's well-intentioned efforts to shield his celebrity dates from the press were ill-advised. During a date with Stark, the porn star whose 1982 affair with Prince Andrew made headlines, Dodi grew angry when photographers accosted them as they left the Pierre Hotel in New York. As their limousine turned onto Madison Avenue and proceeded uptown, Dodi ordered his driver to lose their pursuers. "Floor it," he yelled, and in the ensuing high-speed chase they narrowly missed being broadsided by a yellow cab. Stark was terrified, but Dodi seemed oblivious to the fact that they had narrowly cheated death.

Oddly, Dodi himself was cautious behind the wheel. Although at one time he owned thirty-four Ferraris, sixteen Aston Martins, a Lagonda, and a Humvee, Fayed was uncertain of his own driving skills and never exceeded the speed limit. But as someone who had been watched over and catered to his entire life—first by nannies, then by servants and bodyguards—he had blind faith in the ability of others to carry out his orders. "He always figured," said a friend, "that the professionals he hired knew what they were doing."

Like Diana, Dodi had also taken a stab at marriage.

On the emotional rebound from his mother's unexpected death in 1986, he wed former American model Suzanne Gregard in a spur-of-the-moment ceremony. They separated eight months later. Gregard claimed that, like his father, Dodi lived with the constant fear that he would be abducted and held for ransom. As a result, the former Mrs. Fayed added sadly, "we were always surrounded by bodyguards."

Dodi was becoming known in Hollywood for more than his libido. Despite a $100,000 monthly allowance from his father, Dodi, said one of his former partners in the movie business, "has a reputation for not paying his bills or meeting his commitments." Former employees accused Dodi of stiffing them on wages, and at the time he joined his father and Diana aboard the *Jonikal*, landlords in New York and Los Angeles were suing to collect hundreds of thousands of dollars in back rent. (Dodi blamed an Egyptian named Mohamed Sead for impersonating him, but Sead, who was convicted of fraud in 1997, accounted for only a small percentage of the real Dodi's outstanding debts.)

"Dodi was always generous picking up the tab," said actress Claudine Christian, a longtime friend. "But when it came to real money, the reins were pulled by his father. He was still a little boy." In fact, that is what those in the Al Fayed inner circle continued to call him: "The Boy."

There was also a fondness for cocaine dating back to the 1980s. "He was into cocaine," said Nona Summers, a London socialite who was also an habitual user. "I never did it with him. He didn't tell the truth about many things, but he told me he had done it, that he got himself in trouble and stopped." Another friend from that time recalled seeing a kilo of cocaine in Dodi's suite at the Waldorf Towers in New York. "It was his weekly buy. I was there when the kilo was around, when the cokeheads went into the bedroom."

Whatever his shortcomings, Dodi's ex-wife felt that any woman "would be lucky to have Dodi. He was so romantic and thoughtful. And he didn't take things too seriously. Once during a candlelit dinner he had arranged," Gregard remembered, "the table we were sitting at collapsed, and the whole turkey fell to the floor. We laughed so hard. That was what I loved about him."

It was a similar sort of Laurel-and-Hardy moment that sparked the romance between the Princess and the Playboy. On the afternoon of July 14, Mohamed Al Fayed instructed the crew of the *Jonikal* to drop anchor in Cannes Harbor so that his guests would be afforded a perfect view of the Bastille Day fireworks display. Then he slipped away so that Diana and his son could get better acquainted.

As night fell, white-coated stewards served a lavish

supper as Diana and Dodi, alone on the upper deck, made small talk. "They got on well enough," Debbie Gribble said of those first awkward moments, "but I didn't think anything of it." Until a strawberry rolled off Dodi's plate and landed with a splat at Diana's feet. She scooped it up and then, without warning, threw it at him.

Dodi tossed it back, and within seconds they were in the middle of a full-scale food fight.

Diana, whose sleeveless white summer dress was now dripping with bits of watermelon and grapefruit, "gave him a ripe mango full in the face and one on the back," Gribble said. "They were chasing each other and laughing and giggling like a couple of kids. Then they wrestled a bit and stopped—just staring at each other . . ."

Mohamed and the others rejoined them on deck to watch the fireworks over the water, but, said Gribble, "from that moment on something changed in the way they treated each other." For the rest of the evening they were inseparable. Whenever Gribble turned around, she caught sight of Diana and Dodi deep in conversation. "Dodi couldn't seem to bear to leave her alone. Something had passed between them. Suddenly, they seemed to fit as a couple."

The next day after lunch, Gribble spotted them huddled together. "Everyone else had gone their own way," Gribble said. "Diana and Dodi were still deep in conversation. She was talking about her work and travels in India and Africa and he was enthralled."

William and Harry, meantime, cavorted in the water with Mohamed Al Fayed's young brood or roughhoused with the ever-present Al Fayed guards, several of whom were former Royal Navy Seals. William, already a superb athlete, impressed his hosts by doing swan dives off the *Jonikal*'s thirty-foot-high diving platform. Taking full advantage of these few days away from the watchful eyes of schoolmasters, Wills and Harry also hobnobbed with the crew belowdecks. "They loved being on their own," a crew member said. "They'd help themselves to ice cream from the galley, then insist on doing the wash-up."

While Diana streaked across the water astride a Jet-Ski, clinging to a laughing Prince Harry, Dodi watched from an upper deck. Next to him was his ever-present bodyguard Trevor Rees-Jones, a strapping, twenty-nine-year-old former British army paratrooper.

No one was having a better time than Diana, who reveled in the company of a family that seemed to be as warm and open as the royals were remote and unfeeling. It was not long, however, before harsh reality intruded. On the evening of July 15 news came that Diana's friend, Italian designer Gianni Versace, had been shot to death outside his Miami Beach mansion. Dodi put a comforting arm around her as they

THE DAY DIANA DIED

watched television coverage of the murder and the manhunt for Versace's killer. Given the fate that was to befall both of them that summer, Versace's comment only nine months earlier seemed eerily prescient. At the unveiling of his fall collection in Milan, the designer had stated publicly that when he died he wanted to come back as the Princess of Wales, "the most beautiful and stylish woman in the world."

Determined to cheer Diana up—and in the process ingratiate himself to her children—Dodi rented a St.-Tropez disco for two nights so that she and the children could dance in private. Later, Dodi took them to a nearby amusement park where Diana, Dodi, William, and Harry joyfully rammed one another on the bumper cars. Diana wore her seat belt tightly fastened around her waist, and made certain her sons did as well.

An early witness to what would become one of the century's great ill-fated love stories, Rees-Jones insisted he never told his own wife that the Princess was on board. He just recalled feeling "pleased for the boss and Diana and hoping I could gain them some peace and privacy to enjoy their time together."

Rees-Jones may have been keeping Diana's secret, but he was also keeping a secret from her. She did not know that Kelly Fisher had tracked Dodi down in St.-Tropez, and that now he was sleeping with the model each night aboard the other Al Fayed yacht docked across the bay, the *Sakhara*.

Fisher was also kept in the dark. "I had no idea what was going on," she later said. "Dodi kept leaving me behind with the excuse that the Princess didn't like to meet new people." According to Fisher, during one of those nights he made love to her without any form of birth control only hours before joining Diana aboard the *Jonikal*. "I love you so much," he told her at the time, "and I want you to have my baby."

"Wow, that was a risk," Kelly conceded several weeks later. "I could be pregnant now."

Fisher had a modeling assignment in Nice, and Dodi generously offered her the use of yet another yacht, the *Cujo*, for two days. A converted U.S. Coast Guard cutter, the *Cujo* flew a skull-and-crossbones pirate flag whenever Dodi was on board. By the time Fisher returned to St.-Tropez, Diana had flown home to England with Wills and Harry. Awaiting her at Kensington Palace were four dozen roses and a $12,000 Jaeger-leCoultre gold watch.

On July 22, Diana boarded a flight for Milan, where she attended a celebrity-studded memorial service for Versace. The service marked a reconciliation for Diana and her old friend Elton John. Earlier in the year, John had organized a fund-raising gala for Versace to mark the publication of the designer's book

Rock and Royalty, with Diana as the star attraction. Since a large portion of the royalties was earmarked for AIDS research, Diana had agreed to write the book's foreword—until she realized Versace's book was filled with photographs of nude men alongside snapshots of the Queen and other royals. Worried that "the book may cause offense to members of the Royal Family," Diana withdrew her foreword and backed out of the publication party despite pleas from John. Versace promptly canceled the affair, which was also to have raised money for John's AIDS Foundation, and refunded $400,000 worth of tickets.

Versace got over the brouhaha but "Elton was very upset" with Diana, Natalie Symonds later recalled, "and they didn't speak to each other again until they met at Versace's memorial service." There they sat next to each other in the Versace family pew, and a visibly distraught Diana put her arm around the sobbing John to comfort him. "People," she later said of the emotional moment, "need hugs."

As Diana comforted one old friend at the memorial service for another, Dodi was cruising the Mediterranean with Kelly Fisher. On July 23, they flew back to Paris, and from there Fisher went on to California as originally planned. Now she was flaunting a $230,000 diamond and sapphire engagement ring from Dodi that, strangely, was almost identical to the one Prince Charles had given his bride.

When Diana arrived in Paris the next day, Dodi whisked her away to the Ritz for a romantic weekend. Unnoticed as they entered the hotel lobby through the main revolving doors facing Place Vendôme, they were welcomed inside by Claude Roulet, the hotel's second-in-command.

Roulet escorted the couple up the broad staircase to the right of the lobby, stopping just opposite the Marcel Proust Suite outside Room 102—the $10,000-per-night Imperial Suite. Dodi's and Diana's heels clicked on the black-and-white marble floor as they approached the door. On either side of the fifteen-foot-high door with the oversized gold knobs were Louis XV chairs upholstered in blue velvet. A flower-filled vase sat atop an Empire table with gold legs in the shape of winged sphinxes.

The suite itself consisted of a chandeliered salon, a dining area, two bedrooms, and a huge marble-and-oak bathroom. The cream-colored walls were hung with large oil paintings, the ceiling painted in *trompe-l'oeil,* and the Empire furniture upholstered in red satin. Winston Churchill had stayed in the Imperial Suite, as had Richard Nixon and Madonna. But no one had taken up residence in these rooms longer than German Field Marshal Hermann Goering, who made the Ritz his Paris base of operations during the years of Nazi occupation.

That evening, Diana and Dodi ventured out to

dine at one of Paris's best-known restaurants, Lucas Carton Restaurant on the Place de la Madeleine. To avoid being spotted by the paparazzi, Dodi's permanent Paris driver, thirty-five-year-old Philippe Dourneau, spirited the couple out the back door leading to the Rue Cambon. Ironically, this same tactic had worked the previous September when Prince Charles and Camilla Parker-Bowles secretly rendezvoused at the Ritz. Smuggled out the rear of the hotel, the Prince of Wales and his mistress managed to go undetected during their brief stay. Now the ruse seemed to be working again, largely because the press was still unaware that the Princess was even in Paris, much less at the Ritz.

At Lucas Carton, diners craned their necks to catch a glimpse of Diana and Dodi at a corner table as they lingered over their three-star meal. No one could determine the identity of the man she was with, but their laughter and their body language left little doubt about the intimacy of the moment. "They certainly," said Eventhia Senderens, wife of Lucas Carton's chef Alain Senderens, "seemed to be enjoying themselves . . . There was no fuss. They were left alone."

After dinner at Lucas Carton, Dodi took Diana—as he had Kelly Fisher—to the Windsor villa on the edge of the Bois de Boulogne at 4 Route du Champ d'Entrainement. The exiled Duke of Windsor and his Duchess, the former Wallis Warfield Simpson, had moved into the stone-walled *petit palais* in December 1953 and lived there together until his death in 1972. For the next fourteen years the Duchess continued to occupy the stately residence, living out the remainder of her life in shuttered seclusion.

As the Duchess's health deteriorated, so did the condition of the villa. On her death in 1986, Dodi's father acquired the building and its contents, including all the Windsors' furnishings, paintings, objets d'art, clothing, books, papers, and personal items. After three years, Mohamed Al Fayed had restored the villa to the glittering splendor of the Windsors' 1950s heyday.

By the time the current Princess of Wales got her first glimpse of the place, however, it was empty. After restricting his family to the apartments on the upper floor and maintaining the rest of the house as a shrine to its famous occupants, he had decided to auction off the contents and move the Al Fayeds downstairs. "It has been a very hard decision to dispose of these things I love," Al Fayed explained. "However, I now wish to make more use of the Windsor residence for our purposes . . ."

The famous "Abdication Desk" upon which King Edward VIII signed away the throne for the woman he loved had been packed up and shipped to Sotheby's in New York. So had the tapestries (including the former King Edward VIII's personal banner that

hung in the entrance hall), the Degas, the chinois-
serie, and the Aubusson carpet with ostrich feathers,
symbol of the Prince of Wales, stitched in silver
thread. Captured on horseback by the portraitist Sir
Alfred Munnings in 1921, the then–Prince of Wales
no longer stared across the library at Gerald
Brockhurst's 1939 *Portrait of the Duchess of Windsor.*
Gone too was the menagerie of pug dog artifacts—
silver pugs, ceramic pugs, wooden pugs, glass pugs,
stuffed pugs—that had become the childless couple's
odd obsession.

Still, enough remained for Diana to get a sense of
what had been—and what might be. The cavernous
main hall led into the chandeliered main salon with its
blue, gold, and silver Regency furnishings and
twenty-foot-high French windows that opened out to
the terrace. Turning left, Dodi led Diana into the
mirrored dining room, then to the "Boudoir," the
paneled sitting room where the Duchess penned her
personal correspondence on an eighteenth-century
Chinese-style lacquer secretaire. Just beyond was her
bedroom, empty but bearing the unmistakable stamp
of her walls painted in the shade known as "Wallis
Blue."

Like every English schoolgirl, Diana had been fas-
cinated by the true story of a love so strong it compelled a man to give up the throne of England. But
she was also all too aware that the royals regarded both

the Duke and Duchess with thinly veiled contempt. She would later confess that, as she walked through these rooms for the first time with Dodi, she "could feel their presence in the room—not sad spirits but happy ones, because whatever the rest of the world thought they really were very much in love. And I think they stayed in love until the end . . ."

Diana and Dodi had known each other just eleven days. But already Mohamed Al Fayed was telling his son that—should Dodi choose to live there with the right woman—Villa Windsor was his for the asking.

Their whirlwind weekend over, Diana returned to Kensington Palace. Her attention quickly turned to her sons, who seemed at loose ends in London. Knowing how eager they were to join their father for six weeks of hunting and fishing at Balmoral, she suggested they leave earlier than originally planned. "There's nothing for you here," she told William. "Why don't you go up to Scotland to join your papa a day early?"

Her boys packed off to Balmoral, Diana was soon back aboard the *Jonikal,* sailing overnight from Nice to Sardinia. The Mediterranean, Debbie Gribble recalled, was "as flat as a millpond, the moon was huge and low in the sky, and thousands of stars were out. It was as close to paradise as you can get."

Diana and Dodi laughed and talked as they dined on caviar (her favorite) and pâté de foie gras supplied courtesy of Harrods. The soundtrack from the Academy Award-winning screen romance *The English Patient* played over the yacht's state-of-the-art sound system. "Debbie, have you seen it yet?" the Princess asked her. "You'll cry when you do. I howled."

The crew had its instructions to set the stage for romance. Lights that normally blazed above decks were dimmed, replaced by flickering candlelight. A Sinatra CD replaced *The English Patient* soundtrack. "It was the sort of evening you have in your dreams," Gribble said, "but they still went back to their separate cabins."

Two nights later, Gribble stumbled upon the couple as they were kissing passionately in the main salon before dinner. "You Have Been Loved," one of Diana's favorite songs from George Michael's album *Older,* was playing. "After a few seconds Diana opened her eyes and saw me," Gribble recalled. "She burst out laughing in a loud, high-pitched giggle."

The next morning, Gribble went to make up their cabins and noticed that Diana's bed had not been slept in. Dodi's, she said, "looked like a tidal wave had gone through it." From then on, they made no effort to disguise their feelings for each other.

Their routine varied little for the rest of the cruise. They got up each day at 10 A.M. in Dodi's stateroom, slipped into their bathing suits, and went on deck for a leisurely breakfast of carrot juice, croissants, fruit, and Italian coffee. After breakfast, they both pulled out their cell phones and spent the next two hours catching up with family, friends, and contacts around the globe.

Each day Diana made a point of touching base with her sons and sounding them out on the subject of Dodi. The response from William was always the same. "As long as you're happy, Mummy. That's the important thing." Diana's calls to Debbie Frank, Rosa Monckton, Lady Bowker, and a few other close friends all began with the same breathless announcement: "I've met someone . . ."

Dodi was also sharing the news with a select few—notably his high-powered publicist, Pat Kingsley. Widely regarded as the top press agent in Hollywood, Kingsley numbered among her clients the likes of Tom Cruise, Tom Hanks, and Demi Moore. That he had a press agent at all belied Dodi's oft-repeated desire to remain out of the spotlight. Though he ostensibly called Kingsley only to keep her abreast of the situation, there seemed little doubt that Dodi wanted the world to know.

The remainder of the day was invariably spent swimming or sprawled out on cushions beneath the hot Sardinian sun. Gribble, who brought them iced Perrier precisely every ninety minutes, was "a bit embarrassed" to see Dodi and Diana "draped all over each other, their legs entwined."

Diana squealed with delight when Dodi gave her a diamond bracelet, and when the *Jonikal* dropped anchor in Monaco, they hit most of the principality's major jewelry stores in search of more trinkets. There were more pyrotechnics that night over Monte Carlo, and the couple watched from the top deck—Dodi standing behind Diana, his arms wrapped tightly around her as they gazed up in wide-eyed wonder at the exploding fireworks. The last morning of the cruise, Dodi arranged for two dozen orchids to be delivered to the yacht before they weighed anchor. When the orchids failed to arrive in time for the *Jonikal*'s departure, he left the yacht's tender behind. Hours later, the small boat—with its precious cargo of rare orchids—had managed to catch up to the *Jonikal* on the open sea.

In the past, Diana had—with the exception of airing her marital woes in public—taken extraordinary measures to keep her private life out of the papers. It was different this time. In stark contrast to the publicity-phobic Hasnat Khan, Dodi did not seem at all uncomfortable about the media attention.

Far from it, although it was Diana—and not Dodi—who tipped off the press to their blossoming romance. Determined to make the photographs of their "secret" rendezvous as flattering as possible, the Princess had an intermediary leak the couple's whereabouts to the late Gianni Versace's personal photographer, Mario Brenna.

Without ever actually acknowledging Brenna's presence, Diana and Dodi unselfconsciously romped in the surf, rubbed suntan lotion on each other, held hands, and embraced. All the while an excited Brenna, in full view of his compliant subjects, clicked away. Then they sat back and waited for the inevitable results. "I don't think," Brenna said, "they were entirely unhappy. I caught them hugging each other."

But Dodi had made one serious miscalculation. He had promised to join Kelly Fisher in Los Angeles on August 4 to celebrate her parents' anniversary. When she finally did get in touch with him, Dodi admitted that he was with Diana on the *Jonikal* but concocted a story about Elton John and George Michael being on board as well. If she did happen to see photographs in the papers sometime in the next few days, Dodi advised Fisher to pay no attention to them.

Back home in London on August 7, Diana squeezed into a slinky blue cocktail dress for a date with Dodi at his lavish eight-room Park Lane apartment. "Did you remember?" she asked her butler, Paul Burrell. "My father's gold cuff links? Have you already wrapped them?"

Without saying a word, Burrell handed the tiny box to her. She slipped it into her evening bag, fastened the clasp, and headed for the door. "Don't wait up," she said.

She stepped out of the elevator and into the Art Deco foyer of Dodi's apartment, stopping to admire his collection of baseball caps that covered an entire wall. The living room was modern, with recessed lighting, low tables, and a bright blue curved sofa that could accommodate a dozen or more. Dominating the room was the Princess of Wales herself—a blow-up of Dodi's favorite Diana portrait by internationally acclaimed French photographer Patrick Demarchelier. Seeing it there on Dodi's wall for the first time, Diana tossed back her head and laughed. In addition, nearly every room was strewn with stuffed animals—another reflection of the sensitive man-child who had so endeared himself to the Princess of Wales.

That evening, a pack of photographers waited at 60 Park Lane for the couple to emerge and head for a restaurant or nightclub. Instead, dinner was brought over from the nearby Dorchester Hotel on silver trays by liveried footmen. After dinner, which they ate while sitting on the floor in front of a wall of book-shelves, she reached into her evening bag, pulled out the tiny wrapped box, and handed it to Dodi.

His face lit up when he opened the gift, and he wasted no time taking the cuff links out of the box and holding them up to the light. "They were my father's," Diana said. "I want you to have them."

She had already given him a gold cigar cutter from Asprey's, the London jeweler, inscribed "With Love from Diana." But Dodi knew how deeply she cared for her father and how much she missed him. The cuff links symbolized a new plateau in their relationship.

When she finally did leave Dodi's apartment at 1 A.M., Diana faced a fusillade of flashbulbs. Diana never stopped smiling, but in the pandemonium, her car rolled over a paparazzo's foot.

The next day, she had resumed her campaign against land mines with a trip to war-ravaged Bosnia. She sat down with a volleyball team made up of paraplegics, hugged children whose legs had been blown off, visited clinics and hospitals, and smiled for the cameras when, as she admitted later, "all I really wanted to do was cry."

Sandra Mott, Diana's host on her three-day tour of Sarajevo and Tuzla, tried to lighten things up by sharing makeup tips and talking about their mutual fondness for the romance novels of Danielle Steel. It was clear to Mott, however, that Diana was "lonely." The Princess's mood would change dramatically when, after each grueling fifteen-hour workday, she called Dodi on her ever-present mobile phone. Then, said Mott, "she laughed and laughed with him." And while she dodged reporters' questions about her new romance, on the plane ride home Diana asked for copies of the British tabloids and devoured every word. Diana was, in the words of a friend, "besotted."

One oddly prophetic story failed to make the papers. On August 9, while vacationing on Majorca, Prince Charles was nearly killed when his Mercedes careened out of control on a twisting mountain road. Somehow a crash was averted at the last second, and Charles, trembling, returned to his hotel.

It is doubtful, had Charles's brush with death ever been reported, that anyone would have noticed. On August 10, Diana stepped off the plane from Bosnia just as the *Sunday Mirror* hit the stands. Splashed across its front page was a color (albeit fuzzy) photograph of Diana and Dodi kissing aboard the *Jonikal*. "Locked in her lover's arms," read the subhead, "the Princess finds happiness at last." Inside there were ten more pages of pictures, and more purple prose. "You only have to look at the sensual body language," read the accompanying *Sunday Mirror* piece, "to know that they have found physical and spiritual fulfillment in each other . . ." The paparazzo who was clearly allowed by his subjects to take the photos found fulfillment of another sort: In the span of five days, "the Kiss" shoot, as it came to be known, had brought him more than $1 million in fees.

With the eyes of the world on her, Diana's only

thoughts were of Dodi. As soon as her plane landed at Heathrow she went straight to her hairdressers. Symonds remembered that Diana was "terribly nervous" about seeing Dodi now that their affair was no longer a secret. "Give it plenty of bounce," she shouted at Symonds. "I need lots of bounce."

Despite the fact that she had conquered many of her own demons, from bulimia to suicidal depression, Diana still did not see herself as beautiful. Far from it. The most glamorous and idealized woman in the world was in fact riddled with self-doubt. "She always asked to look like someone else," Symonds said. In 1994 she asked to have her hair cut in the short style worn by Linda Evangelista. But after lunching with Evangelista, she altered her opinion of the model.

"Linda smoked all during lunch," Diana complained, "and she wasn't anything like I thought she would be."

There was one actress Diana held above all others as the epitome of Hollywood glamour. "She *adored* Sharon Stone," Symonds said, "and asked incessantly how she could have the same look. She was crazy about Stone's 'fabulous' face and her sleek hair."

"If I could be anyone in the world," Diana told Rock and Symonds more than once, "I would be Sharon Stone."

The Princess was not so insecure about her looks that she was willing to undergo plastic surgery, however. When stories began appearing in the tabloid press that she had had her nose done, she turned to her friend Anna Harvey and said, "Honestly, if I'd had my nose done, do you think I would have chosen this one?"

The fact that Dodi was less than movie star handsome clearly did not bother Diana. "Elsa," she told her friend Lady Elsa Bowker, "I adore him. I have never been so happy."

Nevertheless, to the world they seemed the unlikeliest of couples. Dodi was, at five feet nine inches, easily two inches shorter than Diana. And while the press persisted in describing him as "darkly handsome," the balding, unathletic forty-one-year-old was, in the words of a former girlfriend, "more of a teddy bear" than some dashing Arab sheik. Several former lovers even went so far to describe him as "inept" and even "pathetic" in bed.

Not that any of that mattered to Diana. From that first day aboard the *Jonikal,* she recognized in Dodi the lonely, abandoned child that made them kindred spirits. She also told Tess Rock that, among other things, she was carried away "by his exotic accent, the way he says Di-yana, you're so naughty!" Their conversations, Rosa Monckton said, "were full of laughter," and when he left a message on Diana's answering machine, she insisted that her friend listen to it so she could hear "his wonderful voice."

For all her apprehension about the Fayed family, Monckton later admitted that at this time Diana was "happy, enjoying herself, and liked the feeling of having someone who not only so obviously cared for her, but was not afraid to be seen doing so."

From the moment her final divorce decree came through, Diana knew all too well that it would take a special kind of man to pursue a relationship with her. "Who would take me on?" she once complained. "I have so much baggage. Anyone who takes me out has to accept the fact that they will be raked over in the papers. I think I am safer alone."

Still, comparisons between Diana and Dodi and another, similarly mismatched couple were inevitable. Diana drew them herself. "Now I understand," she said, "why Jackie Kennedy married Aristotle Onassis."

Jackie had actually been intrigued with the shy nineteen-year-old from the moment she became engaged to Charles. "Jackie admired Diana at first," said Jackie's half-brother, Jamie Auchincloss. "She saw something of her younger self in the Princess. There were many parallels between the lives of Jackie and Diana. Both women were very young when they were thrust center stage, and despite difficult marriages grew into their roles."

Even before Diana's storybook 1981 wedding, Jackie in her role as an editor at Doubleday had been bombarding all her contacts in London with requests for a meeting. It was not easy for Jackie, who had been rudely rebuffed by both Queen Elizabeth and the Duchess of Windsor when she approached them to do their memoirs in 1976.

Once again, Jackie's request was summarily rejected by Diana's faceless, nameless handlers at Buckingham Palace. It is doubtful that the Princess was ever shown the correspondence from Jackie. As time passed and the soap opera that was Diana's marriage unfolded, Jackie's opinion of the Princess underwent a gradual change from admiration to sympathy to disapproval.

The publication of Andrew Morton's *Diana: Her True Story* marked a turning point in the way Jackie viewed Diana. Early on "Jackie respected Diana for rising to the occasion after her marriage," a publishing colleague said. "She thought Di was beautiful, elegant, charming, very stylish, and a wonderful mother. She did not feel the same way about Fergie. Diana and Jackie also shared the problem of having to cope with powerful, philandering husbands. In their approach to this they differed greatly."

Jackie's longtime friend and designer, Oleg Cassini, said Jackie was turned off by the spectacle of Diana "disemboweling herself in public—Mrs. Kennedy would never have done that. Jackie was of sterner stuff made." Following Diana's ritual "disemboweling," Jackie tried a different angle. Now she turned her attention to Camilla. Still the soul of discretion, Charles's mistress turned down Jackie's $2 million book offer.

Diana later confessed to a friend that, when she learned Jackie had died after a brief battle with non-Hodgkin's lymphoma in May 1994, she broke down. At the desk in her sitting room at Kensington Palace, she wrote letters of condolence to John Jr. and Caroline in which she told them their mother had served as her role model.

Jackie almost certainly would have understood why, at this juncture, Diana turned to someone like Dodi Fayed. He was wildly rich, exotic, worldly, fun, romantic, and slightly dangerous. Certainly he was a refreshing change from the bland Anglo-Saxon aristocrats she had spent a lifetime trying so hard to please. And she shared the philosophy Jackie expressed when a friend of hers warned that by marrying Ari she would fall off her pedestal. "It's better," Jackie replied, "than freezing there."

Dodi met the essential criterion: He was totally devoted to Diana, at her beck and call twenty-four hours a day. "Diana was obsessive," Lady Elsa Bowker said. "She wanted the person who loved her to abandon *everything* for her. Very few people are willing to do that." Concurred Monckton: "It is absolutely true that she had found happiness with him. But it was more the fact of having someone there for her twenty-four hours a day. She was unused to this and rather relished it. She was so emotionally insecure that in all her relationships she demanded constant reassurance."

Even so, not everything about Dodi was to Diana's liking. Diana became "truly angry," Monckton said, when Dodi would call with an inventory of the gifts he had purchased for her. "That's not what I want, Rosa," she said. "It makes me uneasy. I don't want to be bought. I have everything I want. I just want someone to be there for me, to make me feel safe and secure . . ."

On August 21, Dodi and Diana boarded an Al Fayed jet and made a quick secret flight to Nice. From there they were whisked by helicopter to Monaco, where they went straight to jeweler Alberto Repossi's shop in the Hotel Hermitage on Place Beaumarchais. Repossi, who advertised his wares in the lobby of the Paris Ritz and had a store on the Place Vendôme, was appointed purveyor to HRH Prince Rainier after he created inscribed gold ID bracelets for the three children of Princess Caroline and Stefano Casiraghi.

Diana sat down and thumbed through the Repossi catalogue until she came to a ring with tiny triangles of diamonds that was part of the jeweler's new "Tell Me Yes" collection. "That's the one I want," she said.

According to Repossi, "Diana seemed to like the young, modern, simple look of our creations, which contrasted with the retro look of her 'royal' jewelry." Despite her early enthusiasm for the ring she saw in the catalogue, Diana asked to put off buying the ring for a few days. She needed time to think.

Things were moving swiftly now. Wanting to know what the future held for her, Diana began searching for answers outside her small circle of friends and advisors. On the advice of her friend Nelson Mandela, she contacted seventy-five-year-old Zulu witch doctor Credo Mutwa, one of South Africa's most respected faith healers and spiritualists.

"I was stunned when I got the call," said the three-hundred-pound Credo, who lives on the Shamwari Game Preserve near Port Elizabeth. "But the more I listened, the more I realized she needed help." At Diana's urging, the witch doctor cast the ancient bones of leopards, lions, and elephants that had been handed down to him from Shaka, the Zulu warrior king.

"What I saw in the bones for her was both wonderful and terrifying," said Credo, who called Diana "Little Sister" when they spoke. "It scared the stuffing out of me," he went on. Credo saw that Diana and Dodi would marry and then leave Britain. "But one of the bones that came up was a 'battleax' that showed a terrible weapon of destruction was poised upon her.

"I saw she would die a terrible death before her happiness would be fulfilled," Credo said. "But I could not tell her. How could I?"

On August 12, a helicopter with Harrods' distinctive green and beige markings set down in a field near the Derbyshire home of psychic Rita Rogers 160 miles outside London. It was the first time Diana had taken any of the men in her life to meet her trusted advisor and friend. With her black bouffant hairdo, heavy makeup and haphazard grammar, the decidedly working-class Rogers seemed an unlikely *éminence grise* for the Princess of Wales. "It took me a year to gain her trust," Rogers later said. "Diana did not need a clairvoyant or a psychic to rule her. She was a very courageous lady in charge of her own life."

But Diana also wanted to know what lay in store for Dodi. They sat down in Rogers's small reading room—the spirit-filled site of all her "readings"— surrounded by photographs of dead children the psychic claimed to have contacted in the afterlife. It was then, according to Rogers, that Dodi's dead mother, Samira, came to her with a message for her son.

"Dodi's mother warned him," Rogers said, "not to go driving in Paris. I saw a tunnel, motorcycles, there was this tremendous sense of speed. It troubled me, and I told him his mother was very concerned for him." And Diana? "The reading was for Dodi, not Diana. I didn't know that she was going to be in Paris with him. I would have warned her as well, but I just didn't see her in the car . . ."

Unfazed by Rogers's grim warning via the ghost of Samira Al Fayed, the couple spent the next two days together in London. With Rees-Jones's help, they were able to elude the small army of reporters who now camped outside 60 Park Lane and sneak away to Harry's Bar, a favorite hangout.

"I got the feeling they had nothing to hide," Rees-Jones said, "and didn't really care." For the most part, Diana did appear to enjoy the media attention. She had, after all, been the one to leak news of the affair in the first place. But Dodi, while far more relaxed about the loss of his privacy than his predecessor Hasnat Khan, occasionally felt the need to flee their camera-wielding pursuers.

"It was quite satisfying giving the press the slip if the boss wanted to," Rees-Jones said. "Dodi would suggest what he wanted to do and if we thought it was totally wrong we would say so.

"But by the end," Rees-Jones added, "it was usually a case of 'get them in the car and GO!' They were both pretty cool about it . . ."

★　★　★

On August 14, while Diana prepared to leave on her Aegean cruise with Rosa Monckton, Kelly Fisher held a tearful press conference announcing her intention to sue Dodi for $440,000, claiming breach of contract. Fisher claimed in the suit that she had given up 90 percent of her lucrative $4,500-a-day modeling career after Dodi promised to pay her $500,000 in two installments before they headed for the altar.

With high-profile feminist lawyer Gloria Allred at her side, Fisher held up the first installment—a $200,000 check that bounced. Thus far, the lawsuit claimed, Fisher had been paid only a "meager" $60,000 in exchange for her "companionship." To prove that they were indeed formally engaged, Fisher flashed her $233,000 diamond and sapphire engagement ring for the cameras. "YOU DODI RAT," screamed London's *Daily Star*.

Dodi never responded publicly to Fisher's charges, but he did deny to members of the Fayed inner circle that he had ever proposed marriage to Fisher. The fact remained, however, that in addition to spending the previous Christmas holidays with her, Dodi had showered Fisher with expensive gifts. These included two Cartier watches, several necklaces and bracelets, and—most significantly—two rings that had belonged to his late mother.

Fisher had only learned of Dodi's affair with the Princess when it hit the tabloids four days earlier. Unbeknownst to Diana, while she and Dodi were conferring with Rita Rogers and sipping champagne in Dodi's Park Lane flat, Dodi's jilted fiancée was peppering Fayed's office with frantic phone calls—only to be rebuffed at every turn.

The final straw came when Fisher read that Dodi was planning on moving with Diana into his newly acquired Malibu mansion—the house he and Fisher had picked out together. "Kelly learned about Mr. Fayed's betrayal not from him, but from 'the Kiss' photo," Allred declared. "It caused her utter dismay, shock, and shame. Mr. Fayed needs to take responsibility for the woman he left at the altar and treated with such total disrespect." Allred went on to say that Fisher was "going public with this because we care about Princess Diana and her future. We would like the Princess, who has suffered greatly in her past, to know of Miss Fisher's experiences with Mr. Fayed so she can make an informed decision regarding her future and that of her children."

Within days, Dodi's jilted fiancée was telling her story in the tabloids. DODI WANTED TO BED ME AND DIANA blared the *News of the World* headline. In the pages of the *Sun,* she took a gratuitous swipe at his masculinity. Dodi was so inept sexually, she claimed, that after they made love she would be thinking "Is that it?"

One by one, Dodi's past lovers stepped forward to

air their grievances. "Dodi seduced me when I was sixteen," claimed actress Traci Lind, who was starring in the television soap opera *Ryan's Hope* when she first encountered Fayed in New York. Lind described Dodi as "insanely jealous," and went on to accuse him of striking her and trying to choke her when she threatened to leave him. "He locked the door of the bedroom and pulled out a 9-mm Beretta and waved it at me. I told myself he won't shoot me in the back, and I wrenched open the door and ran out."

Polo player Broderick Munro-Wilson, a friend of Charles's, branded Dodi a "serial womanizer" who stole his girlfriend. "The poor princess may think she's in love," he warned, "but it's going to be Beauty and the Beast without a fairy tale ending. He'll break her heart."

For the first time, Diana began to harbor doubts about the man to whom she had so impetuously given her heart. "Tess, do you think he's cheating?" Diana asked Rock. "Dodi told me he would never lie to me. But then everyone lies to me all the time."

"Be easy on yourself," Tess answered as she worked on Diana's hair. "Don't listen to what everyone else is saying about Dodi. The important thing is, does he make you happy?"

"Yes," she replied without hesitating.

"In that case," Rock said, "he's got to be good for you. Look, Dodi is young, free, and single—and he adores you. You've got to make your own judgments about him."

"Yes." Diana nodded as she studied her reflection. "You're right."

Determined not to have her romance derailed by the lurid revelations in the tabloids, Diana made the conscious decision to stick with Dodi. "She truly believed," Rock said, "he was as besotted by her as she was by him."

Perhaps. But he did not bother to tell Diana that, while she was traipsing through the Greek isles with Monckton, he had flown to Los Angeles to defuse the Kelly Fisher issue. Photographers swarmed around Dodi as he left his attorney's offices in Century City. "I'm not hiding, I'm not hiding," he insisted as he turned away and sprinted toward his waiting car. Unable to face the press alone, he boarded a private jet and flew back to Diana's side. "People think he was protecting her," said a friend. "It was the other way around. Diana was much, much stronger than Dodi."

She was a magician when it came to molding her own image, fashioning her own mystique. "They keep saying I'm manipulative," she told a friend, "but what is the alternative? To just sit there and have them make your image for you?" But there were moments when even Diana, named for the Greek goddess of the hunt, was overwhelmed. "It's a hunt, Rosa, it's a hunt," she told Monckton, keeping an eye out for paparazzi as they cruised the Greek islands. "Will you really tell people what it is like?"

Diana sought comfort in the sound of Dodi's voice, phoning him from the Greek isles two or more times day. She also called William and Harry regularly at Balmoral, the Scottish castle where the royals always spent their summer holiday. One night she managed to get through to the Balmoral switchboard, only to be told the young princes were out.

Hanging up the phone, Diana, who had a gift for mimicry, arched her eyebrows and sighed. "This," the Princess said, "is what she will be saying now." With that Diana, whose repertoire included imitations of Nelson Mandela, Bill Clinton, and most notably the Queen, launched into a flawless imitation of the operator's Scottish accent. "Och, there goes the Princess of Wales on yet another sunshine cruise."

William and Harry were never far from her thoughts; Monckton recalled that Diana "talked to me constantly about their sons, about her concern to protect them from their position . . . not to be isolated and to be able to live a balanced life." One day they docked at a Greek village called Kipazissi and went to the Greek Orthodox Church. There they lit candles for their children. "Oh, Rosa," she said, turning to Monckton, "I do so love my boys."

There was universal agreement, even among her enemies at "Buckhouse," as Buckingham Palace was called, that Diana was a singularly devoted mother. Now she spoke of having more children. "I've always wanted a little girl," she wistfully told Monckton.

Contrary to later speculation, Diana was not pregnant with Dodi's child—a fact she went out of her way to make abundantly clear to Monckton at the time. The two women were close enough to share even the most intimate details about their bodies, and Diana let it be known that they had embarked on their cruise just as her period began. This was ten days before her last, fatal trip to Paris. Therefore, Monckton would later state unequivocally, "I know that it would have been biologically impossible for her to have been pregnant at the time of the crash."

On August 20, Diana returned to London from Greece and dined with Dodi that night. The next morning she summoned her hairdresser to Kensington Palace. Tess Rock was escorted upstairs by Diana's personal maid, Angela Benjamin, one of the Princess's household staff of six. That evening, Diana was to embark with Dodi on yet another Mediterranean cruise. According to Rock, Diana was "wildly impatient" to leave with Dodi. "She asked me to take special care of her hair, because she wanted to be beautiful for him. Her tanned skin accentuated her eyes, sparkling with excitement and even bluer than usual."

"I think this is it," Diana said. "He's the one!"

Benjamin and the other members of Diana's six-person staff were largely convinced that Diana was about to marry Dodi, move abroad, and begin a new life—perhaps in California. What they did not know was that Diana was actually giving serious thought to embarking on a whole new career.

A year earlier, the Duchess of York had encountered Kevin Costner on a trip to China. When Fergie mentioned that his 1992 film *The Bodyguard* was a particular favorite of her sister-in-law's—Diana had bought the video and screened it repeatedly—Costner mentioned that he was doing a sequel.

"You and Diana would make wonderful lovers on screen," Fergie said. "Why don't you ask her? I'll bet she'd do it."

Fergie later told Diana about her chat with Costner, and the Princess promptly phoned him in Los Angeles. It quickly became clear to Costner that Diana identified with the lonely, hunted pop diva played by Whitney Houston in the original. Costner, in the title role, was totally committed to protecting the star. "Diana longed," said Diana's friend Lady Elsa Bowker, "for someone like that in her own life."

With the backing of Warner Bros., Costner offered Diana the lead role in *The Bodyguard II*. Set in Hong Kong, the film was to deal with a princess who falls in love with her bodyguard after he rescues her from a kidnapper. Costner later recalled that he and the Princess of Wales "talked on the phone about the level of sophistication and dignity that the part would have. It would be tailored for her."

Diana laughed. "Look," she said, "my life is maybe going to become my own at some point. Go ahead and do this script and when it's ready I'll be in a really good spot."

"When I come to you with the script, I'm going to try to be hard to resist," Costner replied. "I'll tell you truthfully this is going to be good or I wouldn't be doing it." Recalled Costner, "She laughed at that."

Costner believed his offer came at a pivotal point in her life. "She wanted to talk," he said. "Her life was complicated. She wanted the right to reinvent herself. But she wanted to be delicate about it."

Toward that end, the project was to remain top secret. Costner's partner, Jim Wilson, set out to craft a role tailor-made for Diana. "We were smart enough to write a role for her that didn't take her beyond her qualifications as an actress," Wilson said. "She very much plays that beautiful princess that she was with the really great political stances that she was taking. It played beautifully into her hand.

"Here's the last person you can fall in love with, and she you, but you know that happens in this world," Wilson added. "So there was definitely a love thing going on between the bodyguard and the princess."

The "love thing," as it turned out, was reportedly to include both a nude scene for Diana and a steamy scene with Diana and Costner in bed. In the original screen treatment Costner, as the bodyguard, is on his routine security check when he sees the master bedroom's door is open. He walks in and, without warning, Diana's character appears out of the shower. "She stands transfixed, just for a few seconds," the treatment reportedly reads, "before she reaches for her robe."

Later, when the Princess's philandering husband is out of town, the bodyguard hears an odd sound and goes to investigate. "Her bed is empty," the treatment reportedly reads. "He hears a noise and spins around" to see the Princess. "Without speaking, he moves toward her and reaches for her. His fingers open the silk buttons one by one . . ."

There was an added inducement for taking on the acting assignment. Diana was to be paid $10 million to co-star with Costner in *The Bodyguard* sequel—money she planned to pour into her favorite charities.

Sadly, the second draft of the script landed on Costner's desk on August 29, just three days before Diana's death. He did not get around to reading it, however, until the day after the crash. "I picked it up and the first thirty pages were totally her," Costner said. "It was dignified, sexy, smart, funny—and I couldn't finish. I stopped. It broke my heart."

As she got ready to leave with Dodi for a third and final time, Diana complained about speculation in the press that she was about to wed. Someone handed her a copy of that week's *People* magazine. Diana and Dodi were pictured on the cover, along with the headline A GUY FOR DI: *In her first real post-Charles romance, Diana takes up with a controversial playboy. Is he a dreamboat—or a deadbeat?*

"Why are they so persistent?" Diana demanded. "They already have me married." She was not, she insisted on several occasions, particularly eager to take the plunge. "I haven't taken such a long time to get out of one poor marriage to get into another," she told society columnist Taki Theodoracopulous. Yet Diana knew she and Dodi were at a crossroads in their relationship. "I know I shall have to decide this week," she told Rock. "I know he's about to pop the question."

Rock cautioned the Princess not to rush into anything. "Don't do anything stupid," she said.

"Don't worry," Diana replied. "I won't do anything stupid."

She was, however, as willful as ever. "No one can tell me how to behave," she told a French journalist that fateful summer. "I work by instinct. That's my best advisor."

At the time, Rock was left with the impression that Diana and Dodi would eventually wed. But Rock's partner disagreed. "Diana had many plans for the future," Symonds said, "but marriage wasn't one of them."

Remarking on the rumors that swirled around Diana, Angela Benjamin told Rock, "Perhaps you're seeing the Princess for the very last time." Those words would haunt Rock for the rest of her life. Because it was.

On August 21 Diana and Dodi flew to Nice and boarded the *Jonikal*. This time they saw no need to keep up appearances, and shared the same stateroom. Dodi gave Diana a small silver plaque with a "love poem" he told her he had written:

As if . . .
I have tried many things, music and cities,
the stars in their constellations and the sea—
When I am not with you I am alone,
for there is no one else,
and there is nothing that comforts me but you.

Diana was, said the *Jonikal's* Debbie Gribble, "very, very touched." But Dodi had not written the poem. In fact, the silver plaque did not even belong to him. When he was dating Tina Sinatra during the

1980s, he noticed the plaque in Tina's living room—a wedding gift from her ex-husband, Richard Cohen.

"He loved it," said Sinatra, who lent the plaque to Dodi so he could make a copy. "After four, five, six years," she said, "I knew I was not going to get it back."

Now the Princess and her playboy seemed more determined than ever to clue the public in on the progress of their sizzling romance. Once again, Diana had tipped off a photographer of her choice—this time Mario Brenna's colleague Jason Fraser—as to precisely where they would be and when as they cruised along the French and Italian coasts. Shots ran in the British tabloids of the couple strolling the beach, and of Diana swinging her leg over Dodi's shoulder as they romped on a Jet-Ski.

Their second night out, the *Jonikal* anchored in the harbor at Monaco so that the couple could return to Alberto Repossi's store in the Hotel Hermitage. This time, Repossi wanted to "create something special, outside of the catalogue, improving the quality by, for example, changing the pierced metal setting for one of studs." Dodi and Diana actually asked Repossi to "expand the collection with some bracelets and some pieces that we would have designed together."

The $200,000 bauble Repossi designed especially for Diana, an emerald surrounded by diamonds, was a classic dinner ring. As far as Repossi was concerned, the piece he was designing would not have been appropriate for an engagement ring. Besides, Repossi stated flatly, "At no time did they tell me that it was an engagement ring." Few people had had more experience than Repossi helping couples pick out their engagement rings. Fevered speculation to the contrary, he did not feel Dodi and Diana fit the profile of soon-to-be newlyweds.

It was agreed that on August 30 Repossi would personally deliver the ring to his store across from the Ritz on the Place Vendôme. That day, a Saturday, Dodi and Diana planned to pick up the ring on their way back to London—and to return to Monaco the following week to confer about the designs for the rest of their collection.

Dodi allegedly called his father from the *Jonikal* to say he was going to propose to Diana, but she apparently viewed the ring only as a symbol of their deepening love. "He's given me a bracelet," she had told Monckton on their Greek escapade. "He's given me a watch. I know that the next thing will be a ring. Rosa," she said with a laugh, "that's going firmly on the fourth finger of my right hand."

Still, Diana took delight in keeping her former in-laws and their handlers at Buckingham Palace on tenterhooks. "They must be going *crazy*," she giggled to a friend. She was right, of course. Ethnic prejudice was still a major factor, but there were other, more legitimate concerns. Dodi brought with him so much baggage, it was argued among the Queen's advisors, he posed a threat to the monarchy itself.

There was, for example, the matter of religion. What were the implications of the Princess of Wales marrying a Muslim, and a Muslim becoming stepfather not only to a future king but also a future head of the Church of England?

Perhaps even more significantly, there was the matter of Mohamed Al Fayed. Diana's prospective father-in-law had already helped bring down one government by confessing that he had bribed several of its leaders in an attempt to gain British citizenship. If the rumors about an impending marriage were true, Al Fayed would be, some British intelligence experts warned, in a position to manipulate the Crown.

Not all the concerns centered on the man who might become a step-grandfather to William and Harry. Dodi, after all, was also a Khashoggi, and his billionaire uncle Adnan had long been a major player in the murky world of Middle Eastern arms deals.

Of course, Diana could have allayed these fears at any time by stating publicly that she had no intention of marrying in the near future. But she preferred to let her nemeses—the "men in gray"—squirm. There was no need to let them know that, for the time being, she was happy enough just being pampered by her new love. "I've been so *spoiled* by him," she had told Lady Elsa Bowker before she left, "so taken care of. These are the things I never, never had."

The *Jonikal* dropped anchor off the picturesque Italian resort of Portofino, the setting for one of the Princess's favorite films, *Enchanted April*. The next morning papers around the world carried photographs of Diana and Dodi lazing in the sun. One afternoon Diana walked out to the end of the long diving platform that jutted out from the *Jonikal* and sat. For thirty uninterrupted minutes, she dangled her feet and, undoubtedly, contemplated her future. A photograph of this rare solitary moment, Mohamed Al Fayed's favorite shot of the Princess, would later hang in his office.

At the same moment, psychic Edward Williams was also alone with his thoughts as he hiked in the hills behind his home in the Welsh town of Mountain Ash, Mid Glamorgan. It was then that Williams, who had predicted the assassination attempts on President Ronald Reagan and Pope John Paul II, was stopped in his tracks.

"When the vision struck me," he later recalled, "it was as if everything around me was obscured and replaced by shadowy figures. In the middle was the face of Princess Diana. Her expression was sad and full of pathos. She was wearing what looked like a floral dress with a short dark cardigan. But it was vague. I went cold with fear and knew it was a sign that she was in danger."

The seventy-three-year-old grandfather was trembling as he told his wife, Mary, about the eerie premonition. "I have never seen him so upset," she said. "He felt he was given a sign and when he came back from his walk he was deeply shaken."

Williams had still not decided what action to take when, on August 26, Lady Elsa Bowker's phone rang in London. "Hello, Elsa?" boomed the voice on the other end.

"Yes, who is this?" Lady Elsa answered.

"Elsa, you don't recognize me? It's Diana!"

Her old friend was stunned. "My God, what did you do to your voice? It's so *strong.*"

"I'm so strong now, Elsa," Diana explained. "I fear nothing. *I fear nothing.*"

The next day, Rosa Monckton called her friend on the yacht. "Yes, bliss. Bye-bye" were the last words Diana would ever say to her.

A thousand miles away, Edward Williams walked into the South Wales police station in Mountain Ash and told the police about his premonition. The officer took Williams seriously enough to file an incident report and pass it along to officers of the department's Special Branch investigative unit. The police log for that day contained the following entry:

On the 27th August, at 14:12 hrs, a man by the name of Edward Williams came to Mountain Ash police station. He said he was a psychic and predicted that Princess Diana was going to die.

In previous years he has predicted that the Pope and Ronald Reagan were going to be the victims of assassination attempts. On both occasions he was proved to be correct.

Mr. Williams appeared to be quite normal.

"I felt I had to do something," Williams said. "An officer I spoke to could have treated me as the local nutter but he was very understanding. I felt better that I had got it off my chest, but the feeling that Diana was in danger didn't leave me . . ."

On August 28, a Thursday, the *Jonikal* dropped anchor off the lushly beautiful Costa Smeralda, Sardinia's Emerald Coast. That night, before feasting on caviar and lobster, Diana raised her champagne glass and toasted her freedom. It was the first anniversary of her divorce.

The next morning the couple took the yacht's launch into the village of Porto Cervo, returning hours later loaded down with dozens of cashmere sweaters. "When Diana said she liked one," Gribble said, "Dodi bought her every color they had in stock . . . She only had to look at a thing and he'd get it."

Lounging on the deck of the *Jonikal* that afternoon

in an aquamarine one-piece bathing suit, Diana spoke by phone with Mohamed Al Fayed between sips of iced Perrier. Harry was going to turn thirteen on September 15. As soon as she returned to London, she told Dodi's father, she had to do some serious shopping at Harrods for birthday presents.

Diana's blissful time with Dodi was once again about to be cut short by the very press they had so zealously courted. That Friday evening they commandeered the launch once again, this time pulling into a beach, where Diana took a dip before they went on to the Cala di Volpe Hotel for a drink. Within minutes they were descended upon by a dozen Italian photographers, forcing them to beat a hasty retreat back to the *Jonikal*. Things came to a head when a scuffle broke out between three paparazzi and several members of the *Jonikal*'s crew.

It was time to go. They decided to abandon ship the next day, board Dodi's private jet, and stop off in Paris on their way back to London.

As far as Diana was concerned, it was just as well. She had been separated from her boys for over a month now, and getting through to them at Balmoral had grown increasingly difficult. Nearly every time she called the castle, the switchboard operator replied in the same thick Scottish brogue that William and Harry were "oot."

"Out killing something," Diana would say wryly to Rosa Monckton as she hung up the phone. But then Diana would become irritated at being portrayed as someone who did not share in the rest of the royals' passion for the outdoors. "After all, I was brought up in that way," she would say. "I hunted when I was young. And it is all part of their heritage." But, she added wistfully, "I do miss them so."

It's worse than sexual abuse.

> —*Diana* on being
> hunted by the
> paparazzi

She is kind, generous, sad and, in some ways, rather desperate. A very shrewd but immensely sorrowful lady.

> —*Carolyn Bartholomew,*
> friend

Duch, how on earth have you survived all these years?

> —*Fergie* to Diana

4

Harry swung the shotgun up, buried the stock in the hollow of his shoulder, squinted through the sight, and squeezed the trigger. The crackle of gunfire rippled down one side of the valley and back up the other. Lowering the barrel, the young Prince rubbed his bruised shoulder as he watched his intended victim—a red grouse—soar to freedom. "Maybe it's your vision," Prince William chided his little brother as they trudged ahead. "Really, have you thought of having your eyes examined?" Wills went on to point out, as he would several times that day, that when he was twelve—Harry's age—he shot fifteen pheasants in a single morning.

Harry had yet to be "blooded"—a rite of passage William had gone through ten months earlier, in October 1996. It was then that fourteen-year-old William shot his first stag and then had his face daubed with the deer's blood by hunting guides. At the time animal rights activists were up in arms, but not William's mother. Diana had also been blooded when she shot her first stag—at thirteen.

The sight of the two princes tromping along the moors with their rifles at the ready would have been utterly familiar to the boys' great-great-great-grandmother Queen Victoria. For, even as their mother plied the warm waters of the Mediterranean with her rich Egyptian boyfriend that summer, Wills and Harry were spending their summer the way generations of royals had before them—amid the rustic splendors of Balmoral.

Victoria and Albert lost their hearts to what Victoria called "this dear Paradise" when they first visited it, and bought the old castle on the banks of the River Dee in 1852 for $50,000. The building quickly proved too cramped for the royal household, so Albert replaced it with a baronial granite mansion the following year.

The Dee River Valley, with its emerald lawns, dark pine forests, glistening groves of silver birch trees, and endless purple savannas of heather, seemed no less a magical place to its current inhabitants. Adding to Balmoral's storybook quality was Riverside Walk, a path along the banks of the Dee punctuated by a series of miniature white suspension bridges.

Over the entire region loomed Lochnagar, with its

eleven peaks soaring over three thousand feet—sentinels mirrored in the dark waters of Loch Muick to the south. The Dee River Valley inspired Lord Byron to write:

England! thy beauties are tame and domestic
To one who has roved o'er the mountains afar;
Oh, for the crags that are wild and majestic!
The steep frowning glories of dark Lochnagar.

The castle itself had changed little since the days of Victoria and Albert. Everything that could be was covered in tartan plaid—linens, curtains, carpets, even the kitchen linoleum and the china. Large oil paintings of Highland scenes hung throughout the castle, occasionally interspersed with portraits of dour-faced Scots who figured in the history of Balmoral. Nowhere, however, was there a sign of John Brown, the servant whose close friendship with Victoria led to rumors of an affair. The statute of Brown she had commissioned after his death was removed from its prominent place by George V and relegated to a remote spot somewhere deep in the woods.

And of course there were antlers everywhere— jutting out above fireplace mantels and over stairways—symbols of the blood sports the royals so loved. "Everywhere you look," said one guest, "dead stags are staring at you."

There are few places in the realm where wildlife is so abundant. A few species here, such as golden eagles and peregrine falcons, are protected. But for the most part, everything at Balmoral is fair game: deer, rabbits, pine martens, polecats, and wildcats—not to mention game birds such as grouse, duck, and pheasant.

Queen Elizabeth was seventeen when, in October 1942, she shot her first stag at Balmoral, using a rifle she had been taught to handle the previous year. She also learned to fish the local lochs and streams that teemed with salmon, pike, and trout.

Although used by the Royal Family only about ten weeks a year—the longest stretch being from the official start of grouse season on August 12 (the "Glorious Twelfth") until early October—Balmoral always marked the beginning and the end of the Court calendar.

Much of their schedule at Balmoral, in fact, was devoted to hunting grouse on the moors from sunup to dusk. The all-day shooting parties tended to resemble a military maneuver—a small caravan of Land Rovers crisscrossing the moors, meeting up at various points with platoons of "loaders" who made certain they never ran out of ammunition and "beaters" to flush out their quarry. There were picnic lunches and barbecues in the field, at which the invariably all-male shooting party might be joined by one of the ladies of the Court. The Queen always nursed a gin and tonic before lunch, whether dining inside or al fresco. "They don't mind serving themselves," observed Prince Charles's valet Stephen Barry. "They don't even mind cooking. But"—in stark contrast to Diana—"clearing up is out."

Inside the castle, tea is a feast of cakes, sandwiches, biscuits, and pâtés. Elizabeth herself periodically refilled the pot from a giant silver kettle. Dinner, always precisely at 8:30, is served from silver salvers by liveried footmen in red waistcoats with shiny brass buttons.

But all the royals—the Queen and Charles in particular—were happiest slogging through plowed fields in their Wellingtons, trailed by Labradors, corgis, Irish setters, and golden retrievers. It was not unusual for a guest to come upon the monarch, a kerchief tied over her graying head, standing over a butcher's block cutting up meat for her dogs.

Her Majesty needed the rest. Even here, she spent hours on paperwork—forced to attend to the infamous "boxes" that followed her everywhere. Blue boxes from the Foreign Office are filled with dispatches designed to keep the monarch apprised of government affairs. The other boxes are red and deal with her upcoming schedule—from tours of hospitals, ribbon-cuttings, and wreath-layings to state visits.

Hewing, as always, to tradition, Elizabeth also fulfilled her obligation as hostess. The social highlights of the Balmoral season were the two Ghillies Balls given by the Queen to thank her estate workers and the locals. Her Majesty, the Queen Mother, Princess Margaret, Princess Anne, and the other royal ladies all wore their Stuart sashes and tiaras.

A detachment from one of the Scottish regiments is sent to guard the Queen each summer. By way of expressing her gratitude, the sovereign made a point of dancing with as many of the soldiers as possible.

Wills and Harry, like their father and their grandfather Prince Philip and all the other Windsor men, wore their tartans and kilts to these affairs. And like the other Windsor men, they were put through their paces—literally—learning Scottish steps such as the Highland Fling.

Diana remembered, as she rather bluntly put it, "shitting bricks" over the prospect of her indoctrination into the lifestyle at Balmoral. But during her early courtship with Charles she seemed to fit right in. One of her favorite pastimes was stalking game in the wild. "We went stalking together," recalled another guest, Patty Palmer-Tomkinson. "We got hot, we got tired, and she fell into a bog, she got covered in mud, laughed her head off, hair glued to her forehead because it was pouring with rain . . . she was a sort of wonderful English schoolgirl who was game for anything . . ."

That all changed after the marriage. They were

ending up their honeymoon at Balmoral when it dawned on Diana that Charles had no intention of ever giving up Camilla. Consequently, Diana would suffer her worst attacks of bulimia whenever she was at Balmoral.

Still, she railed against "this myth that I hate Balmoral. I love Scotland, but just the atmosphere drains me to nothing . . . they just suck me dry, because I tune into all their moods, and boy, are there some undercurrents there! Instead of having a holiday, it's the most stressful time of the year."

The Duchess of York eventually came to share her sister-in-law's ambivalence toward Balmoral and all it represented. But not in the beginning. Diana had just begun her courtship with Charles when the brash redhead "suddenly appeared out of nowhere." Undaunted by the royals, Sarah Ferguson chatted happily with the Queen over lunch at Buckingham Palace and wangled a front-row seat at Diana's wedding.

Soon Fergie, who married Prince Andrew at Westminster Abbey in July 1986, was a favorite of all the Windsors. "I wish you could be like Fergie—all jolly," Charles told his wife. "Why are you always so miserable?"

Already painfully insecure, Diana felt threatened by the zaftig, game-for-anything young woman who did not even seem to mind being ridiculed in the press as the "Duchess of Pork." Outwardly, they behaved like naughty schoolchildren—pushing each other on the ski slopes while an obviously irritated Charles muttered something about "small minds," staging pillow fights, using their rolled umbrellas at Ascot to poke their friends in the backside. "Oh," Fergie later said of this period, "Diana and I were the Thelma and Louise of Buckingham Palace."

In truth, both women would later concede that they were jealous of each other. Sarah felt overshadowed by the glamorous (and reed-thin) Princess of Wales, while Diana was trying desperately to loosen up and become, as Charles put it, "jolly."

Their insecurities could be traced to eerily similar childhoods. Like Frances Shand Kydd, Fergie's mother left her father for another man, remarried, and lost custody of her children. Earl Spencer may have been disappointed that Diana was not a boy, but Fergie's father brought her up as "a tough, strong tomboy." Never allowed to be in touch with what she later called her "feminine self," the Duchess of York concealed her self-doubt beneath layers of bravado.

Fergie, while never suffering from an eating disorder on the magnitude of Diana's, did overeat as compensation for the maternal love she was deprived of as a child. When her mother left, Fergie said, "I became a compulsive eater because of the comfort I needed. I see symptoms of it now. When I have that hole in my heart, I want to eat." (There was another curious link between the two women. Even before Sarah Ferguson married Prince Charles's brother, she and Diana were related by marriage. Fergie's cousin is Sir Robert Fellowes, Lady Jane Spencer's husband and Diana's nemesis at the Palace. Often scolded by Fellowes herself, Fergie referred to her cousin derisively as "Bellows.")

Nevertheless, Fergie seemed right at home at Balmoral; on her first trip she went horseback riding with her mother-in-law the Queen, and went out of her way to win over the Queen Mother by spending several afternoons with her. She was instantly embraced by the Windsors as a welcome breath of fresh air—a breezy antidote to the moody, feckless Diana. "She left me," Diana said, "looking like dirt."

The energetic newcomer could not comprehend what it was that made the Princess of Wales so profoundly, deeply unhappy. "You mustn't worry, Duch," she would tell Diana, "everything is going to be fine."

But things were not going to be fine—least of all for Fergie. Diana watched as criticism of her friend's weight, her clothes, her spending, her raucous behavior, and her mothering skills gradually eroded Fergie's confidence.

The Royal Family had obviously changed its mind about Fergie by the time the Windsors gathered at

Balmoral in August 1991. The Duchess was reprimanded after an episode in which Diana, behind the wheel of a Land Rover, and Sarah, driving the Queen Mother's Daimler, raced each other along the private roads of the estate. Angry at being chastised, Fergie stormed off—leaving Diana to plead with the Queen to give the freewheeling Fergie "room to breathe."

The following January, Prince Andrew and the Duchess of York separated after photographs were published in the tabloids showing Fergie romping in the south of France with Texas oil scion Steve Wyatt. That August 1992 there were even more fireworks when, as the family gathered at Balmoral, photographs were published of a topless Fergie having her toes sucked by yet *another* American. This time the object of her extramarital affection was John Bryan, her so-called financial advisor. Shown the compromising photographs splashed all over the *Daily Mirror,* the Queen summoned Fergie to her study and flew into a rage.

Fergie sat in her usual spot next to Andrew at meals for the next three days ("What do you all do? We all had to come down to breakfast anyway," said Princess Margaret with a shrug.) At holiday's end, the Duchess of York was banished from Balmoral and the bosom of the Royal Family. Forever.

For Wills and Harry, summers at Balmoral were a happy family time—a blur of sun-drenched days spent riding, hunting, and fishing with their father. They also watched videos together and read Kipling together. For as awkwardly stiff as he may have been in public, the private Charles was an affectionate, warm, tactile father who bathed his sons when they were young and continued to hug and kiss them as adolescents. These qualities seemed especially in evidence at Balmoral, away from the byzantine intrigues of Buckingham Palace. It is here, after all, where a sign at the entrance to the drive reads:

SLOW: BEWARE HORSES, DOGS,
AND CHILDREN.

As far as the grandchildren were concerned, things were far less austere than they had been when Charles was a boy. Instead of being forced to bathe in the bone-chilling burns, Wills and Harry were permitted to swim at the local swimming pool or take in a movie at the local theater—so long as the film was deemed suitable for them by the Queen.

To be sure, the boys missed their mother during this time. But they did not miss the pitched battles and bitter scenes that characterized much of their parents' marriage. Many of the worst moments had, in fact, occurred during the family gatherings at Balmoral. In those increasingly rare instances when the

Prince and Princess of Wales were together on family holidays, raised voices and sarcastic asides were the order of the day.

Early on, Wills assumed the role of comforter, stuffing tissues under his mother's door when he heard her crying after a fight with Charles. Soon, his royal bearing was evident. At Diana's first Christmas party after her separation from the Prince, William, then eleven, delivered a polished speech to hundreds of guests. "Sometimes," she would say of her son, "he sounds like a thirty-year-old."

That may well have been because, while she took them to amusement parks and fast-food joints, Diana also exposed them to the less frivolous side of life. "I want them to lead from the heart," she explained, "not the head."

In an effort to make them aware that their world of palaces and kowtowing servants was beyond imagining for most people, she took both boys to homeless shelters, hospitals, and soup kitchens. "I want them to have an understanding of people's emotions, people's insecurities, people's distress and people's hopes and dreams . . . I've taken William and Harry to people dying of AIDS, albeit I told them it was cancer.

"I've taken the children to all sorts of areas where I'm not sure anyone of this family has been before, and they have a knowledge. They may never use it, but the seed is there, and I hope it will grow because knowledge is power."

Diana also made sure that, in their everyday dealings, her sons never failed to express their gratitude to others and never complained. "If someone brought them orange juice when what they really wanted was a Coke," said a friend, "they were instructed to say thank you and drink the orange juice."

When Harry politely asked for something other than what he'd been given, Diana scolded him. "She told him it didn't matter what it was he had wanted; he should simply have thanked the person for what he'd been given," Monckton said. It was that sort of behavior, Diana told him, "that gave the Royal Family a bad name for being difficult." At Disney World and McDonald's, she made them wait in line like everybody else.

At home Diana, like any mother of adolescents, was often correcting their manners. One afternoon she noticed that Harry had left a pile of laundry on a chair. "Oh, Harry, pick up your laundry," she said.

"Don't say 'Oh, Harry,' " he shot back.

Fifteen minutes later, the laundry was still there. "Oh, Harry, I told you to pick it up," Diana snapped.

"It seems to me," Harry replied in a tone familiar to parents of adolescents everywhere, "I asked you not to say 'Oh, Harry.' " Before his mother erupted, the impertinent Prince gathered up his laundry and fled.

It was all part of a concerted effort to bring "the heir and the spare," as they were dubbed by the press, into the modern world. Diana harbored no illusions that theirs was going to be an easy road. "I will fight for my children on any level," she declared, "in order for them to be happy and have peace of mind and carry out their duties."

The precise nature of William's duties seemed to elude the young prince when he enrolled at Eton in September 1995. Registering as "William Windsor," the Church of England's future head turned to his father and asked, "What religion?"

Situated on the Thames in Buckinghamshire, 558-year-old Eton College was a far cry from the spartan Scottish boarding school Charles attended. At Gordonstoun, the mostly middle-class students began each day—even when it snowed—with a shirtless run followed by an icy shower. Charles had been mercilessly hazed by fellow Gordonstoun students who felt that befriending him constituted "sucking up."

At Eton, where students stroll around the ivy-covered campus in tails, William's thirteen hundred classmates were hardly likely to resent his presence in their midst. He may have been the only student with a nineteen-member security detail and a portable transmitter, but he was still one of them. For centuries

Eton had been preparing the sons of Europe's wealthiest and most influential families to assume their proper roles on the world stage, prompting George Orwell to observe that history was "decided on the playing fields of Eton."

William flourished there. A superb student with a flair for French and art, the Prince was also a natural athlete who excelled at rugby, sculling, and water polo. As outgoing with his classmates as he was taciturn with the press, William was popular with his peers. Among his closest school chums were Nicholas Knatchbull, a grandson of the late Lord Mountbatten and a distant cousin of William's, rugby teammate Johnny Richards, and Andrew Charlton, whose father owns a bank.

Boys will be boys, however, and every time a new scandal regarding the royals erupted, someone could be counted on to point it out to William. No sooner had an Italian magazine published nude photographs of Charles than someone—presumably Eton upperclassmen—faxed copies to William.

At the school's four-story Manor House, where he was one of fifty boys aged fourteen to eighteen, William slept in a Lilliputian ten-foot-by-seven-foot room—albeit the only one with a private bath and no nameplate on the door. No posters were allowed in the room, but the inside of William's locker was plastered with pictures of the Barbie Twins, *Baywatch*'s

Pamela Anderson, and his favorite pinup, Cindy Crawford. At William's urging, Diana invited Crawford to tea. When his mother stepped out of the room, William confided to the supermodel, "I want Mummy to be happy at all costs."

Already he could understand what it was like to be under constant scrutiny. At his first teenage dance, William took to the floor waving his hands in the air and generally having a good time. But afterward he told his mother, "Lots of girls tried to kiss me but I didn't do anything because the cameras are everywhere."

Notwithstanding the lack of privacy, William's life was much like that of any teenager. His musical tastes were decidedly mainstream, running to chart-topping groups like Oasis and Pulp. His wardrobe, reflecting his mother's taste in clothes, drew heavily on the Gap and Benetton, augmented with a growing collection of baseball caps and designer sneakers.

Like virtually every other member of his generation, he was an avid fan of video games. He also mountain-biked, and for a time held the record at Chelsea's F1 go-cart track. At Balmoral William, who under British law cannot obtain a driver's license until he is seventeen, often took the wheel of his father's Land Rover.

Now that he towered over the heads of nearly all his classmates at six foot one, the handsome blond

Prince possessed a star quality that was evident to all—especially his media-wise mother. She routinely referred to him as "DDG" ("Drop Dead Gorgeous"). Wills's reaction was predictable. "Oh, *Mum,*" he'd object, "don't say that!"

Out of earshot, Diana would rave, "Isn't he superb! And he's so tall too. The girls will be mad for him!"

They already were. When he was still fourteen, the British teen magazine *Smash Hits* included a centerfold pullout of the blue-blazered Prince. Later, the magazine distributed more than 250,000 "I Love Willy" stickers. His fellow Etonians were soon calling him "Dreamboat Willy."

William hated it. Not only did he possess his mother's natural shyness, he blamed the press in part for wrecking his parents' marriage. During a photo opportunity at Balmoral that August 1997, William and Harry clambered across the rocks with their kilt-clad father. Harry beamed obligingly for the cameras, but much of the time William maintained the downcast gaze made famous by his mother. "Look up, sir. Look up!" would become a familiar cry among those photographers assigned to cover the young Prince. It was not going to get better for them anytime soon. William was even less likely to smile once he returned to school in the fall; it was then, at Diana's insistence, he was scheduled to get his first set of braces.

"William is waiting patiently for the monarchy to be abolished," Diana quipped. "It will make life so much easier for him!" Harry was another matter. In the event his brother did not want the job, Harry was more than willing to step in. "I shall be King Harry!" he declared. "I shall do the work."

Yet despite William's hostility toward the press, Diana was convinced he had the makings of a first-rate monarch. "All my hopes are on William now," Diana said. "I try to din it into him all the time about the media—the dangers, and how he must understand and handle it. I think he understands, I'm hoping he'll grow up to be as smart about it as John Kennedy Jr. I want William to be able to handle things as well as John does."

Toward that end, Diana made sure William was kept apprised of developments from an early age. "She told Prince William in particular more things than most mothers would have told their children," Monckton said. "But she had no choice. She wanted them to hear the truth from her, about her life, and the people she was seeing, and what they meant to her, rather than read a distorted, exaggerated, and frequently untrue version in the tabloid press."

William and Harry had both resolutely refused to take sides in the divorce. To their parents' credit, neither Charles nor Diana pressured them to. Even though his mother had warned him the day before it aired about her bombshell 1995 BBC television inter-view, William was upset by it. And while they knew about their father's affair with Camilla, neither boy had ever discussed her with Charles or had ever even met her.

There were people to turn to outside the family. William's housemaster at Eton, Andrew Gailey, lent a sympathetic ear, as did his wife, Shauna, something of a mother figure to all fifty boys at Manor House. At Ludgrove, Janet Barber, wife of Headmaster Gerald Barber, was a similarly nurturing figure in Harry's life.

Both Princes could always rely on Alexandra "Tiggy" Legge-Bourke, the attractive, fun-loving thirty-year-old nanny hired by Charles to look after them after the separation from Diana. "Both boys adored Tiggy, and she was devoted to them," said a friend of Legge-Bourke's. "She was more like an older sister or a cousin. They teased her and she gave back as good as she got. She brought stability to their world, but she also made them laugh. They needed that."

Diana did not count herself among Tiggy's admir-ers. She grew increasingly resentful when Tiggy hugged William in public and called the Princes "my babies." After Diana complained, Charles instructed the nanny to lower her profile. But when William was confirmed at St. George's Chapel in Windsor on

March 9, 1997, Tiggy sought revenge by drafting a guest list that snubbed Diana's side of the family. By the end of the month, Tiggy was no longer in Charles's employ.

That did not keep her from continuing to see the boys as a friend of the Royal Family. That August 1997, Tiggy was a guest at Balmoral, hunting and fishing and roughing it with the Princes. "She's a country person, which the boys love," said her friend Santa Palmer-Tomkinson. "She's one of the only women I know who can skin a rabbit or gut a stag." On August 28, Tiggy danced with both princes at the Ghillies Ball while the Queen, grinning broadly, clapped to the music.

William was also turning more and more to his grandmother for advice. Although by no means an affectionate woman—she was never seen kissing or hugging anyone, either in public or in private—Elizabeth had a keen interest in preparing Diana's elder son for the throne. During their weekly tea together "Granny" invariably tried to squeeze in a history lesson—showing William a letter written by Henry VIII, perhaps, or a note from Queen Victoria to Disraeli.

The Queen could prove to be a tough taskmaster. At Balmoral as well as at Buckingham Palace and the royal residences at Sandringham and Windsor, anyone who wished to remove a volume from the library was asked to fill out a card and put it in the space the book came from. There was never any doubt as to ownership. Each book contained a nameplate that simply read "The Queen's Book" in flowing script.

When Her Majesty noticed that several bound manuscripts were missing, she called in Scotland Yard. They determined that the missing volumes were still there, only tucked away behind other books. Inside each volume were concealed provocative photographs of Cindy Crawford.

The Queen said nothing to William about the missing books. But in general both she and Prince Philip were harder on William than they were on Harry, or than they were on the Yorks' daughters, Beatrice and Eugenie. As future King, it was simply more important how William was brought up. Paradoxically, he was subject to more criticism and discipline. Thus when, while riding at Balmoral, he left his groom in the dust and returned to the castle alone, his grandmother flew into a rage. "The Queen tore a strip off Prince William," said one witness to the event. "But it was out of concern for his safety. She thought Diana was being foolhardy when she got rid of the Royal Protection Squad, and she didn't want William getting any thoughts."

Whatever affection she may have felt for Diana—and it had been considerable in the beginning—Elizabeth was now glad to be rid of her daughter-in-law.

She had long since come to regard Diana as manipulative, selfish, and irresponsible—a woman who, by virtue of her unpredictable nature and overwhelming popularity, posed a threat to the monarchy itself.

Diana's infatuation with Dodi Fayed confirmed the Queen's worst fears. Elizabeth, said one member of the royal household, "had no patience with this foolish girl who was behaving like a giddy nineteen-year-old, going out with a rich playboy. It was very difficult for her."

Diana had not spoken a single word to the Queen since the divorce. When she opened her last Christmas present from the notoriously penurious monarch—a bar of soap—Diana was in hysterics. Yet she harbored no resentment toward the woman she never stopped calling, simply, "my mother-in-law." No one, in fact, had ever heard Diana utter a single word against the Queen. "And she always spoke to William and Harry about their grandmother with the greatest affection," said Tess Rock.

Diana did not feel so warmly toward her children's great-grandmother. The Queen Mother had never forgiven Edward VIII for abdicating to marry Wallis Simpson—an act that resulted in her own husband becoming King George VI. The Queen Mother had always believed the stress of leading Britain through World War II had contributed to the King's early death at age fifty-seven.

Now the Queen Mother insisted that, by placing her personal happiness above duty to God and country, Diana proved that she was cut from the same cloth as the Duke of Windsor. "She makes no secret of the fact that she loathes me," Diana confided to her sister-in-law Fergie. "The minute I walk in the room, she leaves."

Diana's own grandmother, Lady Fermoy, was one of the Queen Mother's ladies-in-waiting. "Grim and stilted," Diana said of them both. "They are all anti me. My grandmother has done a good hatchet job on me."

One of Diana's cardinal sins of the past was her penchant for upstaging not only Charles but all the royals. During a Christmas get-together at Sandringham in 1993, the Queen was noticeably irked when photographers packed up as soon as they had gotten their shots of Diana, completely ignoring the rest of the family.

Now Diana went out of her way not to upset Buckingham Palace and the gray men who ran it. When it looked like Diana's Jamaica vacation planned for early 1997 might eclipse the Queen's appearance at the Commonwealth Conference in Scotland, the Princess canceled her trip.

The Queen simply regarded such gestures as too little, too late. It was strictly *verboten* for anyone to speak Diana's name in the Queen's presence. And no one, not even Charles, did.

The Duchess of York, although on good terms with her ex-husband Prince Andrew, had similarly been cast adrift by the Royal Family. As their marriages crumbled and they took turns being battered and bashed by the press, Fergie and Diana grew closer than ever.

Until late 1996, in fact, the first person the Princess of Wales called every day was Fergie. They traded advice on men, on child-rearing, and on weight loss—a subject on which the Duchess of York, after years of yo-yo dieting, had become something of an expert. In December 1996, Fergie signed a $1 million contract with Weight Watchers International to become a spokesman for the $1 billion-plus company. In return, the eternally fashionable Diana gave Fergie fashion tips, and—since the two women wore exactly the same size shoe—passed dozens of pairs along to her.

Most important, they bolstered each other's spirits in times of crisis—and they made each other laugh. When Fergie was upset over headlines linking her romantically with tennis champion Thomas Muster, Diana told her to stop worrying. "Take things as they come," she said, "and keep your sangfroid."

It was rare for Diana to have even the briefest of conversations with Fergie without exploding into gales of laughter. "The least word from Fergie had her in stitches," Tess Rock said. "But they shared a lot more than jokes. Diana counted on her to keep her informed about everything."

It was the Duchess of York who paved the way for Diana's interest in astrology and mysticism, introducing the Princess of Wales to a wide range of soothsayers, tarot card readers, clairvoyants, and the like. While Diana never allowed her actions to be unduly influenced by psychics or mystics, Fergie's life was ruled by them.

Just how much Fergie confided in her spiritual advisors became painfully evident in October 1996. For seven years one of Fergie's spiritual gurus, Madame Vasso Kortesis, had—with the Duchess's permission—taped their sessions together. Now anyone could call a special phone line and for several pounds hear excepts of the tapes.

Fergie took legal action to halt the operation, but for four days the conversations spilled over the phone lines and into the tabloid press. This time the public gobbled up Fergie's own graphic accounts of her torrid affairs with Steve Wyatt, John Bryan, and several others ranging from an Irish riding instructor to a London artist to an Arab oil tycoon.

Diana, as always, willingly provided a shoulder to cry on when Fergie called to tell her about Madame Vasso's phone scheme. But the next day it became clear that Fergie had had plenty to say about her sister-in-law over those seven years. In her conversations with Madame Vasso, Fergie confessed her intense jealousy of Diana, whom she sneeringly referred to as "Blondie." The Duchess also predicted that she and Diana would battle for the love of the man they had both met and now lusted after—John F. Kennedy Jr.

No sooner had the Vasso tapes been released than Dr. Allan Starkie, another of the Duchess's psychic advisors, published *Fergie: Her Secret Life*. In his book, Starkie revealed that Fergie resented Diana, and that she dissolved into angry tears whenever the Princess of Wales scored one of her many media triumphs. Starkie also claimed that Fergie felt she was the one who should have married Prince Charles, and that it was her destiny to reign as Queen.

Still, Diana herself had conceded to Andrew Morton that there were times when she had been equally envious of Fergie. The important thing was that Fergie had repeatedly promised Diana that she would be left out of the Duchess's forthcoming memoirs.

Alas, when Fergie's *My Story* was published in November 1996, it contained plenty about the author's sister-in-law. For starters, Fergie admitted that she was relieved when the "Squidgygate" tapes momentarily distracted the British public from her own scandalous affairs. She also wrote that whenever Diana was summoned to Balmoral, the Princess was invariably "teary, reclusive, and out of sorts."

Even this might have been forgiven had Fergie not made one final, unforgivable claim in her autobiography. According to the Duchess, she contracted plantar's warts after wearing a pair of Diana's shoes. The Princess was, said a friend, "furious, because she felt that it tarnished her image."

From that point on, Diana steadfastly refused to talk to the woman she had long regarded as one of her closest allies in the Windsor Wars. Fergie flooded her with pleading letters and phone calls, but to no avail. Diana refused to take Fergie's calls and sent the letters back unopened. "She cut Fergie out of her life," Rock said. "But she missed all the good times they had together."

Even more, she missed Fergie's daughters, Princesses Beatrice and Eugenie. On her bedroom wall next to some framed letters from William and Harry, Diana hung two drawings the Princesses had done for her. They were signed, "For Aunt Duch, with all the love of Beatrice and Eugenie." Occasionally, "Aunt Duch" became emotional about the nieces she had, along with their mother, jettisoned from her life. "I literally adore them," Diana told a visitor to Kensington Palace. "They are the daughters I never had."

Fergie was not the first longtime friend Diana had banished from her life, at least for a time. The Princess did not take criticism well, and often would perceive even the most minor slight as an act of outright betrayal. When Diana called Rosa Monckton from Seoul during an official visit to South Korea with Charles, Monckton advised her to stop sulking. Diana was representing Queen and country, her friend reminded her, and should put aside her personal feelings of resentment toward her husband. "I didn't hear from her," Monckton said, "for four months." Observed longtime acquaintance Vivienne Parry, "I can't think of one friend of hers who wasn't frozen out at one time or another."

Or a relative. Diana had given the proverbial cold shoulder to both of her sisters on several occasions. Charles Spencer was no exception, despite the bond that had been forged after their mother walked out on the family. Still, he never forgot that when he was still a three-year-old crying for his mummy, it was Diana, then six, who made her way down the darkened hall to comfort him.

Educated at Eton and Oxford, Charles Spencer capitalized early on his sister's celebrity. Straight out of college, he signed on as a London-based contributing correspondent for NBC's *Today* show in 1986. Over the next five years, his high-living, club-crawling modus operandi made him fodder for the tabloids. Before he was twenty-three, Fleet Street had bestowed on him the sobriquet "Champagne Charlie."

A womanizer of some renown, Spencer appeared ready to settle down when he married model Victoria Lockwood in 1989. But six months later, as his bride battled alcoholism and anorexia nervosa, Spencer spent a passionate weekend in Paris with old flame Sally Ann Lasson. The resulting *News of the World* headline: DI'S BROTHER USED ME AS HIS SEX TOY.

Champagne Charlie became Earl Spencer when his father died in 1992, the same year Diana and Charles separated. He also inherited a $122 million estate that included Althorp, the ancestral home. The following year Spencer offered his sister the four-bedroom Garden House on the grounds of Althorp. There, he suggested, she could start a new life for herself.

The Garden House was in many ways ideally suited to the Princess of Wales. For once, the omnipresent armed bodyguard who lived at Kensington Palace could be stationed in another building on the estate grounds. The Garden House also afforded its occupant total privacy; it was not visible from any other building at Althorp. "At long last," Diana said happily, "I can make a cozy nest of my own."

But just three weeks later, Spencer called to tell Diana he had changed his mind. He had gone over the security precautions that would have to be taken, and was told that guards and security cameras would have to be placed all over Althorp, infringing on his family's privacy. He also pointed out that Althorp, like other stately homes of England, was open to the public as a way of offsetting the high cost of upkeep. With tourists roaming around, Diana would have to virtually lock herself in her little Garden House several hours out of every day.

Crestfallen, Diana wrote a letter to her brother and begged him to reconsider. He did not respond, and for the next several months there was a frisson between the two. Relations between brother and sister did not remain strained for long. When Diana was photographed topless while vacationing in the south of Spain in 1994, Charles went on the American television program *Inside Edition* to blame the tabloids for the breakup of her marriage to Prince Charles. "I personally believe the British press," Spencer said, "is the biggest cancer in society."

Spencer and Lockwood separated in 1995, but the following year moved with their four children to Cape Town, South Africa, in an effort to patch things up. It was not long, however, before Spencer was seeing South African designer Chantal Collopy. In July 1996 Collopy's husband went public with another *News of the World* confessional. This one was headlined DI'S BROTHER STOLE MY WIFE.

Earl Spencer struck back. In October 1996 he called for a strict privacy law, blasting "the bully boys of the gutter press" for "brutalizing their favorite gallery of stock characters." Once again his big sister, having forgiven him for the Garden House episode, cheered Spencer on.

Yet Diana was not so willing to repair her friendship with Fergie—not quite yet. It is precisely because they had been extraordinarily close that Diana felt so deeply wounded by Fergie's remarks. But even as she put off a reconciliation, Diana marveled at the continuing warm relationship between Fergie and Andrew. "It's incredible that they were never bothered by the divorce," Diana said. "They'll always be together."

Following the Yorks' lead, the Prince and Princess of Wales had also reached a rapprochement of sorts in the year since their divorce was finalized. The acrimony had faded, and Diana had even come to regard Camilla with a sort of detached bemusement.

Prince Charles and his former wife were on the phone with each other two or three times a week, usually chatting amiably about their sons. As with the Queen, Diana took considerable pains not to embarrass or offend her ex-husband. On June 22, 1997, Diana had taken her sons to see *The Devil's Own* starring Harrison Ford and Brad Pitt, and there was an immediate furor in the press over the movie's sympathetic tone toward the Irish Republican Army. She called her ex-husband right away to explain. "I didn't know what it was about," she told Charles. "We just wanted to see a movie, and we picked it out of the paper because William likes Harrison Ford."

Charles told her not to worry; at this stage in their relationship he knew she would not do anything intentionally to embarrass him or provoke the wrath of the Queen. After all they had been through, there was still affection between them. "I know," insisted Tess Rock, "that a special part of her heart still belonged to her husband." Rock recalled arriving at Kensington Palace just after Charles had left.

"Did you see Charles?" Diana asked. "He just left, and guess what?! He was wearing the sweater I gave him for his last birthday. I was so touched."

The turning point had come when Charles and Diana had spent William's first day at Eton together. Gradually, as they shared responsibility for raising their sons, the Prince and Princess became, in Diana's words, "very best friends."

By the summer of 1997, Diana was able to put all her bitter feelings about Charles behind her. "Her love for him never really died," her friend Natalie Symonds said. "Diana seemed to have only good memories of their years together."

Relations between the two had warmed to such an extent that Charles and Diana were planning to make their first public appearance together since William's Confirmation the previous March. The royal yacht

Britannia was about to be decommissioned, and Charles was scheduled to board the ship at Cardiff as part of its farewell tour around Britain. When he called with an invitation for Diana and the boys to join him, she accepted on the spot. "They were both very excited," said a Kensington Palace staffer, "about being seen in public as a family again."

On the morning of August 30, Charles sat in his study at Balmoral and dashed off a note to Diana on the Queen's letterhead. Headed "My Dearest Diana," the note dealt with their mutually agreed-upon plan to have Harry, seemingly less academically gifted than William, stay an extra year at Ludgrove before joining his brother at Eton.

He signed the letter "Lots of love, Charles," and then put it in the Royal Family's internal mail system. A courier picked up the note at Balmoral and took it to Prince Charles's offices at St. James's Palace in London. From there it was to be delivered to Kensington Palace.

"Make sure this goes straight out," Charles said as he handed the envelope to a secretary. "I want the Princess of Wales to have it on her desk when she returns from her holiday. First thing Monday morning . . ."

My boys mean everything to me.
They're my life.

—*Diana*

She was a fighter to the end.

—*Sam McKnight*, friend

5

Riots broke out in West Belfast after the British Government announced its decision to invite the IRA's political wing, Sinn Fein, to take part in peace talks. A fund-raising scandal swirled about Vice President Al Gore, threatening his presidential aspirations for the year 2000. It was revealed that novelist Salman Rushdie, in hiding after Iran's Ayatollah Khomeini put a $1.6 million price on his head, had married for the third time in a secret ceremony on Long Island. At least ninety-eight people were massacred by Islamic insurgents in Algeria, and U.S. Secretary of State Madeleine Albright embarked on a trip to the Middle East in hopes of pulling the peace talks between Palestinians and Israelis "back from the abyss."

As they awakened around 8:45 that morning, Diana and Dodi had no way of knowing that because of them, people would have a hard time remembering that anything else happened that day. At 9:30, Dodi's butler René Delorm served them a breakfast of coffee, orange juice, and croissants on the deck of the *Jonikal.*

At the same moment, Claude Garreck arrived at Paris's Rue des Petits Champs to pick up his friend, Ritz Hotel acting security chief Henri Paul, for their regular Saturday morning game of tennis. As they headed along the right bank of the Seine on their way to their tennis club in suburban Issy-les-Moulineaux, they passed through the Alma Tunnel. "Every time Henri got in a car, he immediately put on his seat belt," Garreck recalled. "He had it on that morning, when we drove through the Alma Tunnel on our way to go play tennis." Traveling at close to seventy miles per hour that morning, they slowed down as they approached the tunnel. "We were watching for radar!" Garreck conceded.

Paul had, as always, reserved a covered court. "Not just because of the rain," Garreck explained, "but because the sun could always get in the eyes of one or the other in the morning." It was typical of Paul. "He was very meticulous," his friend said. "He never left anything to chance. Before he bought a stereo, he'd consult all the specialists, and find out about every detail."

On that sweltering August morning Paul, Garreck recalled, "was in great form." Paul won the first game

I.

"You cannot comfort the afflicted," Diana liked to say, "without afflicting the comfortable." As part of her crusade against land mines, she visited with an eleven-year-old victim at a hospital in Angola, then donned safety gear to stroll through a minefield.

2.

3.

4.

The Princess's gift for mimicry extended to uncannily accurate impressions of the Queen, Bill Clinton, and South African President Nelson Mandela, whom she saw for the last time in March 1997.

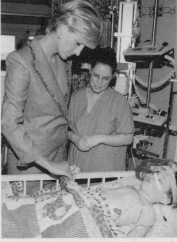

5.

"She'd been hurt too often," said Evelyn Phillips, who knew Diana as a child. "She couldn't stand to see someone else in pain." Diana touched the lives of thousands of children, including this eighteen-month-old girl she visited at St. Mary's Hospital in London.

6.

A beaming Diana (opposite) accepted flowers as she arrived at Christie's in London for a preview of the dresses she was auctioning off for charity. Inside, she gave an impromptu display of what her brother, Charles, called the "laugh that bent her double."

7.

8.

At the height of her affair with Pakistani surgeon Hasnat Khan, Diana visited a Hindu temple in London in June 1997. She wore a red dot on her forehead and went barefoot to join a troupe of ceremonial peacock dancers.

9.

Diana striding past photographers and into Christie's New York, where she briefed Christie's chairman Lord Hindlip on the history of several of her gowns. The June 1997 sale, which was William's idea, raised $3.26 million for charity.

10.

II.

During her
whirlwind trip
to the U.S. in
June 1997, the
Princess had
breakfast with
Hillary Clinton
at the White
House and, later
that same day,
met up with her
friend Mother
Teresa in New
York. The two
humanitarians
died within days
of each other.

12.

At the Tate Gallery's centennial gala in London on July 1, 1997, the Princess of Wales, wearing an eye-popping emerald choker, celebrated a birthday of her own—her thirty-sixth.

Listening to dinner partner Henry Kissinger, Diana hammed it up at yet another charity gala in New York.

13.

14.

By the summer of 1997, relations between Diana and Charles were in many ways better than they had ever been. They both attended William's confirmation.

15.

Diana resented nanny Tiggy Legge-Bourke, at right with Prince Charles in July 1997. But Bourke remained a favorite of William and Charles—and someone they could turn to in times of crisis.

16.

"It's a hunt, Rosa," Diana complained to confidante Rosa Monckton of the paparazzi who surrounded her after she called on a sick friend. "It's a hunt."

17.

JONIKAL

18.

Diana began her affair with Dodi Fayed while on holiday in the South of France. The Princess (above far left), William (center), and Dodi were among those sunning themselves on the deck of the *Jonikal*. Diana took a speedboat ride with Dodi (right), then (opposite) cavorted with Harry aboard a Jet Ski.

19.

20.

21.

Aboard the *Jonikal*, Diana playfully drops ice on unsuspecting victims William and Dodi.

23.

Elton John and Diana repaired their broken relationship when she comforted him at the Milan funeral of murdered designer Gianni Versace on July 22, 1997.

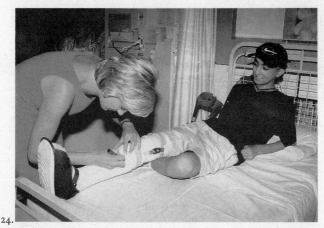

24.

Between vacations with Dodi, Diana kept up her grueling schedule of ribbon-cuttings, dinners, and walkabouts. At a London hospital, she asked to sign the cast of a fifteen-year-old bone cancer patient.

25. While Diana zoomed around the world pursuing her romance with Dodi and campaigning against land mines, Prince Charles and the boys hunted, fished, and communed with nature at Balmoral.

26.

27.

28.

On August 10, 1997, Diana took her anti–land mine crusade to Bosnia. There she comforted a woman placing flowers on the grave of her son, sat on the floor with amputees, and joked with members of the NATO peacekeeping force in Bosnia.

29.
Trying to outrun a photographer, Diana sprinted toward her gym in Earl's Court in London.

30.

The same day Diana dodged the press on the way to her gym—August 21, 1997—Dodi was photographed leaving his Park Lane apartment building. Hours later, they boarded Fayed's private jet and flew to Nice for one last holiday.

Back on the French Riviera for the third time in five weeks, Diana was phoning friends in London with the news that she was in love—but had no intention of marrying.

31.

32.

At the end of the *Jonikal*'s diving platform, Diana found a rare quiet moment alone to contemplate her past and dream about her future. She had one week to live.

Henri Paul enjoying himself at a party in November 1995. By the time his path crossed with Diana's twenty-one months later, he was taking pills for depression and alcoholism.

33.

34.

The $205,400 "Tell Me Yes" ring. Although Dodi apparently intended to propose marriage to Diana the night of August 30, 1997, jeweler Alberto Repossi was never under the impression that it was intended to be an engagement ring.

35.

Ritz security cameras show Diana and Dodi entering the hotel at 9:50 P.M. August 30, after being chased through Paris streets by paparazzi.

36.

After dining alone in their suite, Diana and Dodi waited in a service area with an intoxicated Henri Paul (on the left) before
leaving through the back.

A few minutes before the fatal crash, Diana dashed out the back
door of the Ritz and into the waiting Mercedes. Dodi emerged
from the hotel steps behind her.

39.

Only minutes after their car smashed into the thirteenth pillar of the Alma Tunnel, emergency crews were on the scene. The front of the Mercedes had been obliterated, but the backseat where Diana and Dodi had been sitting remained largely intact.

40.

No one knew that the sole survivor, bodyguard Trevor Rees-Jones (here surrounded by French police) actually had a record of hit-and-run drunk driving.

41.

42.

Diana's butler, Paul Burrell, the man she called "my rock—the only man I can trust," sobbed uncontrollably at the foot of her hospital bed in Paris. Later, before her funeral, he stayed up all night by Diana's coffin telling her stories and the jokes "that always made her laugh."

43.

Four hours after being told their mother had been killed, William and Harry arrived with their father for Sunday church services at Balmoral. "Are you sure Mummy is dead?" Harry asked his father when no mention was made of Diana during the service.

Later that day Charles boarded a jet bound for Paris to claim Diana's body. At first, the Queen objected to any member of the Royal Family making the journey because Diana was no longer technically a "royal."

44.

45.

Outside Paris's Pitié-Salpêtrière Hospital, Diana's sisters Lady Sarah (left) and Lady Jane (center) watched with Charles as the Princess's coffin was carried past a French honor guard to a waiting hearse (below). Over Charles's right shoulder is French President Jacques Chirac.

46.

47. 48.

With his wife, Cherie, and his children fighting back tears, an emotional Tony Blair praised Diana as "The People's Princess" the morning of her death. Attending a party on Martha's Vineyard that Saturday night, the Clintons left after Hillary, according to one guest, "became very upset" on hearing of Diana's death. The President shared his thoughts with reporters on Sunday morning.

49.

Estranged for years, Diana and her mother, Frances Shand Kydd, reconciled in the late 1980s. In her will Diana said that, in the event both she and Charles died, she wanted Frances and her own brother, Earl Spencer, to raise William and Harry.

Tiggy, who had been hunting with Prince Harry (right) a few days before Diana's death, stayed on at Balmoral to comfort the boys. Charles, meanwhile, was so devastated that, in the early-morning hours, he wandered the moors alone and returned with eyes "red and swollen from weeping."

Several acres outside Kensington Palace were covered by flowers left in memory of the woman who had lived there. Onlookers were moved to tears when Charles, William, and Harry appeared at the gates of the palace to look over the flowers, photos, notes, and stuffed animals left by mourners.

The day after the crash, mourners gathered at Place de l'Alma. At Harrods (below), the famous London department store owned by Mohamed Al Fayed, photographs of Diana and Dodi were placed in the window.

56.

By remaining silent and refusing to fly the flag over Buckingham Palace at half-mast, the Queen provoked such outrage that support for the monarchy plummeted. She finally lowered the flag and addressed her people six days after the crash—but only after Charles had delivered an ultimatum.

57.

58.

More than 1.5 million people lined the route of Diana's funeral procession through the streets of London. William and Harry walked behind their mother's coffin with Prince Philip (left), Earl Spencer (center), and Prince Charles.

59.

60.

As they watched the coffin being carried into Westminster Abbey, William cast a sidelong glance at photographers.

Elizabeth II and the Queen Mother arriving at Westminster Abbey for the funeral. At first, the Queen, who had stripped Diana of her royal status, felt she deserved no more than a small, private service.

61.

63.

62.

Sadly, Diana and the Duchess
of York (above) had not
repaired their year-long rift
before the Princess's death.
Mohamed Al Fayed (right),
with his wife, Heini, broke
down during the funeral;
Diana's stepmother, Raine
(below), detested by the
Spencers, was a beaming face
in the crowd.

64.

6-2, but Garreck won the second 6-0. Garreck was thrilled; in Spain, where Paul had vacationed with his friend's family that July, he beat Garreck by a wide margin every time.

They finished up at 11, then drove back to the center of Paris. As was their habit, they went to a kiosk at the Place de la Madeleine, bought several newspapers, and then headed to a boîte called Le Pelican for a drink. Paul would normally have downed a couple of post-game beers, but not today.

"Just make it a Coke," he told the waitress. "I'm in a bit of a rush today."

"Why?" Garreck asked.

"I'm picking up Princess Diana and her friend at Le Bourget," Paul said matter-of-factly, swallowing the last of his soft drink. Acting head of the Ritz's twenty-man security force since Jean Hocquet had resigned two months earlier, Paul desperately wanted the job on a permanent basis. He had already been passed over for promotion once—when his first boss, Joseph Goeddet, was replaced by Hocquet in 1993.

Seven months earlier, Paul had taken charge when U.S. Ambassador Pamela Harriman suffered a stroke after swimming in the Ritz pool. He acted quickly, summoning an ambulance that got her to the American Hospital within minutes. Although Harriman died within forty-eight hours, Paul was commended for his decisive action. Now that he was in serious contention for the job of permanent security chief, he was determined to do whatever was asked of him—and not to make any mistakes.

Garreck drove Paul home and left him at the entrance to his apartment building, just a half mile from the Ritz. Before he got out of the car, Paul told his friend a bad joke. Normally, he joined Garreck's wife and daughter for dinner every Saturday night. But he would not be able to make it tonight. "This evening," Paul said, "I'll surely be getting off work late."

"Well, we'll call each other tomorrow," Garreck said as his best friend got out of the car.

"Yes, we'll call each other tomorrow."

No one knew more about Paul than Garreck, his friend for twenty-one years—two of those sharing a cramped apartment in Paris. Paul was the best man at Garreck's wedding, and was there for Garreck's daughter's First Communion. Yet even Garreck admitted there was much about the man no one knew, nor was ever likely to know.

Balding and stocky, the five-foot-six-inch-tall native of Brittany looked a decade older than his forty-one years. One of five sons born to a municipal worker and a schoolteacher, Paul was an outstanding student and a gifted musician. A pianist whose taste ran the gamut from Schubert and Liszt to Fauré and Brel, he won several contests at the local conservatory. With his long, flowing hair and wild beard, Paul looked every centimeter the French musician that he was in the mid-1970s.

Despite the fact that he took college preparatory courses at the Lycée Saint-Louis in his hometown of Lorient, Paul did not go on to college. His life's dream was to fly Mirage jet fighters in the French air force. Toward that end he learned to fly at the Vannes aero-club, obtained his pilot's license at nineteen, and worked as a flight instructor before enlisting in the military in 1979.

Due to his severe myopia, Paul washed out during flight training at the Rochefort air base. Instead, he was assigned to base security as an ordinary enlisted man. After fulfilling his obligatory year of military service, Paul moved to Paris, where for the next five years he sold boating equipment for a company called Emeraude.

Paul gave up his job after a friend on the Paris police force introduced him to Claude Roulet, second-in-command at the Ritz. At hotel president Frank Klein's insistence, the hotel was in the process of setting up a new security force, and Paul was brought in to help. Once the force was established in 1986, Paul was hired full-time as deputy to security chief Joseph Goeddet.

While his employers saw Paul as reliable, resourceful, and refreshingly competent, several of his underlings described him as bullying and corrupt. "He was Klein's eyes and ears, we all knew it," a bellhop said. "He took delight in intimidating people, making them squirm. The Breton—that's what everybody called him—was in a way sadistic. And he got people fired for small things, like stealing soap or a towel." Another former employee claimed Paul was "on the take and everybody knew it."

In his short time as acting security director, Paul, who spoke fluent English and passable German, had in fact reported several employees for minor infractions. "Henri had many devoted friends—people who loved him," Garreck conceded, "but someone in his position was also bound to have enemies as well." An anonymous letter later found in Paul's desk addressed to the hotel's staff committee said, "You're all deadbeats and thieves, and the Breton is the worst." The note went on to accuse Paul of being "the biggest crook of all," "raking in millions" while he drank "all day long."

They had no way of knowing that Paul was a paid informant for both the French intelligence service DGSE (Direction Général de la Sécurité Extérieure) and France's national police. Paul kept a list of contacts at both agencies in his apartment. He would, an agent said, "verify a lead, or very confidentially keep surveillance on a suspect foreigner."

There was also speculation that Paul might have in

some way been involved in a string of robberies at the hotel—including one in which several display cases in the Ritz's shopping arcade were smashed and thousands of dollars' worth of jewelry stolen.

It also proved highly lucrative for Paul, a skilled fixer well known to hotel regulars, to call in the occasional favor from his contacts on the police force. All of this would have gone a long way toward explaining how Paul, on an annual salary of less than $40,000, had managed to stash *1,000,000* francs (about $200,000) in eighteen separate bank accounts.

Oblivious to this side of Paul's life, his wide circle of friends routinely described the bachelor as a *bon vivant*. He would sit down at the piano and entertain his friends with Chopin and Gershwin. A voracious reader, Paul devoured several books a week—science, history, and current affairs as well as whodunits, science fiction, collections of essays, and books on cooking, the ecology, spiritual healing, and even tattoos.

"He was very strong intellectually," Garreck said of his friend. "He was brilliant and cultivated. He was the ideal friend. Oh, I have other friends, just as charming. But there's not another like him. He was quite rare. He had a curiosity about everything. He was always aware of everything. If you lent him a book, either he had already read it or he had read the reviews. And if he hadn't, he was unhappy. If he wasn't *au courant* about something, it bothered him."

Yet he could scarcely be described as bookish. Bluff, affable, disarmingly outspoken, Paul tended to dominate any social situation. "If you met him once, even for just a few minutes," Garreck said, "you would remember him . . . He was a strong personality."

Always determined to be the center of attention, Paul often made some brash statement just to get people's attention. "He would be perfectly capable," said Garreck, "of turning to some woman he had just met and asking politely 'Is that your real nose?' A lot of people don't appreciate being shocked like that. But he loved it when the person would come back with, 'And you? Is that a transplant, or is your hairdresser on LSD?' He liked someone who had a sense of repartee."

Paul was reckless with more than just his comments. While taking a female friend up for a spin in the single-engine plane he would occasionally rent, Paul let go of the controls and told her to take over. His passenger screamed, unaware that the plane was on automatic pilot. Another time, he aborted a landing at the last minute for no apparent reason, bouncing off the runway and pulling up. Satisfied that his passenger was terrified, Paul circled the field and then landed smoothly. "You should have seen your face," he said, laughing.

For whatever reason, Paul's friends were able to

overlook his brash behavior. If anything, it made him more appealing to them. Certainly he seldom wanted for company. Wednesdays, the gregarious Paul went bowling with a group of friends from his days selling boats. Afterward, they usually dined together at a restaurant called Le Grand Colbert. Paul usually started with beer or a Ricard, the potent yellow anise-based *pastis* aperitif mixed with water. More often than not he ordered seafood (roast red mullet was a particular favorite), drinking mineral water with his meal.

On Fridays, he often lunched with a fellow Breton named Sylvie at Chez Armand, a restaurant in the Palais Royal. The twenty-five-year-old art history major from the Sorbonne and her violist boyfriend rented a studio from Paul, and he encouraged her interest in antique jewelry and paintings.

In addition to his bowling night and his standing Saturday dinner date with the Garrecks, Paul spent several evenings a week at Le Champmesle, a lesbian bar near his apartment building. "He was not an alcoholic," said the Champmesle's owner, Josy Duclos. "He was a regular and usually ordered a Perrier or an orange juice, or a couple of beers if he wasn't on duty. He was conscientious, polite, well-mannered, a joker, and secretive. I knew he was athletic, flew planes, and worked for a millionaire. But that's all I knew."

Outwardly, Paul was the very picture of health.

Only the day before he was to pick up Dodi and the Princess at the airport, he had passed the physical exam to renew his pilot's license. Yet beneath the surface Paul was in turmoil.

It was shortly before Christmas 1988 when Paul met Laurence Pujol, a petite, blond twenty-two-year-old who worked as a secretary in the Ritz's personnel department. Pujol had a two-year-old child, Samentha, and soon Paul had fallen for both mother and daughter. They moved into Paul's run-down fifth-floor walkup in April of 1989.

Paul was, according to his upstairs neighbor Elie Zeitoun, "on top of the world" when Pujol and her daughter moved in with him. "They were obviously very much in love—and I watched as Henri came to adore Samentha."

For the next three years, the trio functioned as a family. Paul was the paterfamilias, caring for Samentha as if she were his own. He bathed the little girl, brushed her hair, took her to the park, played with her for hours on the living room floor, read her bedtime stories. Pujol admitted that she could not have found a better father for her only child.

But there were chinks in their relationship. Even one of Paul's closest friends conceded that he was "a bit of a control freak." Pujol soon chafed under his iron-fisted authority. "He was too much like a mother hen, too paternalistic with me," Pujol said. "I had a hard time dealing with the situation."

To their friends, Paul and Pujol seemed mismatched. "He had a much stronger personality than she did," Garreck said. "There was an equilibrium that was lacking. She was discreet, quiet." Paul, on the other hand, "took up a lot of space."

Feeling smothered by the overpowering Paul, Pujol and her daughter moved out in 1992. But Henri, so accustomed to controlling his destiny, was not about to let the relationship end there. He called them nearly every day, took them out to dinner every couple of weeks, sent them gifts, and even took them to Disney World for Christmas.

"Henri was unwilling to let go," a friend said, "and she was too weak to end the affair. It would have been far kinder to all concerned if she had. Once he got hold of something, he was not the type to ever let go . . ." Soon mother and daughter were back with Paul. Finally, in June 1996, he returned home to his apartment to find that Pujol had again moved out—this time for good—depositing Samentha with her biological father and moving to a small village in Brittany.

Pujol called him on July 6, 1996, to wish him a happy fortieth birthday. Wherever one looked in his tiny apartment, Paul kept framed photos of Pujol and Samentha—poignant reminders of a happier time.

"The door is always open," he told Pujol before saying goodbye. It was to be the last conversation they would ever have.

"At the start of the summer, Laurence suddenly left," said Vincent Martin, a Paris taxi driver and friend of Paul's. "I don't know why. Henri refused to talk about it and seemed to want to bottle it up inside him."

Paul was, added Martin, "a family man suddenly without a family. He was devastated, heartbroken. Henri cared very deeply for Laurence, and he doted on her little girl. He loved nothing more when he was off duty than to take her for a walk."

Paul told a friend, "I miss Samentha so much. I seem to hear her laughter every time I walk in the front door." Now, said neighbor Elie Zeitoun, "he was totally alone. Henri began to change in front of my eyes. In the past, he'd always dressed immaculately and his behavior was above reproach. Now he seemed to let his appearance go—and he started drinking heavily."

Martin, who often went with Paul to the Star Lite Dance Club, confirmed that "when Laurence split, he took to drinking in a big way—beer, wine, Ricard, bourbon, and other spirits. He could hold his liquor, but I worried because it did not lift his mood. He would still be hurting even if he had plenty to drink."

After knocking back five glasses of Ricard at a Paris street cafe called La Vivienne, Paul began crying. "I miss Laurence and Samentha so much my life isn't worth living," he told his friend David Bergeron. "Some days I think about killing myself, but I know it would break my mama's heart."

Bergeron cautioned Paul to stop drinking. "I tried to tell him enough was enough, but he broke down in tears." Outside the cafe, a street musician was playing the violin. As they left, Paul gave him fifty francs ($10) to play the Edith Piaf lament "La Vie en Rose."

"The man was not very good," Bergeron said, "so Henri took the violin and played it himself. He was very talented. Tears were streaming down his cheeks." When he was finished, Paul handed the violin back to the street musician and, Bergeron recalled, "laid his head on the table and wept and wept for Laurence. I had to help him home."

Paul now also went on drinking sprees with former French naval officer Marcel Turgot at another favorite watering hole, Le Petit Rameau. Such out-of-control behavior was, most who had encountered Paul over the years agreed, not remotely typical of the man. "Alcoholic? No, more like a social drinker, discreet, who never drank to excess or made any scenes," said a policeman who had known him for years.

At the cafes and bistros he frequented in his neighborhood and around the Ritz, Paul was for the most part known as the proverbial "social drinker" who would stop after one or two drinks. Typical of Paul's hangouts was Le Bourgogne, a neighborhood cafe-bar not far from the Comédie Française, behind the Palais Royal. Le Bourgogne is near the intersection of the Rue des Petits Champs and the Rue Sainte-Anne, in an area known for its gay bars and Japanese restaurants.

Le Bourgogne itself is small—about ten tables—and neat, the red-and-white tile floor swept clean even when it is snowing out. The back wall is hung with garish oil paintings of Moors. A dozen postcards sent from exotic vacation spots line the wall behind the zinc bar, along with posters advertising Dubonnet and Martini & Rossi.

"Henri Paul was a regular client," said Bernard Lefort, Le Bourgogne's barman. "But he didn't necessarily come in every day. Sometimes three or four days would pass without him stopping by. Sometimes he had a beer, sometimes a coffee, sometimes a Seven-Up. The only thing he never, ever asked me for was a glass of water to take a pill.

"We liked to talk about flying together," Lefort said. "He never talked about his work at the Ritz, but he loved flying. I thought he was a pilot for Al Fayed! He liked speed, but in a plane. I didn't even know if he had a car." As it happened, Paul drove a poky black Austin Mini with an automatic transmission around Paris. But back home in Brittany he kept a Yamaha V Max motorcycle at his parents' house. "When he came back to town," said neighbor Gerard le Flohic, "Henri loved to race around on his motorcycle and show off. It was obvious he loved speed."

Paul took his driving seriously, speed demon or no. Although not often called upon to act as a chauffeur, he took part every year from 1988 until 1993 in the annual Mercedes driving course given near Stuttgart, Germany. He attacked the course with characteristic thoroughness, earning outstanding scores each year.

Dominique Mélo, a psychology teacher at the University of Rennes, insisted that his friend of twenty-five years was "not an alcoholic. I never had any hesitancy about getting into Henri's car with him at the end of a dinner."

Not only was he not an alcoholic, Laurence Pujol insisted, but she claimed never even to have seen him drunk. "Happy, yes," she conceded. "He became quite happy when he had a little too much to drink at a party or on some special occasion. But he never lost control. He knew when to stop. Here was a man who was certified to make an instrument landing in the fog. That kind of person simply does not take unnecessary chances."

But Garreck conceded that Paul's capacity for imbibing was considerable. "He was capable of drinking wine, like everyone [in France]. But you never saw it. Not a sign of inebriation. None." Moreover, Garreck claimed he never saw Paul get behind the wheel of a car in an intoxicated state. "He was someone who was prudent, prudent, prudent. It was imprinted upon his nature." But, Garreck added, "even if he had too much to drink, it would have made him more prudent, rather than excessive in his actions."

Paradoxically, the indefatigably social Paul was also intensely secretive. Even Garreck admitted that his best friend "compartmentalized" his relationships, and that Paul would never have confided in him. "Maybe that's why we got on so well, I never tried to get him to speak of things that bothered him," Garreck said with a shrug. "We liked to laugh together, not torture ourselves with problems. If he'd had the blues, he wouldn't have told me. He never ever said that he was down. Never, never, nothing. Always, 'everything's fine.' Maybe he told others, I don't know."

David Bergeron was one of the few people in whom Paul confided. A week after Paul offered up a tearful rendition of "La Vie en Rose" on the violin, Bergeron found him pouring out his heart to a sympathetic lesbian beneath a gaudy mural of naked women at Le Champmesle. "Here's to the girl who broke my heart," he said, raising his glass in a mock toast. "I was not man enough for her." Then he broke down.

"It was strange sight—a big, strong guy crying his eyes out in the arms of a lesbian," Bergeron recalled. "The guy was in very bad shape."

Paul's problems quickly spilled over into the workplace. At several Ritz staff parties, where he made a joke of walking around the room finishing off other employees' unfinished drinks, Paul was clearly inebriated. Even early in the workday, there were lapses for the man routinely praised as a "consummate professional." Toward the end of 1996, Paul began drinking in the morning and occasionally showed up at the office under the influence. Once he was so intoxicated that, according to one employee, "he fell over in his office and cut his nose."

Things improved somewhat when he began dating an attractive twentyish blond who bore a striking resemblance to Pujol. But, said Josy Duclos, "he found out to his horror that she was seeing another man. They had a terrible fight—and he took off." Paul's world crumbled once more. After that, said another friend, Leonard Amico, "I never saw Henri smile again. He went out of his way to tell other guys how lucky they were to have women in their lives. He obviously envied everyone who had the happiness he'd lost."

By this time, Paul himself was becoming alarmed

at his lack of self-control. "It disturbed him," said Dr. Dominique Mélo, who is married to Paul's friend Dominique Mélo the psychology teacher. (Dominique is a unisex name in France.) Dr. Dominique Mélo was one of at least two female physicians who prescribed medication to Henri Paul for alcohol abuse. "He was afraid of developing a dependence," Dr. Mélo said, "and afraid he would not be able to control the problem alone."

Paul, who was also known to have a hypochondriacal streak, did not hesitate to seek professional help. Soon he was taking Tiapridal, a drug to combat aggressive behavior; Aotal, a medication used to treat alcoholism; the sleeping pill Noctamide; and the antidepressant Prozac. The warning labels on all four drugs state clearly that they are not to be combined with alcohol.

Like most of Paul's friends, Garreck had no idea he was taking pills of any sort. But he admitted that, given Paul's hypochondria, taking prescription medication "would have been totally in character if he were a little anxious about his health, and he had a very stressful job . . ."

In the closing weeks of August, the normally self-possessed Paul let down his guard enough to allow rare, frightening glimpses into a life spinning out of control. At a bar, he boasted about how he would handle himself if terrorists or paparazzi tried to stop the car he was driving. "Most people would try to stop and turn around to avoid them," Paul said. "But not me. I'd drive right at them!"

On August 26, Paul appeared to have reconciled with the twentyish blond. He reserved their usual table at Le Grand Colbert, but she never materialized. Dejected, Paul went back to his lesbian haunt for a comforting shoulder to cry on.

Four days later, as Paul donned his gray suit to pick up Diana and Dodi Fayed at Le Bourget, he was surrounded by images of the woman and the child he had loved and lost. By this time, Marcel Turgot said, "I'm convinced Henri didn't care if he went on living or not."

At 12:30 P.M. on Saturday, Diana and Dodi docked the *Jonikal*'s launch at the jetty behind the Cala di Volpe Hotel and strode through the lobby. Outside, a white Mercedes driven by gray-haired VIP driver Tomas Muzzu waited to take them to Sardinia's bistro-sized Olbia Airport. Muzzu occasionally stole a glance of the Princess in his rearview mirror. Whenever she caught him sneaking a peak, she smiled back. It was a sweltering 90 degrees inside the terminal, and all the flights were inexplicably late.

Gian Franco Pes, who handled private flights at Olbia, had already paved the way for Diana and Dodi to bypass passport checks and drive right onto the tarmac and up to Fayed's waiting Gulfstream IV. Dodi grabbed a briefcase out of the trunk of Muzzu's car and then he and Diana climbed up the stairs and into their private jet.

Sardinian photographers, disguised as workmen, took pictures of Diana and Dodi from the platform of a forklift truck as the couple boarded the plane. He wore jeans, a black jacket, and a black shirt; she was dressed in a taupe pants suit over a black top. They both wore designer sunglasses and grim expressions.

The plane had lost its 1:04 P.M. takeoff slot, so the Princess of Wales and her companion waited on board the plane for another half hour before finally being cleared for departure. Nearby, actress Leslie Caron slumped in the public terminal waiting for her scheduled flight. Caron, the star of such films as *An American in Paris* and *Gigi,* was returning from her vacation home on the island.

Suddenly the stifling calm was broken by the bustle of conversation and movement. Two feet, clad in bright pink bunny slippers, advanced in midair through the airport doors. The slippers were attached to the feet of the ninety-something Marchioness of Dufferin, being pushed in a wheelchair and surrounded by eight English eccentrics. All had been guests at the Marchioness's summer house. "They were all her friends," a wilted traveler commented, "and they were all mad." For once, Diana was up-staged—and grateful for it.

A jeune perdue glacée
Toute seule sans un sou
Une fille de seize ans
Immobile debout
Place de la Concorde
A midi le quinze août.

Hungry, cold, lost
All alone, and broke,
A girl of sixteen
Standing, stock still,
On the Place de la Concorde,
At noon, August fifteenth.

Jacques Prevert, the quintessential Left Bank poet, captured Paris in August in just six lines. Nothing is happening, no one is in town. They have all thronged to the beaches from Deauville to Cannes. To buy a *baguette*—the long loaf of bread that is a staple of the French diet—anyone unfortunate enough to be stuck in Paris must walk several blocks out of his way, since most of the city's bakeries are closed for the annual five-week paid vacation that is every Frenchman's due ever since the Popular Front voted it into law in 1937.

The last week of August 1997, Paris was recovering from the "World Days of Youth," a Roman Catholic youth festival that attracted over one million of the faithful from all over the globe. Strolling around the city in herds of a hundred or more, they picnicked in the Tuileries and frolicked around the fountain on the vast Place Saint Sulpice.

Exactly one week before Diana and Dodi set out for Paris, Pope John Paul II presided over a Mass at Longchamps racetrack attended by more than one million people. His Holiness took the opportunity to offer a belated apology for the Saint Barthélemy massacres of August 24, 1572, when as many as ten thousand Protestants were slaughtered in Paris alone.

During the Mass, the Pope was clearly suffering the effects of the heat wave that had left even the most stalwart Parisians limp. Sidewalk cafes did a booming business as natives and tourists alike engaged in France's national pastime, sipping a Perrier, or a beer, or a cognac, or an *express* as they watched the world drift by. The Federation Française des Spiritueux (French Federation of Spirits) announced that 2.5 *billion* glasses of *pastis,* the powerful drink favored by Henri Paul, had been sold in France so far that summer alone. Whiskey sales were even higher.

It was just another typically uneventful last week in August, as Paris awaited the onslaught of the *rentrée*—when everyone returns from vacation *en masse.* Fire and police brigades, emergency services and hospitals were short-staffed, but no matter.

Nothing ever happens in Paris in August.

At 3:20 P.M. on August 30 the Fayed jet with the green-and-beige Harrods' markings touched down ten miles north of Paris at Le Bourget. Sitting on the runway, Dodi looked out his window and saw that twenty photographers and reporters were waiting to pounce.

Diana did not seem to mind at all. She would have thought it odd had the press *not* been there to greet her. But Dodi's newfound stardom may have gone to his head. They were to spend only a single night in Paris before returning to London so Diana could be reunited with her sons. Determined that this last night not be ruined, Dodi phoned from inside the plane demanding that a police escort accompany them into the city.

Rather than wait on the tarmac and be overrun, they decided to go it alone. Cameras whirred nonstop as they emerged from the jet and climbed down the stairs. With Dodi's driver Philippe Dourneau at the wheel, a black Mercedes 600 sat only feet from the plane, its engine purring. Behind it was a dark green Range Rover.

On her way toward the Mercedes, Diana stopped to greet the ground crew. "She was very friendly," said one. "She said hello to everyone and was full of smiles." Then Diana climbed into the backseat, and as was her habit, fastened her seat belt. (Dodi never wore his, and she did not press the issue with him.) She barely noticed the balding, stocky man in a rumpled suit and thick glasses who strode confidently up to Dodi and stuck out his hand. Fayed was relieved to see a familiar face—someone he knew would take whatever action was necessary to keep the press from tormenting them during their brief stay at the Ritz. In addition to delivering their luggage to the hotel via the Range Rover, it was Henri Paul's job to make sure they got there safely.

Satisfied that Diana and Dodi were tucked comfortably in the backseat, bodyguard Rees-Jones shut the door behind them and slid in next to the driver. The black Mercedes 600 then pulled away from the plane, followed by the Range Rover with Henri Paul at the wheel. Another of Dodi's bodyguards, former Royal Marine Kes Wingfield, rode alongside Paul. Fayed's butler, housekeeper, and a masseur he brought along to treat his bad back were jammed in the back with the famous couple's luggage.

No sooner had the two-car motorcade left the airport and pulled onto the autoroute than the paparazzi—at least four cars and as many motorcycles—joined them in hot pursuit. "Step on it!" Dodi angrily ordered Dourneau. "Lose them."

At his boss's urging, Dourneau moved into the center lane of the three-lane highway and sped up to eighty miles per hour. Diana looked out the window at two motorcyclists zigzagging between traffic as they tried to get ahead of the car.

"My God," she muttered. "They're going to lose control if they keep that up. It's too dangerous. Someone is going to get hurt."

A black Peugeot 205 sedan pulled alongside the Mercedes, then sped up to ninety miles per hour to overtake them on the right. Without warning, the Peugeot swerved in front of the Mercedes and slowed down abruptly—a dangerous maneuver clearly designed to trap the car so the pursuing photographers could swarm around it and get their photographs of Diana and Dodi cowering in the backseat.

At the last minute, Dourneau managed to pull around the Peugeot, and then stay ahead of the pack all the way into Paris. Henri Paul, meanwhile, impressed thirty-two-year-old Wingfield with his driving skills; during the chase he managed to keep a discreet distance behind the Mercedes without sideswiping the Peugeot or any of the daredevil motorcyclists. "All the time they were buzzing around like hornets trying to zoom in front to split the backup car from the Mercedes," Wingfield said. "Henri drove well. He didn't let them get in."

Diana was concerned—not for herself or even for

Dodi, but for the paparazzi on motorcycles. She feared that, caught up in the thrill of the chase, one might lose control and slip under the wheels of a car. "I must admit," Wingfield said, "we weren't concerned about that."

As they approached the center of Paris, Dourneau made a quick turn off the road onto the Porte Maillot exit. "You've given them the slip," Diana told Dourneau as the phalanx of paparazzi continued on the main road behind the Range Rover. "Well done, Philippe."

While Henri Paul continued on to the Ritz with their luggage, Diana and Dodi proceeded to the Villa Windsor. This time, they met with an interior decorator at the Duke and Duchess of Windsor's former mansion. The couple set about measuring for curtains, examining the appliances in the kitchen, looking over plantings in the garden, even going down into the basement to check out the plumbing and heating systems. "They went to look at everything," said Gregorio Martin, who had been the butler to the Duke and Duchess of Windsor and was kept on by the Al Fayeds. "They were going to move in, I think, together—yes. No one spoke of marriage, but they seemed happy."

After forty minutes at the Villa Windsor, they were driven to the Place Vendôme in the center of Paris, where a small mob of photographers now waited for them outside the main entrance to the Ritz. The Mercedes 600 pulled up to the back service entrance on the Rue Cambon at 4:30 P.M., where they were met by a porter in blue livery and ushered inside.

Once safely out of camera range, they were greeted by Claude Roulet, left in charge while Ritz president Frank Klein vacationed in Antibes. Roulet promptly escorted the couple up to the Imperial Suite. Diana walked over to the high French doors that opened out onto a small wrought-iron balcony, pulled back the curtains, and peered outside. Place Vendôme, at its center a bronze column made from twelve hundred canons captured by Napoleon at the Battle of Austerlitz, spread out before her in all its sun-washed seventeenth-century splendor. Below, clustered at the curb, were the enemy—photographers smoking cigarettes, kibitzing, squabbling among themselves and with hotel security.

She had hoped to go shopping for Harry's birthday, but it was obvious that was now impossible. A Ritz employee was dispatched with a list of presents, and would return hours later with several packages—including one that contained the computer play station Harry had specifically requested.

Once ensconced in their hotel suite, Diana and Dodi began to burn up the phone lines, touching base with family members and friends. The first call Diana placed was to her clairvoyant friend Rita Rogers.

As usual, Rogers was screening her calls at home in Derbyshire. "Dearest Rita," the familiar voice said over the answering machine. "Are you there?"

Rogers rushed to pick up the phone. "Yes, hello, Diana. Where are you, my dear?"

"Paris. I'm in Paris with Dodi."

"Paris?" The vision of Dodi somehow facing danger in a Paris tunnel still haunted Rogers. "But what are you doing in Paris?"

"We're just doing a little shopping . . ."

"But Diana," Rogers said anxiously, "remember what I told Dodi."

"Yes, I remember." There was a pause. "I'll be careful, Rita. I promise."

Diana waited for Rita to respond, but the psychic later recalled that at that moment she "went very very quiet," unable to speak.

"I'm looking forward to seeing my boys," Diana said, perking up. "I'm going home tomorrow."

Still nothing. "Don't you worry, Rita," she said again. "I will be careful. I promise."

As they hung up the phone, Rogers felt a chill. She did not, she would later say, feel good about this.

Dodi, meanwhile, was busy telling several people—Ritz president Frank Klein, his uncle Hassan Yassin, his butler René Delorm—that he planned to propose to Diana that very night.

Conversely, Diana went out of her way to reassure

friends she had no intention of marrying Dodi, or anyone, for that matter. Nor would she, as friends had speculated, move out of the country to live with Dodi either in France or in California. "I think in my place, any sane person would have left Britain long ago," she had told a French reporter just a few days earlier. "But I cannot. I have my sons."

That Saturday afternoon, August 30, Annabel Goldsmith telephoned her friend in Paris, concerned that Diana would be "forced into a corner" by all the publicity.

"Don't worry, Annabel," Diana replied. "I'm having a wonderful time, but the last thing I need is a new marriage. I need it like a bad rash on my face."

When she talked to Richard Kay, her friend at the *Daily Mail,* Diana said nothing of marriage—though she did make it clear that Dodi had led her to a crossroads.

"Richard," she said. "I have decided I am going to radically change my life. I am going to complete my obligations to my charities and to the antipersonnel land mines cause, but in November I want to completely withdraw from formal public life." According to Kay, "Diana said she would then be able to live as she always wanted to live. Not as an icon—how she hated to be called one—but as a private person."

Kay attributed Diana's upbeat mood to her Egyptian lover. "She was in love with him," Kay said, "and, perhaps more important, she believed that he was in love with her and that he believed in her. They were, to use an old but priceless cliché, blissfully happy." Kay admitted that he could not say for sure if they were to wed, but concluded that in his view it was "likely." Kay later recalled that, on that Saturday evening, "Diana was as happy as I have ever known her. For the first time in years, all was well with her world."

After speaking with Kay, Diana received the most important call of the evening—from William at Balmoral. The young prince was about to start his third year at Eton, and Buckingham Palace, as part of its agreement with Fleet Street to provide occasional royal photo opportunities, had ordered William to pose at the school for photographers.

But now that Harry was staying behind at Ludgrove an extra year, William worried that such a staged event would overshadow his brother. He did not want Harry to feel left out. Diana agreed. She promised William that, first thing on Monday, she would talk to Prince Charles and they would come up with a plan that would spare Harry's feelings.

That evening Alberto Repossi, having interrupted his stay in Monaco, was scheduled to deliver the "Tell Me Yes" diamond ring to Dodi at the hotel—along with some jewelry for another of his clients who happened to be staying at the Ritz, the daughter of Saudi

King Fahd. But Dodi grew impatient. At 6:30, while Diana was having her hair done in the hotel's beauty salon, Kes Wingfield and Claude Roulet walked over to the Repossi shop on the Place Vendôme. Roulet tended to the paperwork—arranging to have the bill sent to Dodi's father—while they waited for Dodi himself to arrive.

It was less than one minute's walk from the Ritz to Repossi, but Dodi, afraid that he might be recognized if he tried to walk across the street, had Trevor Rees-Jones drive him to the shop in the Mercedes 600. Then the bodyguard stationed himself at the door, keeping a watchful eye on passersby until Dodi emerged with Wingfield and Roulet.

As they wrapped the $200,000 ring he and Diana had selected in Monaco, yet another design caught Dodi's eye.

"She might like this one better," Dodi said, holding this new, larger ring up to the light. "Is it OK if I take both? I'll let her decide."

Unaware that his boss was deciding between two rings worth a total of nearly a half million dollars, Rees-Jones later recalled that he "waited and watched as Dodi bought the ring for Diana. He was so happy." But Dodi never shared his intentions with the man he sometimes called "my shadow." Rees-Jones conceded that at times he felt he was intruding on the couple's privacy. "I didn't like to think about what I was witnessing. I was concerned with who was outside the jewelry store. When Dodi came out he obviously had something with him and he was happy. That's all."

Dodi actually walked out empty-handed. The rings were turned over to Roulet, who delivered them to the Imperial Suite at the Ritz twenty minutes later. At that point, Dodi changed his mind again. He decided not to show Diana the second ring; he would stick with their original choice. Roulet was to take the second $200,000 ring back to Repossi. Meanwhile, Dodi slipped the velvet ring box back into his pocket.

At 7 P.M. the couple left for Dodi's lavish ten-room apartment on the Rue Arsène-Houssaye overlooking the Arc de Triomphe. Once again, they took their favorite escape route through the rear exit onto the Rue Cambon. Henri Paul stood on the curb and watched them speed away with Dourneau at the wheel. Following close behind were Kes Wingfield and Rees-Jones in the Range Rover. Confident that the boss's son and his girlfriend were being well looked after, Paul looked at his watch and decided to call it a day. As always, he took his cellular phone with him.

After spending time in the company of two people who were so obviously in love, Paul probably felt more despondent than ever about his own lost love.

He may also have detected the familiar stirrings of that all-consuming desire for alcohol. Worried what might happen if he began making the usual rounds of his favorite haunts, Paul stopped off in his small office, swallowed two of the Aotal tablets prescribed to curb his drinking, and deposited the empty foil container in a wastebasket next to his desk. The Aotal notwithstanding, that night on the way home he dropped into Le Bourgogne for a Scotch and a beer chaser.

Outside Dodi's apartment, meantime, a half dozen paparazzi were waiting for the couple to arrive. A local store owner watched as Wingfield, Rees-Jones, and two Ritz security guards leapt from the Range Rover and rushed to hold the photographers at bay. A shoving match ensued as Diana and Dodi, flanked by Wingfield and Rees-Jones, rushed from the car into the building.

Amid all the commotion, a Ritz security guard grabbed a camera by the lens and pushed it into the face of its owner, Gamma Agency photographer Romuald Rat. A shoving match ensued. "We went to chat with the paparazzi," Wingfield recalled. "We asked them to give the couple a little distance and respect them and then they might get better pictures later. Just stay back and then you're going to get better pictures because they're going to be smiling and perhaps give you a wave. Some of the photographers were OK with that. They said 'fine.' Some of them wanted to provoke a reaction. We were physically assaulted. We were provoked and poked with cameras."

Stéphane Darmon, a Gamma courier, had been called in from home this Saturday to drive Rat around on his Honda NTV 650 so the photographer would have his hands free to take pictures. While they waited outside Dodi's apartment, Darmon chatted with Dourneau, who bragged about losing the photographers earlier in the day on the ride in from the airport. "He was showing off in a friendly sort of way," Darmon said. "He told me he had been in the business of driving celebrities for ten years. Losing photographers is a game to him."

Dodi's Paris apartment was, if anything, even more lavish than his Park Lane *pied-à-terre*. The marble foyer led into an elegant, high-ceilinged salon with windows looking out onto L'Etoile and the Champs-Elysées. This led into a large sitting room decorated in shades of green. Off a hallway in the opposite direction was the cavernous living room, decorated in shades of pink and beige.

Yet there was no mistaking who lived here. Everywhere were framed photographs of Dodi with movie stars, from Robin Williams to Julia Roberts. The place was filled with television sets—including a large-screen monster in the otherwise elegantly furnished living room—and teddy bears. In the green sitting room, Diana was watched over by a nineteenth-century nude and a three-foot-tall ceramic mouse as she changed for dinner. And wherever she looked—propped sitting in chairs, propped against walls, arranged on tabletops—were stuffed animals.

Dodi took his butler, René Delorm, aside and told him that he intended to propose to Diana after they returned from dinner that evening. The ring was on the nightstand in his bedroom, and Dodi had checked to make sure they had several bottles of Dom Pérignon on ice to toast the big moment. It appeared that Dodi, the eternal man-child with a seemingly bottomless capacity for self-deception, had not even entertained the possibility that she might say no.

But all indications were that Diana *was* going to turn him down. She undoubtedly loved Dodi, but she had gone out of her way to make it clear to those she trusted most that, for the time being, she had no intention of marrying anyone. She pointedly made that declaration not only to Rosa Monckton and Annabel Goldsmith, but also to another close friend, Lana Marks. The fashion designer had talked directly to Diana only days earlier. "Marriage was not part of her plans," Marks stressed, "as she related them to me."

Even more tellingly, Diana did not broach the issue with William during their conversation that afternoon. "She ran everything by William that even remotely affected him," a friend said. "She valued his judgment." If she had intended to take a step toward making Dodi the young Princes' stepfather, she would have sought his approval. Instead, their conversation that day, which lasted less than twenty minutes, dealt solely with William's concerns about Harry being overlooked during the scheduled Eton photo op.

Just a few days earlier, Diana had told another confidante, Lady Elsa Bowker, that she "simply adored" Dodi. But she also made it clear she was not about to marry him. "Diana wanted more children," Lady Bowker said. "She told me, 'Elsa, I want two girls.' But she knew that to marry a Muslim would create enormous problems for William and Harry, and she would never subject them to that. Diana was many things, but she was no fool."

From the moment they arrived in Paris, there was general agreement that Diana had seemed distant, distracted. Dodi's bodyguards and the Ritz staffers were quick to attribute this solely to the carnival atmosphere created by a rapacious press. But while Diana often complained about "the hunt," as she called it, it is unlikely that this alone could have led to Diana looking so deflated. Weighing just as heavily on her mind was the fact that soon she would deal a soul-crushing blow to the one man who was not afraid to declare his love for her. "Maybe marriage was in their future," said another friend. "She did love him and she wanted to go on loving him, but at that moment she knew there was no way she could wed Dodi Fayed."

While she pondered how to best let him down gently, Diana changed out of her taupe pants suit into white pants, a black short-sleeved top, and a black blazer. Now she stood in front of the huge gilt mirror, putting on her gold earrings. The pearl bracelet with the dragon-shaped clasp Dodi had given her dangled from her right wrist.

Dodi, confident that restaurateurs would not be enforcing any strict dress codes in the dead of August, wore jeans, a tan suede jacket over a gray shirt, and cowboy boots that brought him closer to Diana's height. Besides, the restaurant he had chosen for the evening—Chez Benoît, situated on the Rue Saint-Martin not far from the Pompidou Centre—was chic but far from stuffy.

Hoping to throw the paparazzi off their trail, Roulet made a reservation at Chez Benoît for five (Dodi and Diana at one table; Wingfield, Rees-Jones, and himself at another) under his own name. Then he drove ahead to the restaurant and waited for his boss to arrive.

The Roulet party of five never made it. Diana and Dodi left the apartment at 9:30 and headed for Chez Benoît—again followed by a swelling caravan of photographers—only to discover when they got within a block of the place that it was overrun with paparazzi.

Furious that his perfect romantic evening was being irrevocably spoiled, Dodi ordered Dourneau to turn around and head back to the Ritz. For whatever reason, they decided to enter the hotel from the front for the first time today.

"Shit," Dodi muttered as the limousine rolled up to the curb. There were now perhaps twenty photographers waiting in a knot at the hotel entrance, surrounded by as many as fifty onlookers. The broad walkway from the curb to the hotel entrance stretched out before them for what seemed like an eternity. Wingfield and Rees-Jones, who had donned a suit jacket before they left for dinner, now jumped out of the Range Rover and rushed to help Dodi and Diana out of the car and into the hotel.

At first unwilling to get out of the car, Dodi seethed—at hotel security for not clearing a path to the door, and at the paparazzi for trespassing. "Mr. Dodi was more than upset," Wingfield said, "and suggested I should ask these guys to move away because the pavement outside the Ritz is private property."

Diana, meanwhile, soldiered ahead. As she made her way up the walk, Wingfield tried to shield her from cameras that came within inches of her face. "Dodi seemed to be hiding his face with his hand," recalled Pierre Suu of the Sipa Photo Agency. Diana, meanwhile, seemed to be taking things in stride. "She didn't look upset, no," Suu said, shrugging.

Diana pushed her way through the revolving door at precisely 9:50, with Dodi and Rees-Jones following immediately behind. The hotel's Versace boutique was just a few steps from the entrance. While Wingfield later said it looked as if she were "about to cry," other hotel guests who saw her in the lobby that night alternately described her as "radiant" and even "cheerful."

New York-based investment banker Ezra Zilkha and his wife, Cecile, had just left the hotel restaurant and were on the way back to their apartment when they encountered Diana in the lobby. "She was coming in just as we were leaving," Zilkha said. "Even before then we could tell something was going on. Her presence, and I suppose Dodi's as well, had caused quite a commotion among the staff. She smiled and waved. If she was upset or bothered she did not show it." As they walked the few blocks to their apartment between the U.S. Embassy and the Elysée Palace, the Zilkhas commented on the beautiful weather. The temperature was a comfortable 73 degrees, there was a light breeze from the west, and overhead the stars were plainly visible in a cloudless sky. The Princess, they agreed, was fortunate to be in Paris on a night like tonight.

Diana and Dodi walked down the long, narrow

wood-paneled lobby past the garden courtyard on the left and the magnificient tapestries on the right toward L'Espadon ("The Swordfish"), the Ritz's opulent mirror-walled dining room. Here, beneath a ceiling fresco of clouds and massive Baccarat chandeliers, one person could easily spend upward of $200 for a seven-course meal.

It was 10 P.M. and Diana was famished. For an appetizer, she ordered an asparagus and mushroom omelet, to be followed by Dover sole with vegetables tempura. Dodi ordered grilled turbot and a bottle of Tattinger champagne. Just a few yards away, two patrons with large plastic bags at their feet were behaving suspiciously enough to attract the attention of hotel security. The patrons, security surmised, might well have been paparazzi with their cameras concealed inside the bags.

It was all too much for Dodi and Diana, who abruptly left while Ritz staffers discreetly approached the suspicious-looking diners. The patrons, it turned out, were English tourists, and the bags contained cigars.

Dodi asked the maître d' to have their dinner sent up to the Imperial Suite, where they would dine alone. Then, exhausted and hungry, the playboy and the Princess trudged back down the length of the lobby and up the wide staircase to Room 102.

Meanwhile, back in his tiny apartment on the Rue

des Petits Champs, Henri Paul had called in to check on the couple's progress no fewer than a half dozen times since he left the hotel at 7:05 P.M. He was also drowning his sorrows in alcohol.

Arriving home a little before 8 P.M., Paul may have watched television or unwound listening to music on his elaborate stereo system. Or perhaps he amused himself with the electronic flight simulator he had purchased to perfect his piloting skills.

Whatever else he might have done that night, Paul without a doubt took his prescribed doses of Prozac and Tiapridal. And contrary to the warnings on the labels, he drank. In his private bar, police would later find partially consumed bottles of Martini & Rossi white vermouth, vodka, and Suze, a liqueur made of gentian plants. In the refrigerator was an unopened bottle of champagne, but a kitchen cupboard contained three-quarters-empty bottles of Four Roses whiskey and his favorite drink, Ricard. To make matters worse, Paul did not consume any food that evening. In fact, he appeared to have gone without eating all day.

At 9:55, the Ritz's night security manager, François Tundil, called Paul to tell him that Dodi and the Princess had finally retreated to the sanctuary of the Imperial Suite for dinner. By then, Paul had already shaved and dressed and was headed out the door. In his pocket were his credit cards, his keys, a Casio digital calculator, his Ritz and Justice Ministry photo IDs, and an inexplicably large amount of cash—12,560 francs, roughly $2,280. Paul had not been summoned back to the hotel; the decision to return to work, perhaps born of a feeling that only he could handle the rambunctious press, was entirely his.

Paul walked the short distance to Le Champmesle, where his car was parked on the street just opposite the entrance. He stuck his head in the door and, with the keys to his Austin Mini in his hand, waved to Josy Duclos and several patrons seated at the bar. "Good evening, girls, see you later," he said. "I've got to go to work."

There were no cars parked directly in front of the Ritz, but when Paul pulled up to the curb he threw his car into drive and then into reverse, rolling forward and back several times as if trying to squeeze between two invisible cars. When he pushed his way through the Ritz's revolving door precisely at 10:07 P.M., Paul was grinning broadly.

His uncharacteristically exuberant behavior did not impress Wingfield and Rees-Jones, who were grabbing a quick dinner in the Ritz's Bar Vendôme, a cocktail lounge situated just off the lobby to the left of the entrance. In keeping with the quiet elegance of the rest of the hotel, the color scheme inside the Bar Vendôme was muted—the Tudor-beamed ceilings varnished a dusky rose, the chairs upholstered in dusky-rose velvet, the walls covered in a gold-and-brown floral pattern. To the right of the bar was a painting of a man in a rowboat in the style of John Singer Sargent. Another, in the style of Monet, picked up the floral theme. A tall, lanky pianist with a three-day stubble and greasy black curls sat at the bar's baby grand playing Elton John, Marvin Hamlisch, and Billy Joel. During the piano player's ten-minute breaks, the Bar Vendôme was filled with the sound of Muzak.

Paul joined Wingfield and Rees-Jones at the bar where they were eating and ordered one 90-proof *pastis*. Thirty minutes later, he ordered another. Wingfield and Rees-Jones supposedly had no idea that Paul, who ordered the two potent Ricards in front of them and then cut them with water from a carafe, was consuming alcohol. Wingfield later told investigators that he thought Paul was drinking pineapple juice that was so strong it had to be diluted with water. Rees-Jones did not go that far. "He had a yellow-colored drink, then another," he would concede matter-of-factly.

"There was absolutely nothing untoward about his behavior," Rees-Jones remembered. "If there had been, Kes or I would have picked up on it straightaway. That's what we are trained to do. But he seemed perfectly normal to both of us. He sat at the bar drinking some yellow liquid that I assumed was nonalcoholic." While Wingfield and Paul chatted, Rees-Jones "kept a lookout for Dodi and Diana on the staircase."

Between puffs on a cigar and swigs of Ricard, the suddenly boisterous Paul laughed and joked about the day's cat-and-mouse games with the press. Periodically, he would leap up and wander about the lobby, chatting with hallmen and porters in an uncharacteristically effusive fashion.

Several times Paul went outside to taunt the waiting paparazzi. Wild-eyed and grinning incongruously, he joked about his new camera, and about the harrowing ride in from the airport earlier in the day. Even Dourneau admitted that Paul was "more giddy than usual." In the Imperial Suite that night, Diana and Dodi could hear the piano music and the unmistakable sound of Paul's raucous laughter wafting up from the Bar Vendôme.

Wingfield and Rees-Jones may have claimed to be unaware that Paul was drinking right under their noses that night, but Vendôme bartender Alain Willaumez (a.k.a. Patrice Lanceleur) recalled very clearly serving Paul liquor on the evening of August 30—as he had many times before. "It's a well-known fact that Mr. Paul had a tendency to drink," he said. "On several occasions, I saw him drunk inside the hotel."

That evening, the bartender recalled, Paul was "in a state of intoxication, his eyes were shining, he was excited." Weaving on his way out of the bar, he collided with the head barman. Then Paul "staggered right up to the exit" of the hotel.

As for Paul's "tendency to drink," the bartender insisted Frank Klein "knew this perfectly." Another Ritz staffer agreed that Paul "had been boozing a bit and we all knew it. Everyone knew that he drank when he wasn't working."

While the two bodyguards headed upstairs to the Imperial Suite, Paul went out into the street again, this time to fling down the gauntlet. "You won't catch us tonight," he boasted. "Don't even try." As the paparazzi grew more and more impatient, Paul returned a third time to promise them Dodi and Diana would be out "in ten minutes."

"It was weird that he talked to us and was giving us information," Pierre Suu said. "Paul was looking happy and excited. He was saying, 'She will be out in ten minutes,' which was not natural. So we figured something is going on."

The Gamma Agency's Stéphane Darmon recognized from the start that Paul was "playing games with us. He staged two departures, in which Mercedes cars drove round Place Vendôme and came back again. He laughed at us charging off behind them." A crowd had now gathered outside the hotel, and, said Darmon, "they enjoyed it too. In retrospect, he was overly jolly but I did not think about it at the time, especially since I had no idea he would end up driving Diana and Dodi's car."

Rees-Jones and Wingfield were standing in the hallway just outside the Imperial Suite when Dodi suddenly stuck his head outside the door, glanced at his rectangular gold Cartier watch with the maroon crocodile band, and asked how many photographers were in front of the hotel.

"About thirty," Wingfield told him, adding that the paparazzi were themselves surrounded by more than a hundred curiosity-seekers—including two buses filled with British and Hungarian tourists. Then Dodi disappeared inside again, apparently to confer with Diana.

When Dodi came back out fifteen minutes later, Paul was standing with the two bodyguards. The boss told them he wanted to leave the hotel out the back exit—a maneuver that had worked well for them before. This time, however, they would take a different Mercedes with Henri Paul at the wheel. While Wingfield and Dourneau created a diversion in front of the hotel, they would slip out the back with Rees-Jones and leave along the Rue Cambon.

Both men objected to the idea of separating the two bodyguards. "My assessment of the situation when Dodi wanted to leave the Ritz with Diana," Rees-Jones said, "was that we should go in two cars, driving in tandem. There were a lot of photographers and tourists and I thought that would be the quickest way out . . . It would also give us a backup car behind the first Mercedes to put a bit of distance between us and whoever tried to follow."

But Dodi "preferred to leave through the back door with me and Henri Paul," Rees-Jones said, "leaving the usual driver to go out the front as a decoy." Since they had traveled in London and in St.-Tropez with just one driver, Rees-Jones "didn't see the need to make a big issue out of it. I thought it would be better to have two cars, but Dodi was the boss."

As far as using Henri Paul to drive the car, Rees-Jones was "relaxed about that because he was an experienced security man and very experienced at driving in Paris—which I was not at all." The ruse would work only if the reporters recognized at least one of the bodyguards leaving by the front. Besides, the only car available from Etoile Limousine, the firm that provided vehicles to the Ritz, was a 1994 jet-black Mercedes S280 with 26,658 miles on the odometer—a luxury car, certainly, but one that would not accommodate five passengers comfortably.

That was only one of the car's drawbacks. The Mercedes S280 was considerably lighter than the Mercedes 600 (contrary to later reports, neither car was armor-plated) and it did not have tinted windows; the paparazzi would have no trouble shooting directly into the backseat.

There was more. Like the man who was about to take the wheel, the Mercedes S280 itself had a disturbing secret history. The car, license number 688 LTV 75, had been parked in front of the fashionable Taillevent Restaurant on April 20 when it was stolen, then stripped for parts and abandoned outside Paris. Recovered sixteen days later, the car was missing, among other things, the wheels and the tires, the inner workings of the doors, and the electronic "brain" that controls key functions—from the power steering and power windows to the speedometer, the antilock braking system, and the six-cylinder 195-horsepower engine itself. Total cost of repairs: $20,000.

A month after the theft, the car was back on the road. But in June, Etoile chauffeur Olivier Lafaye remarked that a light on the dashboard indicating that the brake linings were worn flashed frequently. The mechanics at the Mercedes garage at Saint-Ouen assured Etoile owner Jean-François Musa that this was probably due to "an air bubble stuck in the circuit."

Today, on the afternoon of August 30, 1997, Lafaye drove a regular client to the airport for a flight to Tokyo and noticed that the light had begun flashing again. There appeared to be no problem with the brakes, but the light kept flashing . . .

There was one last difficulty. The car was a professional limousine, and therefore anyone who drove it had to carry a special five-year permit issued by the Prefecture of Police. Henri Paul, who seemed to have difficulty that evening parking his tiny Austin Mini on a deserted street, did not possess such a license.

As excited as he was by the coming chase, Henri Paul was not alone. Dodi was carried away by the prospect of outwitting—and outrunning—the dreaded paparazzi. In front of the hotel, Dodi's regular driver, Philippe Dourneau, pulled up in the Mercedes 600 and began gunning the engine. Then the Range Rover rolled up—all designed to create the impression that the Princess and her escort would momentarily emerge.

For three of the photographers waiting outside, it all seemed a little too obvious. They drove their motorcycles and small cars around to the rear of the hotel and waited across from 36 Rue Cambon. Above the otherwise nondescript door was a sign that read "Service/Ecole Ritz-Escoffier," referring to the legendary cooking school located on the hotel's lower level. The grimy street, lined with motorcycles and the small cars belonging to Ritz workers, was strewn with coffee cups and plastic wrappers. Repairs were being done on the street right outside the back entrance, so the photographers stood on the opposite side of the street.

At this point, only minutes before leaving the hotel, Dodi called his father in London and explained the plan to him. But Mohamed Al Fayed did not like what he was hearing. "Why don't you just stay where you are and spend the night at the hotel?"

"We can't," Dodi replied. "We're leaving for London in the morning and our luggage is at the apartment. Besides, the ring is there . . ."

"Now look," Mohamed cautioned Dodi, "don't try any tricks when you leave the hotel. Be normal, be nice to the photographers and be nice to everybody. Go out of the front door and say hello. Talk to the paparazzi, they are only doing their job."

Dodi, still seething, would have none of it. But the elder Al Fayed persisted. "You have got nothing to hide," he said. "Relax and enjoy it. Dodi, just help them to make a living." Mohamed hung up the phone shortly after midnight, confident that his son would follow his advice.

Mohamed Al Fayed was tragically mistaken. Paul went ahead of the couple, walking out onto the dimly lit Rue Cambon and waving merrily at the three photographers he saw there. "Paul still had that odd grin on his face," one of them said, "and he was sort of prancing around, preening. It was obvious to us what was about to happen."

Dodi and Diana, followed by Trevor Rees-Jones, left the Imperial Suite and proceeded down the long, narrow hallway carpeted in French blue silk embossed with the Ritz seal, past elaborate Empire period mirrors, hunting prints, and unicorn tapestries toward the back stairway. For the third time, Diana voiced her fears for the safety of the paparazzi on motorcycles. "Mr. Dodi was a little angry because the paparazzi were messing up his holiday and upsetting his girlfriend," Wingfield said. "But the Princess was concerned again that somebody was going to fall in front of the cars. She just wanted them to keep back."

That night Diana was anxious about more than just the safety of the paparazzi. She had never seen Dodi this upset with the press before, and she now knew it was because they were destroying what he had intended to be a very special night. But the Princess had already told Rosa Monckton that the ring Dodi had purchased for her was going straight on the fourth finger of her right hand, and she had confided in others as well that she had no intention of marrying anyone at this time in her life. Now that it became clear he was going to propose, the question of how to turn Dodi down—at least for the time being—without scaring him away must have weighed heavily on her mind.

They paused for a minute in the narrow service vestibule, with its institutional green walls and black-and-white brick floor. On a nearby partition hung hundreds of keys. Just one more time Dodi, leaning against an interior wall, his arm protectively around

Diana's waist, went over the plan with Rees-Jones and Paul, who made no attempt to conceal his glee at the impending game of cat-and-mouse.

The troubled Mercedes S280 with the flashing brake light pulled up to the back door. Within seconds Paul emerged, followed by Rees-Jones. Then Diana, looking blonder, more beautiful, and more world-weary than ever, stepped outside to the all too familiar clicks, whirs, and camera flashes. Following closely behind Rees-Jones, she turned right and walked a few steps down the sidewalk past the construction barriers to the waiting Mercedes. In the distance, at the end of the Rue Cambon, she could see the marquee of the Olympia movie theater. Rees-Jones opened the left rear passenger door and held it as Diana ducked inside the car. Dodi was only seconds behind. She slid over to let him in.

At precisely 12:20 A.M. they sped off with Henri Paul at the wheel, Rees-Jones in the right front passenger seat, Dodi behind the driver, and Diana seated directly behind the bodyguard. None of the people in the car, at this point, had fastened their seat belts. Photographer Serge "Ben" Benhamou hopped aboard his Honda scooter and took off in hot pursuit. Reporter Alain Guizard also witnessed the getaway; he got on his cell phone and signaled his photographer at the front of the hotel that the chase was on. Within seconds, photographers still stuck at the Ven-

dôme entrance scrambled for their cars and motorcycles.

One Ritz staffer who had been observing Henri
Paul's behavior ever since he returned to the hotel
would later describe Paul as being "excited and drunk
as a pig" from the moment he arrived. "He should
never have been allowed anywhere near that car."

Diana and Dodi, who themselves had been drinking champagne that night, were too tired and too
distracted by the day's hectic events to notice that
Paul was intoxicated. After all, they employed bodyguards to pay attention to such details.

On this evening in August, nothing was as it
seemed. Not only was a drunk behind the wheel, but
one of the people in the car that night was actually a
convicted hit-and-run drunk driver. But his name
was not Henri Paul.

It was Trevor Rees-Jones.

How can a picture be worth a life?
> —*Stéphane Darmon,*
> one of the
> motorcyclists
> pursuing Diana in
> Paris

William and Harry will be properly prepared. I am making sure of this. I don't want them suffering the way I did.
> —*Diana*

6

It may be the ultimate irony that, of the four people who got into the Mercedes S280 at 12:20 the morning of August 31, 1997, Diana was the one who should have been driving. She had, after all, driven safely around London with the press in hot pursuit for seventeen years. Sometimes she tried to outrun her pursuers, but for the most part she let them do their job. Never was she known to put her life at risk—or anyone else's. And, as she was proving once again with her oft-expressed concerns for the safety of the motorcyclists, safety was of paramount importance to the Princess of Wales.

On this fateful night, Henri Paul was intoxicated, under the influence of at least two powerful prescription medications, and in the throes of a soul-crushing personal crisis that some felt left him suicidal. The man in the backseat giving orders had been dealing with the paparazzi for only six weeks. And although

Dodi was timid when he was behind the wheel, he had been known to goad his drivers into speeding and jumping red lights.

Doug Thompson was only one of several chauffeurs who recalled being pressured by Dodi to break the law. On June 4, 1997, Thompson showed up at the Beverly Hills Hotel at 7 A.M. to pick up Dodi and take him to Los Angeles International Airport for an 8:15 flight. When he finally got into the car at 7:50, Dodi told Thompson, "Step on it. I'll give you a very big tip if you get me to the airport in time."

Weaving wildly in and out of traffic on the San Diego freeway, Thompson hit speeds of up to ninety miles per hour. Dodi, who did not wear his seat belt, said, "You're going to have to go faster than that." So Thompson pushed his speed up to ninety-five, and managed to get to the airport—usually a thirty-minute trip from the Beverly Hills Hotel—in just fourteen minutes. Dodi tipped Thompson $100. "Later," Thompson said, "Dodi's assistant told me he always pushes drivers to exceed the limit."

What of Diana's last line of defense, Dodi's stalwart bodyguard Trevor Rees-Jones? Incredibly—and unknown to Diana that night—Rees-Jones himself had a drunk driving record. Moreover, only eight years earlier Rees-Jones, now twenty-nine, confessed to causing an accident while intoxicated, and then fleeing the scene.

The neighborhood pub can be a second home for many young British rugby fans, and Rees-Jones was no exception. One night in his hometown of Oswestry, Shropshire, Rees-Jones went through his normal daily routine of downing a few pints with his rugby mates at a local pub. Then he got into his car to drive home.

Only this time, Rees-Jones lost control of his vehicle, skidded, and struck a parked car. Frantic that he would be arrested for driving while intoxicated, he sped away. In less than an hour the local police arrested Rees-Jones, determined that his blood alcohol content was more than twice the legal limit, and charged him with both drunk driving and leaving the scene of an accident. He was fined 300 pounds (about $500) and his driver's license was revoked for one year.

Rees-Jones was not driving the car that night, but he was Diana's last line of defense against Henri Paul. "As far as I was concerned," Rees-Jones said of Paul's peculiar behavior that night, "Paul was on duty and that was that. I had no reason to suspect he was drunk. He did not look or sound like he had been drinking. He just seemed his usual self. He was working. He was competent. End of story. People can come up with all sorts of theories and opinions after the event. But I know exactly what happened because I was there. I can state quite categorically that he was not a hopeless drunk as some have tried to suggest. I like to think I have enough intelligence to see if the guy was plastered or not—and he wasn't. I was quite happy with the situation."

Given his own drunk driving record, Rees-Jones may not have been the best judge, or he simply may have been more tolerant than most. It would have helped if those employees who knew of Paul's drinking problem had warned him, certainly. But the fact remained that many others recognized Paul's impaired condition—including one photographer who called his actions nothing short of "bizarre."

Most important, Paul sat at the bar and consumed two strong-smelling, vividly colored alcoholic beverages right in front of Rees-Jones and Kes Wingfield. Not only was Paul obviously drunk, said bartender Alain Willaumez, but he bumped into someone as he stumbled out toward the lobby. By the time he got behind the wheel of the Mercedes S280, Paul's blood alcohol level was more than *three times* the legal limit. He had also ingested the antidepressants Prozac and Tiapridal in doses high enough to triple the effects of the alcohol. Toxicology tests would later reveal that Paul had not merely gone on a bender that night, but that he was in a state of "moderate chronic alcoholism" resulting from weeks of steady drinking.

As they sped into the night, Diana was riding in a car that had once been stolen and stripped for parts and whose warning lights were flashing, with an improperly licensed driver under the deadly influence of alcohol *and* drugs, a boyfriend who often ordered his drivers to push the envelope, and a bodyguard once convicted of hit-and-run drunk driving.

Diana and Dodi were jostled about in the backseat as the Mercedes sped down the Rue Cambon, past the Hotel Castille, and the Chanel, Celine, Valentino, and Laura Ashley boutiques, past Place Maurice Barre, the Mezza Luna shoe store, and L'Argentier Bar.

In a matter of seconds, Paul had turned right onto the Rue de Rivoli and then stopped at a red light at the Rue Royale, directly in front of the Hotel Crillon. By this time, a half dozen photographers in cars and on motorcycles had managed to catch up, and were gunning their engines in anticipation.

In the past Dodi had instructed his chauffeur to step on the accelerator before the light changed to green, and that is what he did now. Photographers could see Dodi leaning forward in his seat, motioning wildly with his hands for Paul to go. They could also see that even at this point no one in the car, including Trevor Rees-Jones, was wearing a seat belt.

Without warning, the eager-to-please Paul followed his boss's orders and jumped the light, swinging left onto the Place de la Concorde. The car carrying the most famous royal personage of the twentieth century now passed the spot where the guillotine had brought an abrupt and bloody end to France's monarchy.

A fantasyland of fountains, statues, and lights even in the dead of August, the Place de la Concorde is arguably the epicenter of Paris. Standing at the square's famous obelisk, the tourist is afforded an un-obstructed and breathtaking view of the Madeleine Church to the north, the Louvre to the East, the Arc de Triomphe to the west, and the gold-domed Les Invalides and the Eiffel Tower to the south.

Stéphane Darmon, with photographer Romuald Rat on the back of his Honda motorcycle, tried to keep up with the Mercedes. "It zigzagged quite clev-erly through the traffic," Darmon said. Paul had sur-prised his pursuers by jumping the light at the Rue Royale, and now he made another surprise maneu-ver. Instead of turning right and making a straight shot up the broad and fast-moving Champs-Elysées to Dodi's apartment, Paul zoomed straight ahead toward the Seine.

With no more traffic lights ahead, he speeded up even as he made a hard right onto the Cours la Reine ("Queen's Course"), the thoroughfare running paral-lel to the river. On this three-quarter-mile straight-away, the Mercedes picked up speed, leaving the disbelieving paparazzi far behind. Once the car turned onto the Cours la Reine, Darmon marveled, "It just took off—almost supersonic." Now easily exceeding eighty miles per hour, the Mercedes passed through the long tunnel that runs beneath the avenues Winston Churchill and Franklin Roosevelt and the entrances to the Alexander III and Les Invalides bridges. Then they shot out the other end of the tunnel onto the Cours Albert 1st, in the words of one witness, "like a bullet." It was then, Rees-Jones later said, that Diana asked if Paul could go "a bit quicker."

Now rocketing past traffic at over ninety miles per hour—the speed limit in all of Paris is thirty miles per hour—the Mercedes approached the Alma Tunnel, which runs under the entrance to the Alma Bridge. As the car accelerated even further, Diana and Dodi were pressed against the backs of their seats. "The car was flying as it passed me," said taxi driver Michel Lemmonier. "It was like the hounds of hell. There could be only one ending. The poor Princess must have been in terror."

At this juncture, only a matter of seconds before they reached the Alma Tunnel, Rees-Jones made the decision that would save his life: He reached over and hastily fastened his seat belt. Yet of all the people in the car, only the bodyguard had a legitimate reason *not* to be wearing a belt: It is standard procedure for bodyguards not to wear any restrictive safety belts so that they can move quickly in the event of an emergency. "In general, in town I don't wear a seat belt,"

Rees-Jones later conceded, "unless the speed warrants it. When I used to drive with Dodi in London, for instance, we'd drive a slow speed and put on the belts only if we got to a piece of road where the speed warranted it."

Still, it is standard procedure for personal body-guards to insist that the person they are protecting wear a seat belt under all circumstances. "The final say on whether Dodi and Diana wore belts would have been down to them," Rees-Jones later shrugged. "I can only recommend it. You can't make someone wear a belt if they don't want to." Diana, who had spoken so often of feeling safe and protected in Dodi's presence, apparently followed his lead and did not fasten hers.

The question would remain, however: Why, at the last minute, did Rees-Jones buckle up? Because he realized that Paul was driving too fast? Or because he recognized—too late—the one thing about Paul that appeared so plainly obvious to so many others: that Henri Paul was severely impaired by pills and alcohol.

Now Diana could see the chestnut and cherry trees, strung with twinkling white bulbs, and up ahead to the left of the tunnel a large "Bateaux Mouches" sign spelled out in flashing blue bulbs. It is here, parallel to the Alma Tunnel, that thousands of visitors board the famous tourist boats every day.

Above the tunnel itself, on a small square called

Place de l'Alma, is the sculpted gold flame fashioned after the one borne aloft by the Statue of Liberty. Looming to the left: the brightly lit Eiffel Tower, now counting down the number of days to the new millennium in lights forty feet high.

Eric Petel, a twenty–eight–year–old waiter, was riding home from work on his large white motorcycle and was approaching the Alma Tunnel, when in his rearview mirror he saw a car flashing its headlights. "It seemed to be a long way behind me," said Petel, who nevertheless moved to the right to let the car pass. In a split second the car raced past Petel at such speed that, the motorcyclist said, "It made me feel as if I was driving at about thirty miles per hour. But when I looked at my speedometer I saw I was going seventy!"

The driver of another limousine that passed by the Mercedes S280 estimated the car carrying Diana and Dodi was traveling at about 110 miles per hour. The speed limit at the entrance to the Alma Tunnel is the same as it is throughout Paris, thirty miles per hour. "It was going so fast," said Gary Dean, a British tourist standing nearby, "that it gave off a whooshing noise as it approached the tunnel."

Henri Paul had driven through the Alma Tunnel just fourteen hours earlier on the way to his Saturday morning tennis game with Claude Garreck. He had worn his seat belt then, and he had cautioned Garreck to slow down as they both kept an eye out for police radar. Had he not been impaired, he would also have remembered the sudden dip at the tunnel entrance—and the fact that a row of eighteen steel-beamed concrete pillars separated the two rows of traffic running in each direction.

It was a different Paul who rocketed into the tunnel that night, hitting the dip at one hundred miles per hour or more and nearly becoming airborne. With no front wheel traction for perhaps one hundred feet, Paul could not control the car as it careened into the tunnel and suddenly encountered a small white Fiat Uno just ahead of it in the right lane.

At this point the full weight of the Mercedes, catapulted by the dip at the tunnel's entrance, now slammed down on the roadway. This may well have deployed the airbags, at a crucial moment further hampering Paul's ability to steer out of harm's way.

Swerving wildly to the left to avoid striking the Fiat, the Mercedes still clipped the compact car's left rear bumper with its right front bumper. The collision smashed the luxury car's headlight and the Fiat's red taillight, spraying the roadway with broken glass. The Mercedes brushed the third column, pitched to the right, and, as Paul slammed on the brakes and yanked the steering wheel in an effort to regain control, plowed headlong into the thirteenth pillar. It then rotated 180 degrees counterclockwise before slamming into the tunnel wall.

Inside the car, Henri Paul was probably the first to perish—his spinal cord severed by the steering column, his aorta ruptured, his ribs and his testicles crushed, his pelvis and both legs shattered. Dodi, whose legs were horribly fractured in at least seven places, also died instantly of his injuries—principally from massive trauma to the chest and head. Rees-Jones, his life saved by the seat belt he strapped on only seconds before impact, suffered massive facial and head injuries, his jaw nearly ripped off.

As the car literally spun around her, Diana's body followed the laws of physics and continued in its straight line of trajectory. Thus, when the car finally came to rest against the north wall of the tunnel, she was facing backwards on the floor between the front and back seats.

On impact, Diana's earrings were torn away—one landing in the roadway, the other embedded in the dash. The contents of Dodi's pockets—a ticking Breitling chronocraft watch without a band, his gold Asprey cigar cutter, a fawn-colored cigar holder containing a single cigar—ricocheted around the interior of the car. His metal dogtags, inscribed "D. Fayed, type B pos.," were ripped from his throat. The Cartier timepiece with the maroon crocodile band was on his wrist and still ticking, but the Citizen watch Dodi often carried was found broken and lying on the roadway.

Only seconds behind the Mercedes, Eric Petel did not see the Mercedes hit the thirteenth pillar, but was nearly knocked off his motorcycle by the "deafening noise" of the impact. Then he saw the car "bouncing back from the wall and facing me. Not going where it was going, but having bounced back and now facing the other way."

The entire trip—from the back of the Ritz to the moment of impact—had taken less than three minutes. It was 12:23.

The tunnel quickly filled with smoke, perhaps from the tires or from oil leaking onto the hot engine. The motor had actually been rammed backward with such force that the radiator was now in the driver's foot well. The roof in front had been crushed down to the height of the driver's knees. Paul's body pressed against the horn, sounding a shrill alarm that could be heard for blocks. In contrast to the front half of the car, which was smashed in like an accordion, the back of the Mercedes—where Diana and Dodi had been riding—was remarkably unscathed. A white, pink, and blue box of tissues that had been sitting under the rear window just behind their heads had slid slightly off center but was otherwise undisturbed. The trunk had only two scratches on the top. Safety experts would later agree that, had they been belted in, the couple would almost certainly have survived—and probably sustained only moderate injuries in the process.

The Mercedes was still spinning when Petel caught up to it. He hopped off his motorcycle and ran to the knot of twisted steel that had once been a luxury automobile. "When I got to the Mercedes," he recalled, "I noticed the roof was smashed in. The right rear door was partly open, so I looked in and saw a woman." Diana, Petel said, "seemed to have been thrown forward from the backseat and had her head between the two front seats." Her right leg was pinned under the seat beneath her, her left leg propped up on the rear seat where she had been sitting. In a grotesque tableau, Dodi's badly mangled left leg zigzagged across Diana's lap. One of her arms extended across the lower part of Dodi's body, said a witness, "almost protectively." His jeans were slashed open by the metal shards, exposing his genitals.

Petel reached into the car through the partly open door, lifted up Diana's head—her chin had been down, digging into her chest—and brushed the hair off her face. "Her eyelids were fluttering, but she hadn't opened her eyes. I asked her if she was OK and she didn't answer me. Only then did I realize it was Princess Di."

At that point Petel worried that he should have gone directly for help. "I thought, 'Oh, no, I've made a mistake.' And I put her head gently back down without putting it all the way down." After perhaps thirty seconds on the scene, Petel pushed the car door shut, jumped back onto his motorcycle, raced to the nearest pay phone, and dialed the police emergency number.

"There has been a horrible accident in the Pont de l'Alma tunnel," he yelled into the phone. "Princess Diana is in the car!"

The policeman at the other end of the line burst out laughing. "This number is for real emergency calls," he said, "stop wasting our time."

Frantic, Petel hung up the phone and sped to the nearest police station. "They called me a liar," Petel said. "They refused to do anything or even to send someone to check out my story."

After pleading with police for twenty-five minutes, Petel was handcuffed and then held for an hour in a back room before being taken to police headquarters to give a statement. "I was outraged," he later said. "They didn't seem to care about the crash." The next day, Petel would tell his family lawyer what had happened. But it would take five months before French authorities grudgingly agreed to hear Petel's testimony as the first eyewitness at the scene.

Petel was just zooming out of the tunnel to call for help when photographer Romuald Rat and his driver

Stéphane Darmon arrived. Even now, less than a minute had elapsed since the crash.

The bright yellow lights in the white-walled tunnel created an eerie optical effect, transforming orange to pink, green to yellow, brown to gold. As they gazed at the smoking hulk, Darmon said, "it was like hallucinating . . . Everything I remember from this moment, even the sounds, is in slow motion, like in a film. The car was almost facing us, its front end in the wall. There was glass everywhere."

Rat, twenty-four, jumped off the bike and ran for the car. Darmon admits he "just stood there, petrified with horror." At first Rat reacted in much the same way. "At that time, I thought they were all dead," said Rat, who had a first-aid certificate. "I was shocked. For several seconds I stayed back from the car. After a moment, I got hold of myself and went to the car to open the door, because I wanted to see what I could do to try to help them."

Reaching the car he could see from their hideously contorted corpses—eyes open and unseeing, smashed limbs bent at preposterous angles—that Henri Paul and Dodi were dead. The right front passenger door had been ripped off, and Rees-Jones, his white shirt drenched in blood, hung halfway out, moaning in agony.

Rat opened the door that had been shut by Petel and leaned over the Princess "to see if she was alive."

Rat felt Diana's neck for a pulse, but when he touched her she began to stir.

"I'm here," the photographer said to Diana in English. "Be cool. A doctor will arrive." There were small traces of blood coming from her nose and mouth, and a cut on her forehead.

A local resident who heard the sound of squealing tires and shattering glass ran downstairs to check out what had happened. Seeing the carnage, he used his cell phone to call SAMU (Service d'Aide Médicale Urgente), France's state-run emergency medical service.

Meanwhile, a young couple driving in the opposite direction had actually witnessed the crash itself through the maze of pillars. Once out of the tunnel, they pulled over, leapt out of their car, and waved their arms to warn oncoming traffic. One of these drivers had a cell phone, which the woman used to call the *sapeurs-pompiers,* the French fire brigade. But the caller was confused and could not give a precise location. Both the call to SAMU and the call to the fire department had been placed within three minutes of the crash.

While all this was going on, thirty-six-year-old Dr. Frédéric Mailliez and his companion Mark Butt, forty-two, were returning from a birthday party for a friend in suburban Boulogne. Baltimore-born Butt was a manager for Joe Allen's, the Parisian branch of a well-known midtown Manhattan restaurant. The boyish-looking Mailliez, an experienced emergency physician, was employed by SOS Médecins, a private twenty-four-hour on-call medical service. He also worked as an SAMU doctor in Garches, another Paris suburb. Mailliez generally worked twelve-hour days; Butt seldom got off work before 3 A.M. For both men, the Saturday evening birthday party was a welcome chance to unwind.

Mailliez was at the wheel of his white Ford Fiesta marked "Médecin" as he and Butt rode along the Seine en route to their apartment in the 9th Arrondissement. Even they were taken aback by the beauty of the city on this warm summer evening—and by the dazzling monument just across the river on their right. As they approached the tunnel, Butt recalled, "We were talking about the Eiffel Tower. We were looking at it and saying ooo, wow, look at that, it's so pretty. That was the last thing we said. Then we both noticed there was smoke coming from the tunnel." He did not hear the horn; the Fiesta's windows were rolled up.

At first Mailliez thought it was a fire, until he saw the twisted, smoldering wreck inside. Because the car was pointed in the wrong direction, he also assumed it had somehow been traveling the wrong way. Mailliez pulled his car directly opposite the Mercedes and got out. Now he heard the deafening wail of the horn.

Three times before when he was off-duty with Butt, Mailliez was the first doctor on the scene of a serious car accident. "It's getting to be a habit with us," said Mailliez, who told Butt to get out the flashing blue light and put it on the roof of the Fiesta to alert other cars to the accident.

At 12:26, just three minutes after impact, Mailliez, wearing white jeans and a white T-shirt, walked toward the Mercedes. "And when I got there," he recalled, "I thought, shit!" It was obvious at first glance that Paul and Dodi were dead. But Mailliez could see that the blond woman slumped in the backseat and the man in the right front passenger seat were breathing. The doctor lifted Diana's head, but he did not recognize her.

"Rapidly, I take stock of the situation," Mailliez recalled. "I run toward my car, for a little bit of calm, to telephone emergency services for two ambulances with reanimation [resuscitation] equipment." Mailliez, uncertain about which tunnel he was in, pulled out a map to give his precise location. Then he rushed back to the Mercedes with the only piece of medical equipment he had in his bag—Ambu, a mask attached to a portable, self-inflating oxygen balloon. A volunteer fireman, meanwhile, had arrived on the scene and was holding Rees-Jones's head and whispering words of encouragement until the ambulances arrived.

Mark Butt remained back at the Fiesta in case Mailliez needed any other supplies. He watched as more and more people—bystanders as well as photographers—began drifting into the tunnel. American tourist Jack Firestone and his wife, Robin, were returning to their hotel when they passed the scene in a taxi. "Photographers were swarming all over the car, snapping as many photos as they could," Robin Firestone said. "I still feel dirty now when I remember that I saw humans behaving in that way."

Indeed, at this time there were a dozen or more photographers standing to the right of the car, firing off flash after flash and at least partially blinding virtually everyone in the tunnel. An argument erupted between Christian Martinez of the Angeli Agency and Rat, who demanded that his fellow paparazzi restrict themselves to shooting only the car's exterior. While the photographers traded insults, someone draped a blanket over Dodi's exposed parts. Other than that, and Rat's initial efforts to reassure Diana help was on the way, the press took no active part in assisting the rescue effort or comforting the victims.

Two policemen on patrol, flagged down by motorists five minutes after the crash, waded into the fray. "The camera flashes were going off like machine gun fire around the back right-hand side of the vehicle where the door was open," said officer Lino Gagliardone, who blocked off the tunnel and called for reinforcements. When Gagliardone's partner, Sebastien Dorzée, tried to force the photographers back so he could get to the car, they pushed back, showering him and one another with insults.

"It's your fault," one photographer screamed at another. Martinez focused his wrath on the gendarmes who were trying to prevent him from taking pictures of the wreck. "You piss me off!" he bellowed at Dorzée. "At least in Bosnia they let us work!"

The Firestones and other witnesses would claim that the paparazzi not only did nothing to aid the victims, they actually interfered with rescue attempts. But this was not the case, said Mailliez. The young doctor, now leaning inside the car with his knees on the backseat, lifted Diana's head up so she could breathe. He pressed the oxygen mask to her face.

"There were a lot of journalists behind me," he conceded. "Lots of flashes. I felt them very close to me, but they didn't bother me at all. They didn't push me. They never prevented me from doing my work."

As the only doctor on the scene, Mailliez focused his laserlike powers of concentration on the Princess. "My attention is entirely on treating the victims. I think of nothing else. It was such an eerie atmosphere inside the tunnel. The bright lights changed all the colors, and there was an echo that was deafening . . .

But I couldn't be distracted . . . I didn't *care* about the paparazzi. When you're with a patient, you have to shut off everything else."

Mailliez was so focused, in fact, that he never recognized Princess Diana. "I was very close to her, yes—inches from her face and holding up her head so she could breathe into the oxygen mask," he said. "But her face was always in profile, or tilted at angle away from me, so that I never looked at her square in the face. But even if I had, I'm not sure it would have dawned on me who it was. I was too busy doing my job."

The photographers had to continually remind him not to speak French to the injured woman. "Speak to her in English! Speak to her in English!" they kept repeating.

"So I started speaking English to her," Mailliez said, trying to comfort her until help arrived. "She was not really unconscious, but she was not fully conscious either."

Diana opened her eyes and at one point even tried to get up. (There would be later reports in the *Sunday Times* of London quoting Mailliez as saying she had cried, "I'm in such pain. Oh, God! I can't stand this!" But Mailliez flatly denied that Diana ever made these statements.)

Governed by the French medical community's strict code of secrecy, Mailliez later consulted the medical board and was told to say nothing. "I interpreted that as meaning not even to say that she said nothing," Mailliez explained. So when asked by the *Sunday Times* reporter if Diana had spoken, Mailliez likened Diana's situation to that of a skier who has just broken his leg. "All the skier can say is 'It hurts, I'm in so much pain.' Now, I just used that example to show that when you're in pain you don't make grand announcements about the future—you're just thinking about how much it hurts."

Diana did moan and cry, but there were no profound last words for Mailliez to pass on to the world. "When the first-aid givers arrive," he said, "you're not going to begin to tell them about your life, or what you want to will to your children or your grandchildren! You are not going to begin to tell the story of your life." As he worked to save her life, the young French doctor did not stop to decipher what she was muttering between her anguished cries of pain.

At the time, Mailliez actually believed the blond woman would survive. Her condition did not seem grave and, despite the carnage, "there was really very little blood. All the other accidents I came upon were bloodier than this one." The glaring exception was Rees-Jones, whose facial injuries were particularly horrific. "The left side of his face was just hanging down—it was *horrible*," Mailliez said. "Even I was impressed with how gruesome it was."

It took six minutes for the first ambulance to arrive. During that time, Mailliez kept Diana's head up so she could breathe, gave her oxygen, and reassured her as best he could in English that she would be all right. "For me that six minutes was an eternity," Mailliez said. "Because, you know, there is nothing worse . . . it's so stupid . . . to find yourself there when you know exactly what you could do further if you had the right equipment. An emergency physician without equipment and without a team—nurses backing him up and an ambulance—it's like a surgeon without an operating room."

Mailliez, convinced that he had done all he could for the woman under the circumstances, stepped aside and allowed the ambulance crew to take over. The young physician watched a few minutes longer, and then, confident that he was leaving her "in excellent hands," returned to his car. As they drove out of the tunnel, Mailliez told his friend Butt, "The young woman has the best chance of coming out all right." Then they began to wonder why there were so many photographers. Ironically, they decided to take a detour on the way home and drive by the Ritz. "There were a lot of people there," Mailliez said, "sightseers obviously waiting to see someone. But we didn't make any connection, of course. I still didn't know it was Princess Diana, and I didn't think she would die."

There was no way for Mailliez to know that she was hemorrhaging internally. "I didn't even have a blood pressure cuff," he recalled. "No. Not even my blood pressure cuff, that was in my house call bag. I didn't have it with me because I wasn't working that evening. If I had had it with me, I would have known already . . ."

The limp, mangled bodies of Dodi and Paul were extricated from the wreckage. Paul was clearly beyond saving, but rescue workers went through the motions with Dodi. They laid Dodi out near the car and for fifteen minutes tried to restore his vital signs using cardiopulmonary resuscitation. He was pronounced dead at the scene. A bright blue tarpaulin was placed around the car to shield it from onlookers as firemen with electric chain saws cut away at what remained of the car to free Diana, whose right foot remained crumpled beneath the seat. At the same time, the roof was being cut away so that Rees-Jones could be lifted out of the front seat. According to Xavier G., the chief fireman on the scene, it was then that Diana spoke her last intelligible words. "My God," she said, "what's happened?"

Diana groaned as rescuers lifted her out and gently placed her on a stretcher, where she remained in the tunnel next to the wreckage while IVs and breathing tubes were inserted. The stretcher was then slowly lifted up and into the SAMU ambulance. Unlike the

Americans and the British, who practice a "scoop and run" approach to get victims to a hospital as quickly as possible, the French prefer to stabilize patients at the scene. "In the U.S.," Mailliez explained, "you are rushed to the ER, and in France, the ER is rushed to you." Toward that end, SAMU ambulances are really more like emergency rooms on wheels, fully equipped and staffed not by paramedics but by an emergency physician and a nurse. There is also general anesthesia equipment on board so that surgery can be performed on-site.

Once inside the ambulance, Diana was placed on a respirator and given CPR. But her pulse and blood pressure continued to weaken. Rather than move her at this juncture, the decision was made that she be stabilized on the spot.

For the next forty minutes, the ambulance remained inside the tunnel while medics worked frantically to stabilize her. During that time, word of the accident began to trickle out. Philippe Dourneau had arrived at Dodi's apartment in the decoy car, and now he and Kes Wingfield had begun to wonder what had happened to Dodi and Diana. Tipped off by a paparazzo that there had been an accident at the Alma Tunnel, Dourneau rushed to the scene.

At his home in Oxted, Surrey, Mohamed Al Fayed was rousted out of a sound sleep at 1 A.M. and told there had been an accident involving Dodi and Diana.

Fifteen minutes later, after Dourneau called with his firsthand account from the tunnel, Frank Klein relayed the news of Dodi's death to Al Fayed. "I felt," Al Fayed later said, "like somebody had shot both my legs away."

After recovering from the initial shock, he asked, "And Princess Diana? What about her?"

"She is badly injured," Klein replied. More accurately, Diana's condition was being described as "very grave" by medical personnel on the scene.

Paris Police Chief Philippe Massoni had phoned the Elysée Palace to inform them of the accident, but rather than wake President Jacques Chirac, duty officer Christine Albanel phoned the British Embassy. It was 1:45 when British Ambassador Sir Michael Jay was phoned at home with the news that the Princess had been seriously injured in a car crash and was being rushed by SAMU ambulance to Pitié-Salpêtrière Hospital.

"Rushed" was perhaps not the right word. The ambulance did not leave the scene until 1:20 A.M.—nearly an hour after the crash—and then proceeded at a slow crawl to Pitié-Salpêtrière. Nor was Pitié-Salpêtrière, situated 3.8 miles away on the opposite side of the Seine, the hospital closest to the crash site. But it was, on this last day of August, the best equipped and the best staffed to handle such emergencies. It was also the hospital officially designated by the White

House for the treatment of high-ranking U.S. officials visiting Paris, including the President. Moreover, the doctor who would head the medical team treating Princess Diana that night, anesthesiologist Bruno Riou, also happened to be the physician specifically assigned to Bill Clinton in the event of a medical emergency. Shortly after Diana's ambulance left the tunnel, a second ambulance carrying Rees-Jones left for Pitié-Salpêtrière.

Dr. Riou had just been making what he thought was his final round in the hospital's intensive care unit when his pager went off at 1:15. Riou dashed downstairs to the basement operating theater, where he joined the hospital's chief anesthesiologist Dr. Pierre Coriat, head emergency surgeon Jean-Pierre Benazet, and the respected cardiovascular surgeon Dr. Alain Pavie. Initially, they were not told the identity of their first patient. But at 1:30, as they were putting on their green surgical gowns and scrubbing up, the medical team was told that they would be operating on Diana, Princess of Wales.

As reports came in from the doctors treating Diana's injuries in the ambulance, the prognosis looked increasingly grim. It did not help, critics would later say, that the ambulance crept along—with its flashing blue lights, wailing siren, and motorcycle escort—at under five miles an hour. "I remember that they were going very, very, very slowly," said photographer

Pierre Suu. "You could practically walk beside it." (Mailliez later conceded that perhaps the ambulance should have gone faster. "You have to go fast," he said, "but you have to arrive with the patient *alive*.")

Less than thirty seconds from the hospital, Diana suffered cardiac arrest. The ambulance came to a full stop on the Austerlitz Bridge as the medical personnel on board scrambled once again to resuscitate her. Electric paddles were used to shock her heart back to life. Then "external heart massage"—CPR—was once again administered by physicians who did not realize that she was bleeding internally from a tear in her left pulmonary vein. The standard techniques they were using to pump blood to the brain and other organs may in fact have made the problem worse.

Finally, the ambulance carrying Diana rolled slowly through the hospital's main gate, past rubble from a construction site, and up to the emergency entrance. It was 2:01. The trip from the tunnel, which would normally have taken seven minutes, had taken forty minutes. It had been ninety minutes since the crash.

At about the same time the stretcher was removed from the ambulance and Diana was carried to the operating room, Sir Michael Jay conferred with Police Chief Massoni and French Interior Minister Jean-Pierre Chevènement upstairs.

The ambassador sat down with his wife Sylvia in

the makeshift situation room that had been set up on the second floor and began making calls. "The Queen must be informed at once," he said. Sylvia Jay looked up the number of Balmoral in the personal phone directory they carried with them and dialed the number.

Britain is one hour behind France, but it was still after 1 A.M. at Balmoral. The entire household was asleep when the switchboard lit up with Ambassador Jay's call. The Balmoral operator whose Scottish brogue Diana had so deftly imitated answered and put Sir Michael through to Robin Janvrin, the Queen's deputy private secretary. Janvrin, awakened from a sound sleep, took a moment to digest the news. He had not even known that Diana was in Paris.

Janvrin listened, incredulous, as he was told that Dodi Fayed had been killed and the Princess of Wales seriously injured. Rather than go directly to the Queen, Janvrin told the operator to connect him with Prince Charles's room.

Out fishing all day with his sons, the Prince of Wales had buttoned up his blue cotton pajamas and crawled into his large four-poster bed around 11:30 P.M. Of all the Windsors, Charles required the least amount of sleep—managing to slog through his brutal schedule of public appearances by catching the occasional catnap in planes, cars, even at the dinner table. But at Balmoral, he went to bed exhausted after a full day of physical exertion, and there he remained for eight hours straight.

The phone rang several times before Prince Charles, a notoriously heavy sleeper, reached for the phone at his bedside. "I'm sorry to awaken you, sir," Janvrin said, "but I've just received a telephone call from Sir Michael Jay in Paris. It seems there's been an accident. It appears the Princess of Wales has been injured, sir . . ."

"An accident in Paris? Diana?" Charles had been aware that Diana was stopping briefly in Paris on her way home to London. But, still half-asleep, he struggled to put the pieces together. Once he did, Charles sat bolt upright in bed. He quizzed Janvrin for what few details he had, and then told Janvrin that he would personally inform the Queen.

But the first person Charles spoke to after learning of the accident would not be his mother the Queen, or his father Prince Philip, or either of his own sons. The first person Charles contacted after being told of the accident was the one person he always turned to in times of crisis—Diana's long-time rival, Camilla Parker-Bowles. As she had so many times in the past, Charles's mistress, sound asleep at her country home in Wiltshire when the phone rang, offered her lover a sympathetic ear. They both agreed that Dodi's death was a terrible tragedy, but that Diana, who of late had been in such superb physical condition, would be fine.

It was only after talking with Camilla that Charles asked the switchboard operator to put him through to the Queen. The phone next to Her Majesty's bed rang minutes after Diana arrived at the hospital. Unlike her son, the Queen was a light sleeper and fully alert from the instant she picked up the receiver. He had to tell her only once that there had been an accident in Paris, that Dodi Fayed was dead and Diana had been injured.

Charles and the Queen agreed that it would be best to let William and Harry sleep. More would be known about Diana's condition in the morning, and the boys would be in a better position to deal with the news that their mother was in the hospital recovering from injuries sustained in a car crash. With that, the Queen asked Charles to inform her if there were any major developments, hung up the phone—and went back to sleep.

Charles, meantime, got dressed, went into his private sitting room, and turned on the radio. At 2:06, the first reports of the accident began trickling in to Britain's Radio 5.

At the four-bedroom home he maintains in his constituency village of Trimdon Colliery, Tony Blair answered the phone. The Prime Minister was, an aide later said, "shocked and anxious" when news of the accident was relayed to him. Dreading the worst, he tried to get back to sleep, but couldn't.

In Tuscany, where she was vacationing with her two small daughters, Beatrice and Eugenie, the Duchess of York was awakened by a call from London. She was told that Diana and Dodi had been in a car accident in Paris, and that Dodi had been killed. At first, no mention was made of Diana's injuries.

It had been nearly a year since the two old friends had spoken. As much as she missed her closest confidante—not to mention her little nieces—Diana still had not forgiven Fergie for saying in her memoirs that the Duchess had contracted plantar's warts from a pair of the Princess's shoes. Her letters kept coming back unopened and her calls to Diana were never returned. But Fergie had persisted, confident that the woman she called "Duch" would someday cave in as she always had in the past.

The minute she heard the news of Dodi's death, Fergie's first thought was of comforting her old pal. She dialed Diana's mobile phone and left a message that her friend would never hear. "Duch, I'm here," Fergie said, "how can I get to you?"

As word of Diana's condition began to filter back to her, Fergie made frantic efforts to charter a private plane to take her to Paris. "I just wanted to be at her side," she said, "to be there for her . . ." Ironically, the Duchess had signed a $1 million contract with

Weight Watchers and had already taped a series of television commercials that were soon to begin airing in the United States. In them, Fergie playfully proclaimed that losing weight was "harder than outrunning the paparazzi."

Six time zones away, Bill and Hillary Clinton were among the guests at a party on Martha's Vineyard. Exactly three years earlier, Diana had stunned even the Vineyard's celebrity-weary inhabitants when she vacationed there as the guest of the Brazilian ambassador's wife.

This summer, despite persistent rumors that the Princess would materialize at any moment, the Clintons had dominated the social season. The party that evening was their tenth in thirteen nights on the island, and the guest list seldom varied. Among the regulars: *Washington Post* publisher Katharine Graham; novelist William Styron and his wife, Rose; Washington power broker Vernon Jordan; columnist Art Buchwald; singer Carly Simon; television journalist Diane Sawyer and her husband, director Mike Nichols; Ted Danson and his wife, Mary Steenburgen.

It was shortly after 9 P.M. Eastern Time when the President and First Lady were told of the crash in Paris. "They were concerned," said one of the guests. "But from the first reports it sounded as if we were talking at the very worst about a broken bone or two." The party continued, with a small knot of people in the study monitoring the situation on CNN.

At Pitié-Salpêtrière, four senior nurses had joined the surgical team awaiting Diana's arrival. By the time Diana was wheeled into the operating room, she was ghastly white; all the blood had drained from her face. Although they had a half century of experience between them, two of the nurses actually became "physically sick" at the sight of the Princess, said a hospital spokesman. "They had been told she was coming in and of course they often operated on crash victims. But seeing the most beautiful woman in the world lying on the operating table in that state was something they could never have been prepared for."

As soon as he saw her, Dr. Riou knew she was bleeding to death internally. Within seconds, Diana again suffered cardiac arrest. She was immediately hooked up to a heart-lung machine. If they were to have the slightest chance of saving Diana, they would have to open her chest, determine the extent of her internal wounds, and try to repair them.

Within a few minutes, the doctors were staring into Diana's chest and shaking their heads. Her thoracic cavity had filled with blood gushing from the rupture in the left pulmonary vein—the main vessel connecting the left lung and the heart. Given the nature of the injury, the CPR performed in the ambulance had in all likelihood only made matters worse.

Diana's blood pressure was dangerously low, her organs, starved of oxygen by the massive blood loss, irreparably damaged. The nurses moved swiftly, inserting a tube into the chest and draining it of blood so Pavie could sew up the lacerated vein. There was more heart massage—this time as the doctors took turns squeezing Diana's heart in their hands, trying to get it to resume pumping on its own. They used the electric paddles again to jump-start her heart, along with massive doses of stimulants injected directly into the cardiac muscle.

Nothing worked. There had been hope that, given Diana's age and level of fitness, her heart would still respond. So they refused to quit. For almost two hours, they kept trying until—at 3:45 A.M.—Riou finally told his team there was nothing more to be done. He sutured up the large incision in her chest, and the heart-lung machine was switched off. A soul-killing silence descended over the room. Riou officially pronounced Diana dead at 4 A.M.

Doctors and nurses kept their composure inside the operating room. But once they were in the hallway, several nurses broke down in tears. Although it was theoretically possible to repair the kind of lesion Diana suffered, hospital officials insisted that this particular injury was so rare no one to their knowledge had ever survived it.

At Dodi's Paris apartment, the household staff was

summoned to the living room and quietly told that their boss and the Princess of Wales had been involved in a high-speed crash—and that both had been killed. A collective gasp went up from the small group, several of whom fled the room in tears. Debbie Gribble, who had watched the love story unfold as chief steward aboard the *Jonikal*, was among a handful of employees who accompanied Diana and Dodi to Paris. "Everyone was in a state of shock," she said. "I couldn't believe it. Only a few hours earlier I'd been with what I'd thought was the happiest couple in the world."

Thirty minutes later Diana's brother-in-law and nemesis, Sir Robert Fellowes, called Pitié-Salpêtrière from Balmoral wanting an update on the Princess's condition. Charles had been glued to Britain's Radio 5, which at 3:30 London time was broadcasting that Diana had suffered a concussion, a broken arm, and cuts to one of her thighs. One "eyewitness" was quoted as saying Diana walked away from the crash. "At this point there was no suggestion," recalled Radio 5's Peter Allen, who would soon break the news to Britain's listening public, "that she was in serious danger."

So Fellowes, believing as Charles did that the worst Diana had suffered was a concussion and a broken arm, was not prepared for what he was about to hear. A British Embassy official at the hospital got on the line and, his voice breaking, told Fellowes Diana had died. As strained as relations had been between Diana and the Queen's disapproving private secretary, Fellowes—who also faced the unenviable task of breaking the news to his wife, Diana's sister Lady Jane Spencer—was shattered.

Now Fellowes, telephone still in hand, turned to Prince Charles and told him his ex-wife was gone. What the Prince of Wales did then stunned even Fellowes. Charles unleashed a howl of anguish that brought members of the royal household running from other parts of the castle. Then he buried his head in his hands and wept. "Who would ever believe me if I described the Prince's reaction?" the British official on the other end of the line recalled. "He uttered a cry of pain that was spontaneous and came from the heart, before breaking into uncontrollable sobs."

Seeing that Charles was too distraught to speak, Fellowes then informed the Queen. Although Fellowes later claimed that the Queen was "clearly very upset" at hearing the news, others at Balmoral were not sure. While those around her made no effort to conceal their grief, the Queen betrayed an astonishing lack of emotion—even for the notoriously reserved monarch. Prince Philip, who had made no effort to disguise his contempt for Diana, seemed as ever his remote, chilly, self-involved self.

Given her own unyielding sense of propriety, the Queen was miffed at Charles's unabashed display of personal pain. It was a side of her son Elizabeth had always looked upon with disdain. In 1974 when Charles served as an officer in the Royal Navy, a seaman aboard his ship HMS *Jupiter* was killed in a similar car crash. The Prince telephoned home in tears. "Charles," the Queen said wearily, "really must learn to be tougher."

If he craved a reassuring hug or words of sympathy, he was not about to get either from the Queen. Even as a boy Charles turned to his nannies for maternal warmth and comfort. Where Diana flew at her sons with her arms outstretched after the briefest absence, Elizabeth would greet her little boy with a handshake after they had been separated for months.

Now Charles called Camilla a second time. She had also been listening to the radio and, like Charles, believed that Diana had suffered relatively minor injuries. Choking back tears, Charles told her Diana had been killed.

"Oh, those poor, poor children!" Camilla said of William and Harry, whom she had actually never met. She would later tell a friend that, despite the tensions of the past, she too was overcome with emotion and began to cry. It had already dawned on both Charles and his mistress that Diana's death would turn the public against her and virtually destroy their prospects of ever marrying. But for now, they were simply coping with the shock.

"Forget about me," Camilla told Charles, "and concentrate on the boys. They need you."

At first Charles considered going in to wake up William and Harry immediately—to hold them and console them in a shared moment of grief as Diana herself would have done. But the Queen saw no reason to disturb her grandsons' sleep. What would it accomplish? There was nothing they could do; their mother was in God's hands now.

Charles acquiesced to his mother's wishes. He would tell them in the morning. But how? The boys' belongings had already been packed for the trip to London. They had expected to attend the usual Sunday services at Crathie parish church in Balmoral and then meet Mummy at Kensington Palace. They had not seen their mother in more than a month, and over dinner had spoken of how eager they were to see her again.

It was hard enough on Charles, who was perhaps more devastated by Diana's death than he would have ever imagined, to be faced with consoling her sisters over the telephone. Both wanted to rush to her side as soon as possible. Her death was tragedy enough. But that she died in a hospital outside the country and away from her loved ones was, said a Spencer family friend, "more than her sisters could bear."

Jane, especially, was upset by the fact that there were no family, no friends with her in her last moments—and none with her now. "Poor Duch. She is all alone there," Jane wept. "We can't leave her alone!" It was agreed that both Lady Jane and Lady Sarah would board a Royal Air Force jet in Aberdeen and fly to Paris. They would then accompany Diana's body back to RAF Northolt, the royal air base northwest of London. Diana's sisters had conferred with their mother and brother, and all agreed that the funeral should be a private Spencer family affair.

The first issue at hand was what role, if any, Charles should play. Without hesitation, he had told Lady Sarah and Lady Jane that he would accompany them to Paris and escort Diana's body back home. But the Queen would have none of it. After conferring with her advisors, she told Charles that it would be inappropriate for him even to be at RAF Northolt to meet the plane, much less fly to Paris to claim her body.

But Charles stood firm. With the backing of the Prime Minister, who would be in constant touch with him by telephone throughout the week, the Prince argued forcefully that there would be a public backlash if no member of the Royal Family made the trip to Paris. Reluctantly, the Queen gave her son permission to make the trip.

Diana's mother had been alone at her home on the

remote Scottish Isle of Seil when she was told. A nephew and several friends rushed to Frances Shand Kydd's side to comfort her. "She was," said a neighbor, "practically catatonic." Raine, the stepmother Diana once called "Acid Raine" but had recently come to accept, called the hospital when she learned of the accident and was told the Princess had died. As a member of Harrods International Board of Directors, she tried to get word to Mohamed Al Fayed in England. There was no need. Within an hour of learning that Dodi had died Al Fayed, convinced that his son and the Princess had been assassinated, had helicoptered to Paris. He was standing just one floor above the operating room the moment Dr. Riou officially pronounced Diana dead.

Al Fayed did not linger at Pitié-Salpêtrière. As his limousine turned right down the Boulevard de l'Hôpital and across the Austerlitz Bridge toward the morgue, Al Fayed may already have been concocting his own *fin de siècle* potboiler—a love story in which his son was prevented by dark forces inside Buckingham Palace from becoming stepfather to the future King of England.

At first, it would be reported that a French official he knew approached him at the hospital and introduced him to a paramedic who had worked on Diana at the scene of the accident. This anonymous individual presumably told Al Fayed that Diana, while floating in and out of consciousness, muttered her last words. Later Al Fayed would claim that it was an emergency room nurse who approached him and, covering her hospital badge so she would not be accused of violating France's stringent medical secrecy laws, whispered the Princess's final wishes.

"This nurse said she recognized me and had something important to tell me," Al Fayed claimed. "But she was insistent that nobody would know her identity because it was unethical of her to pass on confidential information from an operating theater. I understood, and agreed never to reveal who she was."

Diana's last words, according to Mohamed Al Fayed: "I would like all my possessions in Dodi's apartment to be given to my sister Sarah, including my jewelry and my personal clothes, and please tell her to take care of my boys.

"For me to have a message from a mother through a nurse to her children was so important because Diana lived for nearly two hours in the operating theater. She felt that she was going, she wanted to give a message for her kids."

Al Fayed, who six months later would be arrested for rifling the safe-deposit box of a business competitor, went so far as to indicate that the first name of the nurse was Michelle—the given name of an operating room nurse who normally would have been working that night. But unbeknownst to Al Fayed, schedules had been shuffled for the month of August and the mysterious "Michelle" was not on duty that fateful night. When she did arrive at the hospital at 7 A.M., the nurse who supposedly had listened to Diana utter her last words the night before learned of the accident for the first time. "She hadn't been watching television or listening to the radio since the night before," Thierry Meresse, the hospital's communications director, said. "The nurse Al Fayed supposedly spoke to never existed."

Al Fayed also neglected to take into account another important fact: At the crash scene, Diana had been intubated—a breathing tube inserted down her throat and into the trachea. "There was absolutely no way," said one of the doctors who treated Diana that night, "that she could have said *anything*. It would have been impossible."

It was not yet 4 A.M. in England, and the world was hours from waking to the terrible truth. Charles spent most of the next two hours alone in his sitting room, his sobs audible to aides standing in the hallway. At 6:30, the Prince pulled on a sweater and went for a solitary walk along the moors. When he returned, according to a member of the household staff, Charles's eyes were "red and swollen from weeping." Over the next few hours, said Diana's friend, Lady Bowker, "Prince Charles realized he had always loved her—he fell in love with her in retrospect, if you will. He never expected something like this to happen, and now he was overcome with remorse."

At his modest suburban home, a restless Tony Blair had still been unable to get back to sleep when the second call came through at 3:30—the same moment Charles was learning of Diana's death. The Prime Minister also wondered how he would tell his sons, Euan and Nicholas; they had met Diana and played with William and Harry at Chequers only six weeks before. Sitting up in bed, Blair prepared a brief statement over the phone with his press secretary, Alastair Campbell. "This is going to produce real public grief," he told Campbell, "on a scale that is hard to imagine."

At 5 A.M. two of the surgeons who had fought so hard to pull Diana back from the brink of death— Pavie and Riou—faced the press alongside Ambassador Jay and French Interior Minister Chevènement. Riou's opening statement was jarringly brief:

"Last night in Paris, the Princess of Wales was the victim of a high-speed road accident. She was immediately taken under the care of the Paris SAMU, which carried out initial resuscitation efforts.

"Upon her arrival at the Salpêtrière Hospital, she manifested an extremely grave hemorrhagic shock, originating in the chest, quickly followed by cardiac arrest.

"An emergency thoracotomy revealed an important wound in the left pulmonary vein.

"In spite of the closing of that wound and an external, then internal, heart massage of more than two hours, no circulation could be reestablished and she was pronounced dead at 4:00 A.M."

On Martha's Vineyard, a gasp went up from those gathered around the television set when CNN confirmed that Diana had died. The President, mouth agape, shook his head in disbelief. Hillary Clinton, said a guest, "looked like she got the wind knocked out of her."

Like millions of mothers around the world, the First Lady thought first of the children. "How awful," Hillary said, her eyes brimming with tears. "She lived for those boys. What will they do without her? How terrible . . ." Stunned and, according to one journalist at the party, "obviously distraught," the Clintons promptly departed.

In Italy, Fergie halted efforts to charter a plane for Paris. It was too late. She faced the same dilemma as the others—how to tell Beatrice and Eugenie that their Aunt Duch was gone. Inconsolable, she also had to cope with the sad truth that she and Diana never repaired their rift. "Whatever happened between us," she said as she wept, "I always thought of her as my best friend and I always loved her. At times she was my only friend in the Royal Family, the only one I could talk to. She had a wonderful heart. I've lost a sister. There are no words strong enough to describe the pain in my heart."

Nothing, of course, would compare to the pain experienced by the two young men Diana called "my dear, dear boys." Another friend of the Princess, Lord Archer, pointed out that "the rest of us have lost a superstar and a very important ambassador. But the children have lost their mother. Our hearts should go out to them first."

Shortly after 7 A.M., Charles knocked gently on William's bedroom door. To Charles's surprise the young Prince, who had clearly outgrown yet another pair of pajamas, was already awake. Charles entered the room, sat on the edge of the bed, and told him what had happened that morning in Paris. Then father and son did something unthinkable to past generations of royals—they held each other and cried. "I knew something was wrong," William said. "I kept waking up all night."

In their last conversation, William told his mother that he was worried that a photo opportunity at Eton might upstage Harry. Now, as the reality of Diana's death began to sink in, the protective big brother wished there were some way to spare Harry's feelings. But there wasn't. When Charles and William went to

Harry's room and broke the news to him, all three Windsor men wept unashamedly.

Charles then led the boys to a sitting room where the Queen and Prince Philip were waiting. Sitting on a couch with his sons on either side of him, Charles gave them what few details he could, and assured them that the doctors in Paris had done all they could to save their mother. The Queen did not hug her grandsons. And however shaken she may have been, there was never a moment when Her Majesty lost her composure. Over their usual 9 A.M. breakfast, however, the Queen and Prince Philip did tell the boys how "terribly sorry" they were that the boys had lost their mother. She also informed her grandsons that in her opinion it would be best if they remained with the rest of the Royal Family at Balmoral for a few more days.

Diana's former mother-in-law also saw no particular reason to distrupt the royal Sunday schedule. While Charles suggested that William and Harry might wish to grieve at least for the first few hours in the privacy of their own rooms, the Queen thought otherwise. She wanted the family to attend church as usual that morning. For the Windsors, Her Majesty was determined that life proceed as normally as possible.

"Granny," as William and Harry called the Queen, was concerned about the impact of Diana's death on the young Princes. To spare them any further upset, she temporarily banned newspapers from Balmoral and ordered that televisions and radios inside the castle not be turned on.

Governing her thoughts, as always, was the future of the monarchy—what effect the tragic events of that Sunday would have in shaping the future King. If the early stories were true that Diana had been chased to her death by paparazzi, then there was a danger that William—already wary of the press—might shrink from his public duty. By showing up at church with the rest of the family only hours after being told of their mother's death, William and Harry would prove to the nation that that was not going to happen. It was also the sort of stiff-upper-lip show of unity, strength, and dignity in adversity the Royal Family prided itself on.

Less dignified, perhaps, were the questions the Queen had begun asking almost immediately upon learning of Diana's death. It was at this time—while her son, her grandsons, and the world at large still reeled from the enormity of the human loss—that England's Queen demanded to know if Diana was wearing any royal jewelry when she died. And if so, she ordered that it be returned immediately.

While William and Harry, incredibly, were being required by the Queen to prepare for church, the public slowly awakened to the stomach-turning news.

Rita Rogers, who had spoken with Diana only eight hours before the crash, now sat in her Derbyshire home staring blankly at the television set. She had warned Dodi that he faced danger in a tunnel in Paris—that there would be motorcycles—"but I never saw Diana in the tunnel," she mumbled to herself over and over again that day, "I never saw her in the car . . ."

In Mountain Ash, Wales, where he had told police on August 27 that Diana was in mortal danger, psychic Edward Williams had not been able to shake the feeling of impending doom. "I felt better that I had got it off my chest," he said, "but the feeling that Diana was in danger didn't leave me. When I switched on the TV Sunday morning and I heard she had been killed, I felt sick to my stomach. Princess Diana's destiny was somehow in my hands and I didn't do the right thing." What of his August 27 warning? Taken seriously enough to be passed along by the local police, it awaited action on the desk of the Special Branch officer.

In Paris, Dr. Frédéric Mailliez had had a difficult time getting to sleep. The young emergency physician knew that, given his limited resources, there was only so much he could have done for the blond woman in the tunnel, but still . . . "There's a frustration," he said, "that maybe you could have done more. Eventually I fell asleep, but with this strong feeling of helplessness."

Mark Butt was another matter. Mailliez's companion, still shaken by what he had seen in the Pont de l'Alma tunnel—even at some distance—could not sleep. At the same time William and Harry were being told, Butt poured a cup of coffee and turned on CNN.

"And the first thing I heard was that there was an accident, and that Princess Diana was dead. And that it was an accident in Paris. And that it was at the Pont de l'Alma tunnel. So then I knew what it was." Butt's knees buckled.

"Frédéric! Frédéric!" Butt shouted as he ran into Mailliez's room. "It was Diana! It was Diana!"

Mailliez, who admits he has "a hard time getting up," shot out of bed and ran to the television. "Oh my God," he said, trying to drink it all in. "My God."

It was 7 A.M. before a timid aide decided to wake up French President Jacques Chirac and tell him that Princess Diana had been killed not far from the Elysée Palace. "Lady Di? You mean the Princess of Wales? Pont de l'Alma? She was in Paris?"

It took a moment for it all to sink in, but once it had he dictated a statement to be read to the press: "I have learned with deep emotion of the brutal death of Lady Diana. She was a young woman of our times, warm, full of life and generosity. Her tragic death will be deeply felt because she was a familiar figure to all of us. In these terrible hours, I think of her family and especially her children."

In Martha's Vineyard, a somber President Clinton stepped before the television cameras to offer his nation's condolences. "We liked her very much," the President said, speaking for himself and the First Lady. "We admired her work for children, for people with AIDS, for the cause of ending the scourge of land mines in the world, and for her love for her children, William and Harry. We can only hope that her work will go forward and that everyone who can will support her two fine sons and help them to have the life and future that she would want."

Former British Prime Minister Margaret Thatcher said that with Diana's death "a beacon of light had been extinguished." The Princess's friend Nelson Mandela praised her as "an ambassador for victims of land mines, war orphans, the sick and needy throughout the world." Pope John Paul II, described by aides as "deeply saddened," offered special prayers for Diana at the Vatican.

No statement by a world leader would be more heartfelt than Tony Blair's. Before leaving for church services that morning, the Prime Minister called Balmoral to express his condolences to the Queen and the Prince of Wales. Charles's voice broke as he spoke with Blair, but Elizabeth, even under these extraordinary circumstances, was her usual composed self. Hanging up the phone, Blair had already begun to wonder if the Queen understood how much Diana was loved—and the national catharsis that would almost certainly be triggered by news of her death.

It was a message he hoped to convey to them when he spoke to the British people for the first time that morning at 10:28. "I feel like everyone else in this country today, utterly devastated," said Blair, choking back tears as he spoke to reporters on the steps of the twelfth-century stone chapel he attended in his parliamentary district. "Our thoughts and prayers are with Princess Diana's family and in particular her two sons, the two boys. Our hearts go out to them. We are today a nation in a state of shock and in grief that is so deeply painful for us.

"She was a wonderful and warm human being, though her own life was often sadly touched by tragedy. She touched the lives of so many throughout the world with joy and comfort. How many times shall we remember her in how many different ways—with the sick, the dying, with children, with the needy. With just a look or a gesture that spoke so much more than words, she would reveal to all of us the depth of her compassion and her humanity.

"You know how difficult things were for her from time to time, I'm sure we can only guess at," Blair mused. "But people everywhere kept faith with Princess Diana. They liked her, they loved her, they regarded her as one of the people. She was the people's princess, and that's how she will stay, how she will remain, in our hearts and in our memories forever . . ."

As he recapped Blair's brief speech, BBC television anchor Martyn Lewis tried to maintain his composure. "You keep your emotions under control but I was in danger of going," Lewis later said. "Blair's words were very powerful. I had to pause for a few seconds to pull myself together."

Mother Teresa, who only two months earlier had met with Diana at one of her Missionaries of Charity settlement houses in the Bronx, joined the chorus of praise for her friend. "Diana," she said simply, "had a beautiful spirit."

Just five hours before she hurtled to her death in the Alma Tunnel, Diana had told her friend Annabel Goldsmith that she needed another marriage "like a bad rash on my face." Now, in a self-described state of denial, she jotted down happy memories of the times Diana would drop in on the weekend for lunch. "I will miss that fresh little voice on the telephone," she scribbled in her diary, "always rather humbly asking me if we were busy at the weekend. I will miss her radiant smile as she burst through the door—it was always a burst—and hugged us all, so full of life and happiness at the thought of a few hours' escape from what I know to have been a lonely existence. I felt I was there for her to have a bit of fun and relaxation and love."

Captain James Hewitt, the former cavalry officer who had betrayed Diana by revealing the most intimate details of their clandestine affair in a book, also felt compelled—however misguidedly—to share his feelings. Standing on his front lawn, Hewitt told reporters that he, "like the rest of the country," was "still in shock over the tragedy. The world has lost a very special person who touched the hearts of millions. On a more personal note, I would like to say how much I liked and admired her. I loved her and will miss her very much."

One of the male admirers she occasionally categorized like greyhounds by "trap" number, George Michael, waxed surprisingly eloquent about his friend's passing. Together, they had helped raise millions for AIDS treatment and research. "I truly believe some souls are too special, too beautiful to be kept from heaven," Michael said, "however painful it is for the rest of us to let them go."

At the time of her death, Diana and Cindy Crawford had been working on a secret project. At William's urging, the Princess had once arranged for Crawford to come to tea at Kensington Palace. In recent weeks, Diana had been hatching a plan to bring the boys on holiday to Switzerland when Crawford was hosting a golf tournament there.

Now Crawford's main concern was for the Princes. She called Balmoral and asked to speak to William, but the Queen had ordered that all calls be held. "He will be in pieces," Crawford said of William. "He adored his mother. He considered her to be his best friend."

Yet, amid the eloquent statements of loss and bereavement, little was heard from the Royal Family itself. Buckingham Palace had issued only one terse sentence on the subject:

> The Queen and Prince of Wales are deeply shocked and distressed by this terrible news.

On this wet and gloomy Sunday in Scotland, three black Rolls-Royce limousines pulled in front of Crathie Church, just across the River Dee from Balmoral, at precisely 11:13 A.M. The small stone church was built in 1895 to replace a series of churches on the site dating back to the ninth century, and had been attended by generations of British monarchs.

The Queen Mother, ninety-seven, arrived in the first car, dressed in black and accompanied by Prince Andrew and Princess Anne's son Peter Phillips. Her trademark greatgrandmotherly smile remained perfectly in place. Already she had reminded her daughter that Diana, at the time of her death, was no longer officially a royal.

In the back of the next limousine were William and Harry, seated on either side of their father. The boys wore dark suits, Charles a gray jacket, a matching gray vest, and kilts. While the Prince of Wales clasped his hands in front of him, the boys stared grimly out the window. As they got out of the car, said an onlooker, Diana's sons looked "shocked and pale, but calm."

Queen Elizabeth, also in black and wearing a broadbrimmed hat, rolled up in the next limousine with Prince Philip at her side. Both stared, unspeaking, straight ahead. As they walked up the steep steps to the church entrance, Elizabeth turned to look briefly into the crowd of people that lined the walkway. The look, said one tourist, was "the look you always see—you know, sort of supercilious. If she was upset, you sure couldn't tell it. Prince Charles's attention was on William and Harry. They kept starting at the ground and never looked up. Harry looked saddest of all."

The Reverend Robert Sloan welcomed the Royal Family at the door, but only Charles stopped to chat with him. Sloan was "struck by the way they seemed to be bearing up. It was clear they had gone through great grief and trauma."

With Sloan looking on, a visiting minister, the Reverend Adrian Varwell from Benbecula in the Outer Hebrides, conducted the service. Varwell went ahead as planned with his sermon, liberally peppered with jokes by Scottish comic Billy Connelly (who, ironically, played Queen Victoria's Balmoral confidant John Brown in the film *Mrs. Brown).* Varwell also talked about the unsettling experience of house moving. At one point, the minister held up a plastic bucket with a hole in it that he used to feed his goats and sheep. The Reverend Varwell likened the leaky bucket to "people who waste God's love."

The hymns had not been changed, nor the prayers said every Sunday for the Royal Family. The Queen, her family, the Prince of Wales, and Princes William and Harry were, as usual, mentioned by name. But not Diana.

Incredibly, no mention was made of Diana or her death during the royal church service at Crathie that morning. Princess Diana was not mentioned, a church spokesman explained, because "the children had been awakened just a few hours earlier to be told of the death of their mother and we did not wish to disturb them further." Diana's death was ignored, the Reverend Sloan insisted, "to protect the boys."

Protect the boys? With the two people in the world who meant the most to her sitting in the royal pew, churchgoers were amazed that not a mention of their mother was made. At one point during the service, Harry turned to his father and whispered, "Are you sure Mummy is dead?" Charles did not reply.

"It must have been the only place in the world," said one parishioner, "where Diana's death wasn't the only thing anyone could talk about. It was absolutely amazing. What could her boys have been thinking? I wouldn't have been surprised if they both jumped up and screamed what is going on? I know I felt like doing that."

But the failure of anyone in the church to mention Diana was neither misguided nor a simple oversight. Asked specifically if she wanted any changes made in the sermon that morning in light of the tragic events in Paris, the Queen said categorically, no. Nor did she ask that Diana's name be reinstated—at least this once—in the prayers for the Royal Family. She had personally seen to it that Diana was stripped of her royal status at the time of the divorce, and her edict that Diana's name not be spoken in her presence had yet to be officially rescinded. "Sheer common sense," said royal observer Marianne Macdonald, "suggests she was indeed not sorrowing for Diana."

A tall, attractive young woman was waiting for

William and Harry when they returned to the castle. The boys flew into the outstretched arms of Tiggy Legge-Bourke. To be sure, there had been considerable hostility between Diana and their high-spirited former nanny. So much, in fact, that Diana had demanded that Charles take her off the royal payroll. But the boys remained fond of the tomboyish Tiggy, and had come to view her less as a mother substitute and more like a fun-loving big sister. Unbeknownst to Diana, she had spent the last two weeks of August as a guest at Balmoral and had planned to fly home to Wales that weekend.

Her grudge against Tiggy aside, Diana knew that, with the exception of Charles, the emotionally constipated Windsors were not about to comfort the Princes with warm hugs and tender words. But the down-to-earth, distinctly unstuffy Tiggy could be counted on for just that. Now, with the express consent of the Queen, Charles pleaded with Tiggy to stay. That afternoon she moved into a cottage on the castle grounds. Tiggy would remain on call for William and Harry "as long as they need me," she reportedly told Charles.

"Good," Charles replied, his voice breaking again. "Their mother would have wanted that."

As Tiggy comforted the Prince's now-motherless children, Diana's butler and confidant Paul Burrell walked into the second floor room at Paris's Pitié-Salpêtrière Hospital and broke down as he saw her body for the first time. And outside in a hospital corridor, the British consul was seeking an answer to the Queen's persistent question: "Where are the jewels?"

Whoever is in distress can call on me. I will come running wherever they are. It is my destiny.

—*Diana*

They adored their mother and she loved them passionately. I can hardly bear to think about them.

—*Rosa Monckton*

7

"I had always believed the press would kill her in the end," Earl Spencer said to reporters gathered at the gates to his Cape Town home. "But not even I could imagine that they would take such a direct hand in her death as seems to be the case. It would appear that every publication that has paid for intrusive and exploitative photographs of her, encouraging greedy and ruthless individuals to risk everything in pursuit of Diana's image, has blood on their hands today. Finally, the one consolation is that Diana is now in a place where no human being can ever touch her again. I pray that she rests in peace."

Spencer's bitterness toward Fleet Street was understandable. After all, he had been the subject of so many scandalous headlines independent of his sister that he fled to South Africa in the vain hope of repairing his shattered marriage. Of course, Spencer also neglected to mention that for years he himself had been a high-flying television correspondent, and that Diana—to her credit—had played the media like a Stradivarius.

Still, in the absence of any other villains, the press would certainly do for the moment. At the scene of the accident, Paris police took six photographers—Serge Arnal, Nikola Arsov, Jacques Langevin, Christian Martinez, Romuald Rat, and Laszlo Veres—into custody, along with Gamma motorcycle driver Stéphane Darmon.

They were handcuffed, loaded into a police van, and taken to the nearest precinct station for questioning. At the station, the photographers were fingerprinted and strip-searched. Although twenty rolls of film had been confiscated, police also conducted a thorough cavity search—just to make sure that no photographer had concealed a roll in his rectum. After mug shots were taken, the hapless paparazzi were tossed into a dank holding cell.

The men were interrogated for hours, and then hauled in front of Judge Hervé Stephan. The judge felt there was evidence that the photographers' reckless actions during the chase might have contributed to the crash. At the very least, there was evidence that they might have violated France's Good Samaritan law by failing to come to the aid of the victims.

Later, three more photographers who had left the scene before the police roundup—Serge Benhamou,

Fabrice Chassery, and David Oderkerken—turned themselves in. All ten were placed under formal investigation—the French equivalent of being criminally charged—for "involuntary homicide and nonassistance to persons in danger."

Ultimately, the charges would prove groundless— the pursuing photographers neither caused the accident nor, according to Dr. Mailliez, in any way interfered with efforts to treat the victims. And as distasteful as it may have seemed to bystanders at the time, their responsibility was to record on film what was a legitimate news event.

But for the first twenty-four hours after the crash, it was open season on the press in general and tabloids in particular. Someone scrawled PAPARAZZI ASSASSINS on a concrete abutment above the Alma Tunnel. In front of Kensington Palace, Diana's home, a crowd jeered reporters who were there to describe the scene. "You've hounded her to death!" one shouted at a BBC correspondent. "Happy now?" a bus driver yelled, applauded by the mob as he showered reporters with blistering expletives. Reporters unfortunate enough to be stationed in front of Buckingham Palace and at Balmoral were spat at, called "murderers," and even threatened with physical violence.

Mohamed Al Fayed, meantime, was on a timetable of his own. As soon as he learned Diana had died, Al

Fayed left Pitié-Salpêtrière for the morgue. When the sheet was pulled down to reveal Dodi's face, his father later claimed that he was surprised how serene his son looked. "I could see that Dodi was at peace," he said. "He had such a beautiful smile. He looked like a little boy again." Al Fayed did not mention that there was a gaping wound above Dodi's right eye, and that the rest of his face had been badly cut in the crash.

The man who had gone to such lengths to become a British citizen wanted his son to be buried on English soil—and, in accordance with Muslim custom, within twenty-four hours of his death. But this Sunday in August Al Fayed's minions would have to work miracles to secure the documents needed to bring Dodi home in time. That morning, as he waited in his office at the Ritz for Dodi's body to be released from the morgue, the man they had all feared broke down in front of his startled executives. By noon, Dodi's casket was loaded onto Harrods' Sikorsky S-76 and, with his father strapped into the seat next to it, flown back to England.

Before he left Paris, Al Fayed visited Dodi's apartment near the Arc de Triomphe and told butler René Delorm that he wanted everything in the apartment untouched—a shrine to his fallen son. Al Fayed did, however, remove one item personally: the $200,000 "Tell Me Yes" ring that Dodi had intended to give Diana that night. The ring, which Mohamed Al

Fayed brought back to London, was later placed in a Swiss safe-deposit box along with several love letters Diana had written to Dodi.

Delorm undertook the heartbreaking task of gathering Dodi's personal things together, and asked Debbie Gribble if she was up to packing the Princess's clothes away. "It was so sad, I couldn't help crying while I did it," Gribble said. "I just pulled her black leather bag onto the bed and got on with it."

Gribble painstakingly packed away the cashmere sweaters Dodi had bought Diana in Sardinia—most of them still in their plastic wrapping—as well as the handmade shoes, Diana's shorts, and T-shirts. She carefully folded Diana's beige suit and her Armani jeans.

The Princess had not brought much in the way of toiletries—some Chanel, some Estée Lauder. "There didn't seem to be enough there for a whole life," Gribble mused. It was then, she said, that the enormity of the tragedy suddenly hit her. "I couldn't stop the tears from flowing."

But Gribble said the hardest things to pack were the very last items she slipped inside Diana's black leather bag: a photograph of William and Harry hugging and the silver-etched love poem Dodi had given her. "That," Gribble said, "broke my heart."

All this time, Diana's nude body lay beneath a sheet in a small blue-walled room just above the entrance to Pitié-Salpêtrière Hospital's Gaston Cordier wing. When British officials called the Ritz to locate the Princess's clothing, they were shocked to learn that all her belongings had been shipped back to England by Al Fayed. It was then that the mad scramble began to find some suitable garment in which to dress Diana—the bizarre search that ended when Ambassador Jay's wife, Sylvia, offered one of her own black cocktail dresses.

Less than twelve hours after Diana was pronounced dead, rumors of every conceivable sort were already running rampant. An early report that a small quantity of cocaine was found in the car proved to be totally unfounded. So too was the story that a necklace had been stolen from the wreckage. Diana was not wearing a necklace that evening, as was clearly visible in all photographs and videotape taken of her that evening.

Although there was not a shred of evidence pointing to a murder plot, the inevitable conspiracy theories began to take root before the mangled Mercedes was placed on a flatbed truck and removed from the tunnel. In Egypt, a nation which had taken considerable pride in the budding romance between the Princess of Wales and one of their own, there was a general consensus that the couple had been assassinated by British Intelligence.

This assassination theory would, in the days immediately following the crash, be offered up as fact by some of the Arab world's leading journalists and commentators. "The British intelligence service killed them," wrote prominent Cairo writer Anis Mansour in the respected daily newspaper *Al-Ahram*. "They could not have let the mother of the future king marry a Muslim Arab." Libya's Moammar Gadhafi accused the French and the British of "arranging" the crash.

Why would England's Establishment want Dodi and Diana dead? Presumably to prevent the mother of the future King from converting to Islam, or from giving birth to Muslim children who would be half-siblings to the sovereign. But even if she were to marry, there was no need for Diana to convert—both Mohamed Al Fayed's wife, Heini, and Dodi's first wife, Suzanne Gregard, remained Christians. As for the children from such a union, they would have no claims on any royal titles, and as such pose no threat to the monarchy.

In fact Diana, whose phenomenal popularity had long vexed her former in-laws, would certainly come under attack for marrying a foreigner—not to mention the Egyptian playboy son of one of the most notorious wheeler-dealers in Britain. The idea of Diana losing some if not most of her broad-based public support could not have been entirely unappealing to her enemies at Buckingham Palace.

Then there were the multitude of variables that

evening that would seem to render any assassination scenario implausible: the abrupt departure from Chez Benoît and the unexpected return to the Ritz, the last-minute switch of drivers that put a severely impaired Henri Paul behind the wheel, the decision on the couple's part not to fasten their seat belts, the seemingly arbitrary nature of the crash itself, and its uncertain outcome. Any murder plot that could take into account all this and more would, said Margaret Thatcher, "stretch credulity. It's all ridiculous. Complete rubbish." Nonetheless, so long as the mysterious Fiat Uno remained unaccounted for, the questions—and the wild speculation—would continue unabated.

While scores of outrageous conspiracy theories were floated on the Internet and in newspapers throughout the Arab world, a very real crisis was brewing in the United Kingdom. In the wake of Earl Spencer's bitter attack on the press, Diana's family wanted a private funeral. The Queen saw no reason to deny the Spencers their wish. Diana was, after all, no longer married to Charles and therefore not technically entitled to any special treatment.

But the unprecedented global outpouring of grief Prime Minister Tony Blair had predicted had already begun. From Washington, D.C., to Tokyo to Moscow, thousands of mourners stood in line for hours to sign books of condolence and leave floral tributes at British embassies and consulates.

Nowhere, of course, was the pain more keenly felt than in Britain. In the streets of the capital, total strangers hugged one another and entire families sobbed openly. Outside the royal palaces, mourners had already begun laying down a floral carpet that would eventually cover several acres of central London. At Kensington Palace, many knelt and prayed, while others crumpled to the ground in tears. Most simply wandered in stricken silence.

The Prince and the Labour Party leader had been friendly ever since Blair's election as Prime Minister. So Blair did not hesitate to call Charles aboard the Paris-bound RAF jet and tell the Prince it would be a "fatal mistake" to allow plans for a private funeral to proceed. "The people," he warned Charles, "simply will not stand for it."

Employing Sir Robert Fellowes as their go-between, Blair and Charles managed to convince the Spencer family that Diana's funeral would have to be, in part, a national event. The Queen, however, proved a more formidable challenge. Not even Fellowes's importuning could budge Her Majesty. On the subject of a public funeral for the woman she had taken pains to banish from the Royal Family, the monarch remained implacable. "There is," she said, shrugging, "no precedent for it."

Indeed, the monarchy was ruled by precedent—and never more so than when it came to funerals.

Should the Queen or Queen Mother die, all the arrangements are already in place. The guest lists to these events are updated as various heads of state are replaced or die. At least once a year there is a predawn rehearsal of the Queen Mother's funeral procession through the streets of London. And when they travel, all royals bring along mourning clothes, in case a family member dies and they must rush home for the funeral.

In determining the size and nature of Diana's funeral, there was sufficient precedent for a private royal funeral, attended only by members of the extended Royal Family, their children, and their spouses. Again, Blair and Charles were convinced that would leave the public feeling cheated and resentful of the monarchy. A full state funeral was intended only for kings and queens, but by order of the monarchy and a vote in Parliament could be extended to such exceptional figures as Winston Churchill. The third, and most likely, alternative was a ceremonial funeral usually reserved for members of the family who also hold high military rank (such as Lord Mountbatten), the consort of the monarch, or the heir to the throne. After weighing the options, Blair and Charles decided that what England needed to see was "a unique funeral for a unique person." Ultimately, the job of persuading the Queen to change her mind would fall squarely on her son's shoulders.

At 6:51 P.M. local time, the RAF transport with its distinctive red tail and the Union Jack emblazoned on the fuselage touched down at Northolt. As the world watched on television, Diana's coffin, still draped in the *ancien régime* lions and harps of the royal standard, was taken from the plane. Then a hatless RAF honor guard, ceremonial swords sheathed and moving in funeral lock-step, slowly carried the coffin toward the waiting hearse. Bringing up the rear: a burly, lantern-jawed sergeant, cradling a spray of white lilies in his arms and clearly fighting back tears.

Prince Charles, Lady Sarah and Lady Jane, Tony Blair, and other dignitaries stood watching in total silence; the only sound was from flags fluttering in the stiff breeze. Paul Burrell later told Lady Elsa Bowker that he had "never seen Prince Charles like this—so devastated, upset, eyes red from crying. He is in total shock."

At Northolt, the Prime Minister continued to lobby for a public funeral on the grand scale. He cornered Lord Airlie, who as lord chamberlain would coordinate the arrangements. To Blair's relief, Lord Airlie agreed that the event would have to be "a mixture of the traditional and the modern"—much like Diana herself.

"Yes," said Blair, who cleared his calendar solely to deal with this crisis. "But how do we convince the Queen?"

The *Sturm und Drang* over Diana's funeral arrangements was of little concern to Mohamed Al Fayed. That night, in keeping with Muslim custom, Dodi's body was wrapped in three lengths of white cloth before being placed in his coffin. Then, escorted by two police cars and a motorcycle, the hearse carrying Dodi's black-draped casket proceeded to the domed Central Mosque in Regent's Park. The twenty-five-minute service—conducted with Dodi's coffin facing toward Mecca—was attended by fifty mourners, including top executives of the Fayeds' far-flung business empire and Egypt's ambassador to Great Britain. Diana's last love was then driven twenty-five miles southwest of London to Woking, where he was buried at Brookwood Cemetery.

No members of the Royal Family deigned to pay their respects at Dodi's funeral, but the Queen did send her condolences via messenger from Balmoral. "It was a most kind, warm, and generous letter of condolence," said Al Fayed's spokesman Michael Cole, "and Mr. Al Fayed and the whole family are truly grateful."

At the same time Dodi was being laid to rest, Diana's body was at a private mortuary being autopsied by the Fulham coroner. After the autopsy, she was clothed in a simple, long-sleeved black coat dress designed by her friend Catherine Walker. The Princess had purchased the dress only three weeks before, and had never worn it.

The photograph of William and Harry that had been placed in the coffin by nurses at Pitié-Salpêtrière Hospital was placed back in Diana's folded hands, as were the photo of her father and the rosary given to Diana by Mother Teresa. (In yet another ironic turn of events, the revered nun would die of a heart attack at age eighty-seven on the eve of Diana's funeral. That same day Sir Georg Solti, who had planned to conduct a special BBC concert in honor of Diana, also died unexpectedly. He was eighty-four.) Mohammed Al Fayed sent the silver-engraved love poem Dodi had given Diana on the *Jonikal* to St. James's— unaware that Dodi had actually "borrowed" the poem years earlier from his then-girlfriend Tina Sinatra—and asked that it also be placed inside the coffin. The offer was declined.

Diana was then moved to the Chapel Royal at St. James's Palace, just a few hundred yards from Buckingham Palace. In another twist of fate, her body now lay in state in the palace she professed to hate. St. James's housed the offices of the Prince of Wales, and as such was a stronghold for her husband's friends. St. James's was one of the two places (Buckingham Palace being the other) where "the enemy," as she called them, actively plotted against her.

Diana's butler Paul Burrell spent this night as he

would every night until her funeral—sitting by the coffin, reading aloud from her favorite books, telling her stories and the jokes that had made her double over with laughter. Burrell told Diana's hairdresser Natalie Symonds, "I just don't want her to be alone."

To the amazement of most Britons, the Queen chose to remain holed up with the Royal Family at Balmoral, 550 miles from the epicenter of her nation's grief. Since television sets at Balmoral remained switched off by royal command, Diana's sons were among a handful of people who did not watch the touching moment when Diana's body arrived home on British soil.

That Sunday evening at 8:30, less than seventeen hours after Diana was pronounced dead and ninety minutes after her body arrived back on British soil, the Windsors sat down to dinner as usual. Presumably to avoid "upsetting" the boys, the Queen never mentioned Diana but instead steered the conversation toward hunting—specifically the deer-stalking party scheduled for that week. When he arrived at Balmoral from London later that evening Charles, dumbfounded by the notion that the family planned to stick to its original schedule, demanded that the stag hunt be canceled.

William and Harry, exhausted and still in a state of shock, went to bed right after dinner. Before William retired, however, the two brothers spent over an hour together in Harry's room consoling each other.

At Eton and Ludgrove, meantime, the boys' class-mates worried about how to behave toward the motherless Princes. "It will be your duty never to mention her," one father advised. "You must pretend that nothing has happened and just carry on." One of William's former masters at Eton allowed that what happened to his mother was "a terrible tragedy. But Prince William is not a little boy. He cannot grieve forever; he must learn to take it."

In a strange twist of fate, the only person their father could turn to for consolation was his longtime mistress Camilla, now unquestionably the most hated woman in Britain. Only one month earlier, after the fiftieth birthday party Charles threw for her to over-whelming public approval, a poll showed that 68 per-cent of Britons felt that Charles and Camilla should marry.

To maintain the momentum, Camilla had planned to cohost a charity ball on September 13 to benefit the National Osteoporosis Society. Some of England's biggest celebrities—including Emma Thompson, Mick Jagger, and Joan Collins—were scheduled to at-tend. So, too, was the Prince of Wales. It was to be the first appearance of Charles and Camilla at a major public event—and a major step in the direction of marriage.

Camilla immediately canceled the ball, and the vacation she had planned with Charles at Balmoral for late September. In a single stroke, her prospects of ever marrying Charles and becoming Queen seemed to evaporate. "Diana's death has set Charles and Camilla back years," royal watcher Judy Wade observed, adding that if they were seen together any time in the coming months, "it could be the end of them. The public simply won't tolerate it."

Meanwhile, much of the city was engulfed in a fragrant tide of flowers; in addition to the bouquets left at palace gates and monuments, blossoms were tied to lamp posts, trash bins, park benches, and even tree branches, creating an exotic Garden of Allah effect. So massive was the outpouring of sorrow that much of it spilled over to Dodi. Mourners flocked to Fayed's grave at Brookwood Cemetery, leaving flowers, notes, stuffed animals, and snapshots. And many if not most of those who paid their respects to Diana with flowers and notes were careful to include Dodi's name in their prayers.

At Harrods, Mohamed Al Fayed ordered that the 11,500 lights that normally illuminate the building's elaborate Victorian exterior be turned off in Dodi's memory. One of Harrods' front windows, normally reserved for mannequins draped in the latest designer fashions, was turned into a Dodi and Diana shrine, complete with silver-framed photographs of the couple.

From his London home, Mohamed Al Fayed issued word through Michael Cole that he wished to deal with his grief in private. But on Monday morning his operatives went on the attack, promising a civil suit against the photographers who had been taken into custody at the scene. It was an opportunity for Cole, a blow-dried former anchorman for BBC television, to indulge his distaste for the tabloid press. In a statement as inaccurate as it was crass, Al Fayed's spokesman likened the paparazzi to "Apache Indians swarming around a Wells Fargo stagecoach." Cole claimed there was "no doubt in Mr. Fayed's mind that this tragedy would not have occurred but for the press photographers who have dogged Mr. Fayed and the Princess for weeks."

In a startling turnabout, Al Fayed suddenly found himself on the defensive when the medical examiner in Paris released its first toxicology reports. They showed that Henri Paul's blood alcohol content was three times the legal limit—roughly the equivalent of downing nine ounces of whiskey. The accuracy of the tests was immediately challenged by those loyal to Al Fayed, so they were done again. And again. Not only did subsequent forensic testing prove beyond a shadow of a doubt that Paul was drunk, but they detected high levels of the antidepressant Prozac and

Tiapridal—the powerful prescription medications Paul had been secretly taking to treat his chronic alcoholism.

According to a Ritz employee identified in sealed police reports only as "Frédéric L.," about an hour after they left, word of the crash had filtered back to the hotel. Frédéric L. heard about it "from the regular parking valet on duty. He was completely undone. He said, 'There's been a very serious accident with the Princess Diana. It's very serious for the Ritz.' Then one of the security guards said something I didn't understand until some time later: 'It's a terrible thing to drink. Drinking and driving kills.' Very shortly, we were told to speak to no one of it."

Ritz bartender Alain Willaumez confirmed that it "was well-known that Henri Paul had the tendency to drink." Hotel president Frank Klein, Willaumez took pains to reiterate, "knew this perfectly." Yet the bartender related that, the day after the accident, Klein pressured him not to tell police he had served Paul two glasses of *pastis* the night of the accident. Instead, Klein asked him to back up the bodyguards' claim that Paul was drinking "fruit juice" the night of the crash. "For the good of the Royal Family," Klein allegedly said, "you must maintain this version."

At Pitié-Salpêtrière Hospital, meanwhile, hospital administrators were fighting off attempts by Al Fayed to pick up the critically injured Trevor Rees-Jones by helicopter and transport him to a private hospital in England. Although he was sitting inches from Diana and Dodi at the time of the crash, Rees-Jones would be one of the last people in the world to know they had been killed. For ten days he remained in a coma, his mother, Gil, keeping vigil at his bedside.

Eventually, it would fall to Trevor's mother to break the news to him. "There is no easy way of saying this, Trevor," she said, taking his hand, "but Diana and Dodi were both killed in the crash and so was the driver, Henri Paul. You were the only survivor."

"It was like a hammer blow," Rees-Jones later said of that moment. "I just sat there in total shock. I felt terrible. I just assumed that everyone else was OK too. It never crossed my mind that I was the only one . . ."

It would take over a month for doctors to rebuild his face, using his wedding photos as a guide. "They had the whole wedding album in the end," Rees-Jones later said, "and studied each picture of me at different angles to reconstruct my features." Ironically Trevor Rees, who became Trevor Rees-Jones when he married Sue Jones, had just separated from his wife after two years of marriage.

Even such pivotal issues as the cause of the crash paled in comparison to the crisis triggered by Diana's death. The British people were in a downward spiral of despair over the loss of their beloved Princess, and yet the Royal Family was nowhere to be seen.

Clearly, the Queen had not the slightest inkling how deeply her subjects loved the woman the Palace had long viewed with thinly disguised contempt. The mountains of flowers around the palaces grew day by day, and by Wednesday over 750,000 people had waited patiently for up to twelve hours to sign condolence books at St. James's Palace. In a measure of the nation's grief, the number of condolence books opened at St. James's grew from four to sixteen to forty-three—in comparison to only five books put out for mourners when the hugely popular King George VI died.

Buckingham Palace, where police at first refused to allow mourners to leave flowers at the gates, became a focal point of the growing resentment toward the royals. When every other flag in the kingdom was flying at half-mast, the public demanded to know why the flag over Buckingham Palace was not. In keeping with protocol, the flag flew over Buckingham Palace only when the sovereign was in residence. The Queen saw no compelling reason to make an exception in this particular case.

That, in turn, begged the question, why *wasn't* the Queen in residence? Why did the Royal Family choose to remain in Scotland when tens of thousands of their people were pouring into London? And why—when other world leaders praised Diana and her humanitarian accomplishments—had Britain's own Royal Family chosen to remain so conspicuously and icily aloof?

Even the most ardent monarchists were moved by the Queen's passionate indifference. "They have blood on their hands," none other than *Burke's Peerage* managing director Harold Brooks-Baker said of the Royal Family. "They found a modern woman to be the mother of Charles's children and when they couldn't handle her, they kicked her out. They finally succeeded and today they stand guilty. Here was a victim of the monarchy. Diana died a martyr. We can only hope her death brings about another kind of palace rebellion. The House of Windsor is in desperate need of a major overhaul, and if it doesn't get one soon, I fear for the very existence of the monarchy in Britain."

Constitutional expert Anthony Barrett agreed. "A stunning reversal has taken place," Barrett said. "The monarchy must bow its head, or it will be broken. We, the people, will henceforth define how they should represent us. The Princess cannot be replaced. It's as if the country is crying, 'Diana is dead! Long live democracy!' No longer will the nature of the country be decided from above and delivered to a grateful public."

Pauline Ford, a retired nursing home manager from Coventry, echoed a swelling sense of outrage. "If it wasn't for them," she said of the Royal Family, "Diana wouldn't be dead. This has turned me into a republican. We shouldn't have one [a monarch] after this Queen." London cabbie Mick Boreham agreed. "Diana's death was a chance for them to get in touch with the people they'd lost," Boreham said as he left a bouquet outside Kensington Palace. "It's too late now. After the funeral a lot of anger is going to go their way. This must be what a revolution feels like."

Soon, polls were showing two out of three Britons believed Diana's death would bring down the monarchy. Others, disregarding the simple fact that William had no particular desire to ever ascend to the throne, called for Charles to step aside in favor of Diana's elder son.

SPEAK TO US MA'AM—YOUR PEOPLE ARE SUFFERING trumpeted the *Mirror*. The *Daily Mail* demanded LET THE FLAG FLY AT HALF MAST, while the normally ultra-loyal *Express* pleaded SHOW US YOU CARE. The *Sun* joined in the chorus with WHERE IS OUR QUEEN? WHERE IS HER FLAG?

Back at Balmoral, Her Majesty dug in. The flag at Buckingham Palace had not flown at half-mast for Winston Churchill. It would not fly at half-mast for a woman who, in Elizabeth's view, had betrayed and undermined the monarchy. "It is unlikely the Queen liked her very much," admitted a member of Charles's inner circle. "How could she after Diana had gone on television and said the sort of things she did about her son? The Queen is a mother after all."

Prince Charles had already stood up to his mother's hidebound advisors on the issue of the funeral procession to Westminster Abbey. To accommodate the 1,500,000 who were expected to line the route, Charles insisted that it be doubled to two miles. Fittingly, then, the cortege would begin at Diana's home, Kensington Palace.

At virtually every step, Charles leaned on Blair and the Prime Minister's savvy press officer Alastair Campbell for guidance. "Charles knows that the Royal Family must change," a senior Labour MP said at the time. "The only trouble is that, unlike Tony Blair and unlike Diana, he does not instinctively understand how that should happen."

There was one royal who *did* "instinctively understand," and on whom Charles would also come to depend. In the year before her death, Prince William had become one of his mother's most trusted advisors. The hugely successful auction of her gowns had been William's idea, and he had urged her to go ahead with her anti-land mine campaign despite criticism that arms control was beyond the ken of the Princess of Wales. William, who like his mother had a keen ear for gossip, shared what he learned with the Princess—including secrets gleaned from his Eton classmates concerning some of the most powerful families in England and the Commonwealth.

Each afternoon Charles, William, and Harry walked for several hours around the Balmoral grounds, with the Prince of Wales's Jack Russell terrier Tigger in tow. Away from his mother's loyal courtiers, Charles briefed the boys on the details of the funeral, voiced his concerns, and asked for their input.

It was enough for Harry, not yet thirteen, just to cope with the loss. But William wanted "to know," in the words of one senior member of the royal household, "about the telegrams, who has written and what they are saying. He is not shying away from what he sees as his responsibility."

Neither was William reluctant to share his views. He told his father he did not understand why the flag over Buckingham Palace was not flying at half-mast for his mother "if that is what the people want." Nor did he fathom the Palace's initial reluctance to expand the procession route to accommodate mourners. And while he loved the peace and seclusion of Balmoral, William asked his father the salient question:

"Why are we here when Mummy's in London?"

From the outset, William insisted on one thing: Whatever the details of the funeral itself—no matter how long the route or what the conditions—both he and Prince Harry would walk behind their mother's funeral coffin in the procession.

"It is just too sad for words," one of the Queen's courtiers said of the young Princes. "But everyone is struck by Prince William's strength of character. He really is a remarkable young man who has shown he has great courage."

Much of William's time at Balmoral was spent explaining things to Harry. "It is touching," a royal insider told veteran British journalist Robert Jobson, "how William and Prince Harry have pulled together when their world is falling apart. Diana would have been very proud. They are very, very brave."

With public pressure mounting, the Palace continued making concessions. The Queen permitted the Union Jack at Windsor Castle to be flown at half-mast—something done previously only upon the death of the sovereign.

But on the issue of flying the flag half-mast at Buckingham Palace, Her Majesty refused to bend. The Queen and Prince Philip now planned to make a fleeting visit to London for the funeral at Westminster Abbey, and then return the same day to Balmoral. That way they would not set foot in Buckingham Palace, and the flag would not be raised.

Publicly, Blair defended the Royal Family for trying to provide a "haven" for the young Princes in their hour of grief. But privately the Prime Minister told Charles that, unless his mother moved quickly to show the people she shared in their loss, the harm to the monarchy would be irreparable. Nothing less than a heartfelt address to her people on the eve of Diana's funeral would suffice.

"I wish I could blame the courtiers, but I can't," a member of Blair's inner circle told a reporter for the London *Sunday Times*. "The Queen was unknowing and unyielding. She has been very severely jolted by the public reaction. It took an alliance of the Prime Minister and the Prince of Wales to make her budge."

Clad in kilts and pink knee socks, Charles angrily confronted his mother, warning her that both he and Blair now believed there was a strong possibility the Queen would actually be booed at the funeral—or worse. Given the level of resentment toward the Crown, there was now concern for Her Majesty's safety.

For the first time, Charles delivered a flat ultimatum to his mother: The Queen must give the order to fly the flag over Buckingham Palace, and she must speak directly to the nation. Otherwise, Charles would go on television with an address of his own— an outright apology for the Windsors' apparent callous disregard for the people's suffering.

Impressed by her son's passion—and the fact that he had the full backing of the Prime Minister—the

Queen acquiesced to his demands. It had not, she would later concede, remotely occurred to her that Princess Diana was loved and admired every bit as much as Churchill—apparently even more so.

Several hours later, the Queen, Prince Philip, Charles, and his sons ventured outside and greeted well-wishers at the entrance to Balmoral. As they examined the bouquets left at the castle gates, Harry held tight to his father's hand.

Bowing to her son's demands, the Queen departed Balmoral for London the next day, Friday. When she finally arrived at Buckingham Palace at 2 P.M., the royal standard, which flies only when the monarch is in residence, was at long last raised. Halfway up, it stopped. The crowd burst into applause. But moments later, the flag continued its journey to the top of the pole. It had merely gotten stuck. Facing an angry crowd outside the palace, British television reporter Anthony Holden suggested that the Queen may not have wanted the flag to fly at half-mast, "but God did."

By way of damage control, the Queen and her husband ventured outside the gates of Buckingham Palace to survey more of the flowers left in honor of Diana. The response from the crowds, still angry that the flag over the palace was not flying at half-mast, was tepid. But at Kensington Palace, the appearance of William and Harry amid the oceans of flowers left at their mother's former home proved profoundly touching. As the diffidently handsome Prince William thanked the crowd, hundreds of women reached out simply to touch him. Scores, overcome with emotion, dissolved in tears after kissing his hand.

There was one thing remaining for the Queen to do if she was to keep her promise to Charles. With the throng of mourners clearly visible from the palace balcony behind her, Elizabeth II looked intently into the lens of a television camera and tried to win back her subjects. "What I say to you now as your Queen and as a grandmother," she began, "I say from my heart. First, I want to pay tribute to Diana, myself. She was an exceptional and gifted human being. In good times and bad, she never lost her capacity to smile and laugh, to inspire others with her warmth and kindness. I admired and respected her for her energy and commitment to others, especially for her devotion to her two boys." The Royal Family had remained in relative seclusion at Balmoral, she explained, merely to help William and Harry cope with the "devastating loss" of their mother. The Queen, it was generally agreed, had never given a more convincing performance.

No one who knew Diana will ever forget her. Millions of others who never met her, but felt they knew her, will remember her.

—*Queen Elizabeth*

If I had to define my role, I'd be inclined to use the word messenger.

—*Diana*

8

"Mummy, Mummy, look," said the little girl standing outside Kensington Palace on Saturday morning. She pointed at the flag-draped coffin atop a gun carriage, pulled by six horses of the King's Troop Royal Horse Artillery and flanked by a dozen beaver-hatted Welsh Guards. "It's the box with the Princess!" Her mother was embarrassed, but others in the crowd smiled warmly at the girl and patted her head. A banner stretched across the palace lawn. "No one can hurt you now," it read. An even more poignant message was printed on a card that poked out of one of the white wreaths atop Diana's coffin. It had been addressed by Harry and read, simply, MUMMY.

Alongside Prince Philip, Earl Spencer, and Charles, the young Princes marched solemnly behind the gun carriage bearing their mother's body. Even Harry, dwarfed by the large men around him, cast a giant shadow in the slanting late summer sunlight. Clearly unable to look at the coffin, William stared at the ground before him, eyes shielded by a his trademark blond fringe.

Behind the men in Diana's life walked five representatives from each of the 110 charities the Princess had supported. Many were members in good standing of her loyal "wheelchair brigade"; others hobbled on crutches. None of these people ever thought they would be marching in a royal procession. Diana would have it no other way. These were her people.

As the cortege passed Buckingham Palace, the Queen, standing outside with her family, bowed her head in tribute. For a breathless moment in history, time froze. "That's right," muttered an elderly man in the crowd. "That's right."

No single event in history had ever been witnessed by so many people at one time. Across the globe, an audience of more than 2.5 billion watched the solemn progress of Diana's cortege through the silent streets of London and the funeral service at Westminster Abbey.

The procession itself evoked bittersweet memories of her first procession sixteen years earlier, when the world watched the radiant young Princess and her dashing new husband waving from their glittering carriage like characters in a fairy tale. Now, letters scrawled on a pink ballet slipper that had been tied to the gold-filigreed gates of Kensington Palace captured the moment. "You were a Cinderella at the ball," the message read, "and now you are Sleeping Beauty."

Inside the thousand-year-old Abbey itself—which holds the tombs of Mary Tudor, Elizabeth I, and Mary of Scotland—it seemed somehow oddly fitting that Diana should make her official exit surrounded by the ghosts of England's most headstrong queens. As much as any of her ancestors, Diana had profoundly altered the course of British history—standing up to the monarchy in life and now in death, forcing it to adjust to a new, more egalitarian millennium.

Indeed, the two thousand mourners gathered inside the Abbey that sunny September morning ran the gamut from film, rock, and fashion stars to world leaders to cancer survivors, battered women, and land mine victims. And though the Palace had objected to a rock star performing in Westminster Abbey, Elton John's heartfelt tribute to his friend, "Candle in the Wind 1997," reduced a number of mourners—including Prince Harry—to tears. Originally an *homage* to Marilyn Monroe, the song's lyrics were revised for Diana. It would quickly become the biggest-selling single of all time.

There was undeniable beauty in this moment of final farewell. While Big Ben tolled outside, sun flooded through stained glass windows, dappling the Gothic arches with an ethereal display of light and color.

There was also drama. In his moving and pointedly provocative tribute to his sister, Earl Spencer renewed his attack on the press. "I don't think she ever understood why her genuinely good intentions were sneered at by the media, why there appeared to be a permanent quest on their behalf to bring her down. It is baffling," he said. "My own and only explanation is that genuine goodness is threatening to those at the opposite end of the moral spectrum. It is a point to remember that of all the ironies about Diana, perhaps the greatest was this—a girl given the name of the ancient goddess of hunting was, in the end, the most hunted person of the modern age."

The Earl went on to say there was no need to "canonize" her because to do so "would be to miss out on the very core of your being . . . For all the status, the glamour, the applause, Diana remained throughout a very insecure person at heart, almost childlike in her desire to do good for others so she could release herself from deep feelings of unworthiness . . ."

Then Diana's brother flung down the gauntlet before the House of Windsor itself. With the sovereign seated only a few yards away, Queen Victoria's palm-sized diamond bow brooch glittering from her lapel, he praised Diana as "the very essence of compassion, of duty, of style, of beauty . . . Someone with a natural nobility who was classless and who proved in the last year that *she needed no royal title to continue to generate her particular brand of magic.*" Charles went ashen when the Earl pledged to Diana in the name of the Spencers that "we, your blood family, will do all we can to continue the imaginative way in which you were steering these two exceptional young men so that their souls are not simply immersed by duty and tradition but can sing openly as you planned." Hillary Clinton, seated in a pew near the Royal Family, gasped audibly at Spencer's remarks. The Queen Mother looked startled, but the Queen, staring straight ahead at the coffin, remained as inscrutable as ever. Prince Charles, whose own deeply felt grief over Diana's death surprised even him, beat his fist against his knee.

Spencer's voice began to crack with emotion as he thanked God "for the small mercies he has shown us at this dreadful time. For taking Diana at her most beautiful and radiant and when she had joy in her private life. Above all we give thanks for the life of . . . the unique, the complex, the extraordinary and irreplaceable Diana—whose beauty, both internal and external, will never be extinguished from our minds." Outside, tens of thousands watching the service on jumbo television screens burst into thunderous applause. The sound was clearly audible even through the stone walls of Westminster Abbey, and soon those inside—including William and Harry—began to clap. As the sound of applause welled up from the rear and washed over Diana's coffin, the Queen, her husband, and her children sat in stony silence.

In that moment, the people had made irrevocable their choice of Diana over the royals. They chose her warmth over their chilly indifference, her breath-of-fresh-air informality over their implacable stuffiness, her humor over their witlessness, her soul-stirring need to make a difference over their age-old, bred-in-the-bone, paralyzing fear of change.

Ultimately, Diana was not so much the English rose among the thorns of the Royal Family as the seed of a new beginning. She was the Princess of Wales who became the People's Princess and the Queen of Hearts. And now she was also the Lady of the Lake, buried on an island called the Oval in a pond on the grounds of Althorp.

What inspires such deep universal feelings of sorrow and loss? Certainly Diana was a mind-spinning tangle of contradictions: beloved by millions yet sadly alone; dazzlingly regal yet down-to-earth; skillfully manipulative yet disarmingly direct; worldly yet naive; brave yet riddled with doubt; self-loathing yet proud; needy herself yet boundless in her capacity to give. In revealing her own flawed humanity, Diana proved that she was everything—and nothing—like the rest of us.

August 31, 1997. No wars ended or began that day. Nor did any natural disasters strike. There were no earth-shaking discoveries made, no records shattered, no feats accomplished. Yet it was a day that both stunned and united the world like few others in history. It was the day Diana died.

EPILOGUE

When *The Day Diana Died* was published on the anniversary of the Princess of Wales's tragic death, it created an instant international sensation. For the first time, the public was afforded a behind-the-scenes glimpse of the Royal Family and how each of its members behaved in those hours surrounding what would turn out to be the most famous car crash in history. Many were moved by Charles's reaction, unaware of the extent to which his ex-wife's death left him, in the words of Diana's butler Paul Burrell, "destroyed." No less unexpected was the way in which Charles, who had seemed to be an aloof and distant father, comforted their two sons and fought to make sure their mother received the royal funeral she deserved.

Conversely, the public was shocked and outraged at the Queen's seemingly callous disregard for the Princess and for the fragile emotional state of Diana's two young sons. It seemed utterly incomprehensible that the Queen's first question, directed to British diplomats on the scene at Pitié-Salpêtrière Hospital, dealt not with the cause of the accident that took the Princess's life, her medical treatment, or whether she suffered, but with the disposition of any royal jewels that might have been in Diana's possession. "Where are the jewels?" was trumpeted in headlines around the world as a clear indication of Her Majesty's lingering resentment toward the rebellious Princess of Wales, even in death.

Equally mystifying was the Queen's insistence that her grandsons attend church only hours after their mother's death, and that Diana's name not be mentioned during the service. Her Majesty's initial opposition to having a member of the Royal Family accompany Diana's body home, her reluctance to interrupt her Balmoral vacation to join mourners in London, and her steadfast refusal to fly the flag at half-mast over Buckingham Palace all served to fuel lingering public resentment.

The Queen would be forced to admit she had seriously miscalculated the depth of the British people's affection for Diana, and in the process placed the monarchy in jeopardy. Over the next two years, she made a concerted attempt to win back her subjects, going so far as to visit a pub for the first time (although she declined to drink) and ride in a London cab (another first). More substantively, Her Majesty released certain previously top-secret financial records of the Royal Family and did not oppose Prime Minister Tony Blair's proposal to end primogeniture, making the monarch's eldest child—not just the eldest son—heir to the throne. Elizabeth even decreed that in the future all curtsying and bowing to Royals should be strictly voluntary.

But the disturbing revelations contained in *The Day Diana Died* threatened to set back the Queen's aggressive campaign to win back her people. In an unprecedented move, Buckingham Palace issued a formal statement denouncing *The Day Diana Died* and its author. Yet, tellingly, the Queen's spokesman did not specifically deny any of the facts contained in the book. "They only respond when it's true," said one former Palace official, "and when you've struck a nerve."

While *The Day Diana Died* soared to the top of the bestseller lists—media coverage of the first anniversary was exceeded only by the exploding Monica Lewinsky–presidential impeachment scandal—intense pressure was brought on sources who had cooperated in the writing of the book to disavow their stories. None did. Realizing that the book had rankled the Queen, the royal photographer whose stunning portrait of Diana, William, and Harry appeared on the cover withdrew permission to use the shot. The cover was hastily redesigned to include another, equally haunting photograph of Diana.

While Buckingham Palace scrambled to repair the Queen's image, the official inquest into the crash plodded on. Investigators in Paris interviewed the owners of more than 3,000 white Fiat Unos but failed to locate the car that brushed against Diana's limousine that night. To further complicate matters, several new theories were offered to explain why the Mercedes veered into the tunnel wall.

There was new evidence that upon grazing the Fiat Uno, the air bags in the Mercedes may have deployed prematurely and with such explosive force that Henri Paul lost control of the car. There was also new forensic evidence indicating that Paul had high levels of carbon monoxide in his blood that night—enough to cause headaches, dizziness, and disorientation.

The most sensational theory held that it was no accident at all, but, rather, an assassination carried out with consummate skill by British Intelligence. Mohamed Al Fayed believed from the beginning that Dodi and Diana had been murdered by elements of Britain's Establishment who could not accept a Muslim as the stepfather of a future King of England. Al Fayed had gone so far as to offer a one-million-pound reward to anyone who could prove it.

The assassination theory got a boost when Richard Tomlinson, a former agent with MI6, Britain's foreign intelligence agency, charged that the fatal crash in which Diana and Dodi died had all the earmarks of a government-sanctioned hit. The chain of events that night was "one of the classic assassination scenarios practiced by British Intelligence," he said. Tomlinson also testified before the French magistrate overseeing the investigation, Hervé Stephan, that Henri Paul was a paid informant for British Intelligence.

In the end there was no evidence whatsoever to substantiate the assassination theory. The investigation did reveal, however, that MI6 and other agencies of the British government kept a close eye on the Princess before and after her divorce.

Astoundingly, so did several United States intelligence agencies. A request filed under the Freedom of Information Act revealed that the CIA, the FBI, the Defense Intelligence Agency, and the National Security Agency have secret files on Diana totaling more than 1,000 pages. The NSA alone had amassed 39 separate documents containing 124 pages detailing activities of the Princess of Wales in the year before her death. To obtain this information, which remains officially classified on the grounds that its release "could reasonably be expect to cause exceptionally grave damage to the national security," these agencies monitored her every move within the United States and even eavesdropped on the Princess's telephone conversations.

Among other things, the government files contain hours of taped conversations between Diana and one of her closest confidantes in the United States, Lucia Flecha de Lima, wife of Brazil's ambassador to Washington. Several times a week, the Princess would call Flecha de Lima and pour out the most intimate details of her life—from her love affairs to her plans for William and Harry to her skirmishes with the Royal Family.

Most disturbingly, this information was immediately shared with British Intelligence and used, said one of Diana's closest friends, "to systematically destroy her. I believe what happened in that tunnel was an accident. But government agents did use whatever information they could find to try and discredit her."

In January 1999, French authorities ended their sixteen-month-long investigation by concluding that Diana and Dodi died essentially as the result of a drunk-driving accident. Henri Paul, under the influence of two powerful antidepressants and with three times the legal limit of alcohol in his blood, was solely to blame for the tragedy.

Accordingly, criminal manslaughter charges against the paparazzi who had pursued Diana's car into the tunnel were dropped. For its part, Ritz Hotel management would not be criminally prosecuted for its failure to provide a qualified—and sober—driver that evening.

Civil suits were another matter. Bodyguard Kes Wingfield claimed that after he refused to appear in a documentary advancing Al Fayed's theory that Diana and Dodi had been murdered, he was pressured to quit. Wingfield sued for breach of contract, and Al Fayed settled out of court.

That did not keep Dodi's father from publicly blaming Wingfield and sole survivor Trevor Rees-Jones for the death of Dodi and Diana. Al Fayed insisted that the two bodyguards should not have let Paul get behind the wheel, and that they should have made certain the lovers were wearing their seat belts—just as Rees-Jones was wearing his.

Al Fayed was no less outspoken in his disdain for the Establishment. When Diana's mother, Frances Shand Kydd, shunned him as they arrived to testify before Judge Stephan in Paris, Al Fayed stood on the courthouse steps and hurled invectives at her.

In truth, Shand Kydd had grown distant from her grandchildren—this despite provisions in Diana's will stipulating that the boys' maternal grandmother play a major role in their upbringing. Instead, her attempts to spend time with William and Harry were rebuffed. "The Spencers," said a friend of Diana's, "are treated with the same disregard as they always have been."

Conversely, Charles, devastated by the loss of Diana, grew even closer to his sons. In addition to trips abroad together, weekend family outings, and the occasional rock concert, Charles now engaged in previously unheard of public displays of affection. Where once there was only chilly formality between Charles and the young princes, he now regularly hugged them in public. Once, before boarding separate planes for a vacation in Greece, Charles was even photographed standing on the tarmac, kissing William good-bye.

The British public warmed to the visibly kinder and gentler Charles, and it showed in the polls. While his approval rating plummeted from 82 percent to 41 percent over the five years prior to Diana's death, by 1999 fully 63 percent said they felt Charles "would make a good king."

Charles, in turn, grew ever more confident—confident enough to resume the campaign aimed at making his relationship with Camilla Parker-Bowles more acceptable to the British public. She had already won over Diana's boys. In June 1998, Prince William arranged to meet "Mrs. P.B.," as she was now called by Charles's inner circle, over tea at the princes' apartments at St. James's Palace. Leaked to the press as a "chance encounter," the meeting was nothing of the sort. "William had heard about Camilla for years from his mother," one of Diana's friends said. "He was eager to see for himself what all the fuss was about. In the end, William discovered he rather liked Camilla." A few weeks later, a similar meeting took place between Camilla and Harry at Highgrove, Charles's country house. Like his brother, Harry warmed to the informal, sometimes self-deprecating woman Diana had nicknamed "The Rottweiler."

Nevertheless, Annabel Goldsmith, Lady Elsa Bowker, and other friends of Diana's felt the meetings were a betrayal of the Princess's memory. "Diana had more or less come to accept Charles's love for Camilla," one said. "But that doesn't mean she would have approved of her becoming a stepmother figure to her boys. Not at all. Diana would have been very upset that the woman who destroyed her marriage and made her life hell was now being embraced by her sons. And so soon after her death."

Nor was the Queen ready to accept Camilla. She continued to avoid any public function Camilla might attend, ordered her courtiers to shun Mrs. Parker-Bowles (one, Robin Janvrin, infuriated Charles by declining to attend the same private tea at which she was introduced to William), and let it be known that any marriage plans would meet strong opposition from the Crown. Still, Camilla remained, in the words of Charles's former private secretary Richard Aylard, the "non-negotiable part of his private life."

By early 1999, Camilla moved into York House,

the Prince of Wales's five-bedroom residence within the walls of St. James's Palace. When they weren't in London together, Charles and Camilla spent weekends at Highgrove. "They have settled into life," said one of the Prince's aides, "like any other married couple of twenty-eight years."

Increasingly, it seemed not a question of whether Charles and Camilla would actually marry, but when. "We all know that a Prince of Wales with a girlfriend is fine," an aide pointed out, "but a King with a girlfriend is tricky."

If the Queen remained steadfast in her opposition to marriage, the Church of England seemed willing to bend. Where the Church has once forced a King to abdicate because of his intention to marry a divorced woman, Wallis Simpson, it now appeared that they would not stand in the way of Charles if he wished to wed Camilla. The Bishop of Durham even went so far as to say it was "more desirable morally" for them to marry. (At about the same time, another British cleric strongly denounced the "cult of Diana" and branded the late Princess "immoral" because of her extramarital affairs.)

If Charles and Camilla did choose to marry—and it seemed increasingly likely—Camilla would be consort rather than Queen once Charles ascended the throne. For the time being, she relished her status as royal mistress. A portrait of her great-grandmother, Alice Keppel, mistress to Charles's great-great-grand-father King Edward VII, hung in a prominent spot in her Wiltshire home, and Camilla invariably wore Keppel's jewelry whenever she attended formal functions.

William and Harry, meantime, were not eager to see their father remarry and appeared satisfied with the status quo. In fact, with their mother gone and the Spencers reneging on their promise to be an integral part of the boys' lives, William and Harry were now more Windsor than Diana had ever allowed them to be. By way of grooming the future King, the Queen made certain that William join her for tea, either at Buckingham Palace or Windsor, at least once a week.

The absence of Diana's humanizing influence on the princes' upbringing became clearly evident to the Princess's friends. Instead of spending weekends with their mother visiting homeless shelters or amusement parks, the boys now spent weekends in the country with their father and his mistress. They had always preferred hunting, fishing, and riding at Balmoral to their mother's hectic social life in London. Now, with the tomboyish nanny Tiggy Legge-Bourke on hand to serve as a big-sister figure, William and Harry seemed to be adjusting astonishingly well to their mother's sudden death.

Given William's close relationship with his mother, Diana's friends were especially surprised at how well he handled the tragedy. The once-effervescent Harry, in contrast, initially withdrew after his mother's death, becoming more moody and introspective. After joining his brother at Eton, however, fourteen-year-old Harry reverted to his old exuberant self.

The healing process was accelerated by the British press, which kept a respectful distance from Diana's children in the months following the crash. That did not keep William from becoming, much to his apparent chagrin, a heartthrob on a global scale. "DDG—Drop-Dead Gorgeous," as Diana used to call him, soon rivaled Leonardo DiCaprio as the reigning teen idol, landing on countless magazine covers.

Two years and several conspiracy theories later, the world was still sorting out Diana's legacy. No one person had raised more money for charity during a lifetime, and in death Diana's name proved an even more powerful draw. But even the fund bearing her name became mired in controversy.

First, there was the questionable nature of some of the endorsement deals arranged by the fund. While much of the money came from the sales of Elton John's "Candle in the Wind 1997," postage stamps, and collectibles bearing Diana's likeness, there was a public outcry when the fund allowed Diana's name and image to sell margarine.

Then there were the disclosures that $800,000 had been paid to the fund's lawyers for twelve weeks' work, and that two fund directors—Michael Gibbins and Diana's sister, Lady Sarah McCorquodale—spent $20,000 of the fund's money on a single trip from London to New York aboard the Concorde.

The fund's management made its biggest public relations blunder in January 1999 by firing Diana's longtime butler and confidant Paul Burrell from his job as fund-raising events manager. The man Diana frequently called "my rock," who could not be consoled when he first saw her body in Paris, was given $5,000 in severance pay. "He was redundant," the fund's chief executive, Andrew Purkis, said of Burrell. "So I have no apologies for that."

The reason given for Burrell's unceremonious sacking was equally unfathomable. With nearly $140 million in its coffers, Purkis claimed the Princess of Wales Fund was simply no longer interested in soliciting new contributions. Yet the fund was also blasted for being too slow in distributing those funds. As of February 1999, it had reportedly distributed less than $25 million. Incredibly, the United States–based organization that was responsible for Diana's historic crusade against land mines was denied money from the fund bearing her name because it was an American—and not a British—group.

For all the controversy and revisionism, there is one immutable fact: For millions around the world, the memory of that fateful day in Paris remains piercingly vivid—poignant testimony to the life of one young woman who, for all her flaws, changed the world.

ACKNOWLEDGMENTS

My wife, Valerie, and I had hosted a small dinner party on the evening of August 30 and were bidding goodbye to our friends when our eldest daughter came running downstairs with the news that Diana had been killed in a car crash. For the next fifteen minutes, five people who collectively had lived through World War II, Korea, the assassinations of John F. Kennedy, Martin Luther King Jr., and Robert F. Kennedy, Vietnam, Watergate, the explosion of the space shuttle *Challenger,* and a series of both natural and man-made disasters too numerous to mention, stood staring at our television set in disbelief. Then, shaken by the sudden death of someone they had never met, our guests departed to follow the story from the sanctuary of their own homes.

The scene was being replayed in millions of homes across America and around the world, as people who had watched Diana metamorphose from a shy school-girl to the most celebrated woman of the century tried to come to grips with a death that seemed mindless yet strangely fated. It seemed too eerily co-incidental that Diana, like the other stunning blonde who married a dashing prince, would die in a car crash. But that she would die at the height of her beauty and fame appears, in retrospect, to be something we should have known would happen all along.

Not that I could have ever foreseen the outcome back in the 1980s, when as senior editor of *People* magazine I edited numerous cover stories on the royals in general and Diana in particular. My personal favorite of these was the cover story we ran on the July 21, 1982, birth of Prince William. Just in case, we had two covers designed and ready to run—one with the headline IT'S A BOY!, the other proclaiming IT'S A GIRL!

For a fourth time, I am blessed to be working with one of the finest teams in the publishing industry. I owe a particular debt of gratitude to Willam Morrow editor in chief Betty Kelly for instantly recognizing that the Princess of Wales's tragic death was an event quite unlike any other, and for her passionate commitment to seeing that the whole truth about Diana's final hours be told. Once again, my thanks extend to my whole second family at Morrow—particularly Bill Wright, Michael Murphy, Paul Bresnick, Jacqueline Deval, Sharyn Rosenblum, Patricia Alvarez, Rebecca

Goodhart, Maria Antifonario, Ben Schafer, Brad Foltz, Debra Weaver, Lisa Queen, Fritz Metsch, Lorie Young, Kathy Antrim, and Camille McDuffie of Goldenberg-McDuffie Communications.

Ellen Levine has been my agent and friend for fifteen years now, and during that time has held my hand through the birth of an astonishing sixteen books. I have, quite simply, run out of adjectives to describe the depth of my gratitude, respect, and affection for Ellen—and for her wonderfully talented associates Diana Finch and Louise Quayle.

The Day Diana Died would not have been possible without my research associates Janet Lizop in Paris and Hazel Southam in London. Both consummately professional journalists with extensive contacts in both cities. Hazel and Janet produced much of the research and conducted many of the interviews that shed new light on the Princess's death and its aftermath.

I am grateful, as ever, to Jeanette and Edward Andersen for their wisdom and support. My wife, Valerie, knows all too well just how indispensible she is and has always been to me. For putting it all in persepective, my thanks to my daughters, the brilliant and beautiful Kate and Kelly. They take after their mother.

Additional thanks to Dr. Frédéric Mailliez, Thierry Meresse, Lady Elsa Bowker, Béatrice Humbert, Jeanne Lecorcher, Claude Garreck, Mark Butt,

Rémi Gaston-Dreyfus, Peter Allen, Grigori Rassinier, Andy Radford, Penny Walker, Ezra Zilkha, Michelle Lapautre, Jeanette Peterson, the Countess of Romanones, Paula Dranov, Bernard Lefort, Jean Chapin, Fred Hauptfuhrer, Patrick Demarchelier, Rosemary McClure, Aileen Mehle, Evelyn Phillips, Betsy Loth, Tom Freeman, Michael Shulman, Debbie Goodsite, Cathy Cesario Tardosky, Valerie Wimmer, Joy Wansley, Miriam Lefort, Oleg Cassini, Cecile Zilkha, Lawrence R. Mulligan, Gered Mankowitz, Gianni Versace, Lee Wohlfert, Barry Schenck, Tobias Markowitz, Cranston Jones, Wendy Leigh, Ray Whelan Jr., Brad Darrach, Susan Crimp, John Marion, Charles Furneaux, Dudley Freeman, Steve Stylandoudis, David McGough, Vincent Martin, Deborah Eisenman, Norman Curry, Jeannette Walls, Julie Grahame, Yvette Reyes, Bob Cosenza, Ian Walde, Kevin Lamarque, Manuel Ribeiro, Andrew Campbell, David Bergeron, Sabu Quinn, John Stillwell, Gary Gunderson, Tanya Waght, Stefano Rellandini, Alain-Philippe Feutre, Michael Crabtree, Wolfgang Rattay, Mick Magsino, Marcel Trugot, Joe Greensted, Farris Rookstool, Francis Specker, Steven Lee, Chris Helgren, Patrice Fitch, Pitié-Salpêtrière Hospital, SAMU, the Gunn Memorial Library, the New York Public Library, the Silas Bronson Library, the BBC, Channel Four Television Ltd., the Litchfield Library, Kensington Palace, the New Milford Library,

Brown's Hotel, The Princess of Wales Memorial Fund, the Lansdowne Club, The Institute of Charity Fundraising Managers, the London Library, the Press Association, the Southbury Public Library, the Brookfield Library, the Boston Public Library, the Ritz Hotel, the *Times* (London), the Woodbury Library, the Bancroft Library of the University of California at Berkeley, Archive Photos, Corbie-Bettmann, Globe Photos, DMI, Sygma, AP-Wide World, Retna, Sipa, Big Pictures U.S.A., Reuters, the Associated Press, Design to Printing, and Graphictype.

SOURCES AND
CHAPTER NOTES

The following chapter notes are designed to give a general view of the sources drawn upon in preparing *The Day Diana Died*, but are by no means all-inclusive. Given the highly sensitive nature of the investigation into the Princess's death, many European law enforcement and medical sources insisted on anonymity. The same applied to certain key sources at Buckingham Palace as well as friends and acquaintances of the Royal Family who agreed to cooperate only if they were assured that their names would not be mentioned. The author was privy to confidential police reports and depositions that proved invaluable in reconstruting Diana's final moments. Obviously, there were also thousands of news reports and articles concerning Diana published in the seventeen years prior to her fatal accident—which in itself may have generated more news coverage than any single event in modern history. These reports appeared in such publications as *The New York Times, The Washington*

Post, *The Wall Street Journal*, *The Boston Globe*, the *Sunday Times* (London), the *Los Angeles Times*, *The New Yorker*, *Vanity Fair*, *Time*, *Life*, *Newsweek*, *Paris Match*, *Le Monde*, *U.S. News & World Report*, the *Times* (London), *The Guardian*, and *The Economist*, and carried on the Associated Press, Knight-Ridder, Gannett, and Reuters wires.

CHAPTERS 1 AND 2

Interview subjects included Dr. Frédéric Mailliez, Thierry Meresse, Béatrice Humbert, Jeanne Lecorcher, Rémi Gaston-Dreyfus, Penny Walker, the Countess of Romanones, Mark Butt, Grigori Rassinier, the Reverend Canon Andy Radford. Published sources included "Farewell, Diana," *Newsweek*, September 15, 1997; "The Final Hours," the *Sunday Times* (London), September 7, 1997; Annick Cojean, "The Final Interview," *Le Monde*, August 27, 1997; Joe Chidley, "From the Heart," *Macleans*, September 15, 1997; "Lady Dies," *Liberation*, September 1, 1997; "Driver Was Drunk," *Le Monde*, September 3, 1997; "Charles Escorts Diana Back to a Grieving Britain," *The New York Times*, September 1, 1997; Andrew Morton, *Diana: Her True Story* (New York: Simon & Schuster, 1997); "Spread It Around," *Sunday Mirror*, November 9, 1997; Pascale Palmer, "I Gave Diana Last Rites," *The Mirror*, October 23, 1997; Rosa Monckton, "My Friend Diana," *The Guardian*, September 8, 1997; "Flashback to the Accident," *Liberation*, September 2, 1997; Tess Rock and Natalie Symonds, "Our Diana Diaries," *Sunday Mirror*, November 16, 1997; Howard Chua-Eoan et al., "A Death in Paris: The Passing of Diana," *Time,* September 8, 1997; "Diana: The Man She Really Loved," *Point de Vue, Images du Monde;* and "Diana, Investigation of the Investigation," *Le Point,* September 13, 1997.

CHAPTERS 3 AND 4

For these chapters, the author drew on conversations with Lady Elsa Bowker, Fred Hauptfuhrer, Peter Allen, Charles Furneaux, Farris L. Rookstool, Gered Mankowitz, Evelyn Phillips, Lee Wolfert, Brad Darrach, Aileen Mehle, Oleg Cassini, Thierry Meresse, Jeanette Walls, Béatrice Humbert, Doris Lilly, and Wendy Leigh. Among the published sources consulted: David Ward, "Prince's Pride in His Sons," *The Guardian,* September 20, 1997; John Coles and Shekhar Bhatia, "A Heavy Drinker with a Taste for High Life," *The Express,* September 3, 1997; Tina Brown, "A Woman in Earnest," *The New Yorker,* September 15, 1997; Clive Goodman, "Diana and Dodi: The Untold Love Story," *News of the World,* December 7, 1997; "Diana: Stop the Rumors!" *Point de Vue, Images du Monde,* November 5–11, 1997; "Remembering Diana," *People,* September 15, 1997; Cosmo Landesman, "Michael Cole Speaks," the *Sunday Times* (London), May 10, 1998; Sally Bedell Smith, "Dodi's Life in the Fast Lane," *Vanity Fair,* December 1997; "Diana, Princess of Wales 1961–1997," *The Week,* September 6, 1997; Rosa Monckton, "Time to End the False Rumors," *Newsweek,* March 2, 1998; Robert Lacey, *Majesty* (New York: Harcourt Brace Jovanovich,

1977); Hugh Vickers, *The Private World of the Duke and Duchess of Windsor* (London: Harrods Publishing, 1995); Sarah Bradford, *Elizabeth* (London: William Heinemann, 1996); Richenda Miers, *Scotland's Highlands & Islands* (London: Cadogan Books, 1994); Stephen P. Barry, *Royal Service: My Twelve Years as Valet to Prince Charles* (New York: Macmillan, 1983); and Harry Porter, "Her Last Summer," *Vanity Fair,* October 1997.

CHAPTERS 5 TO 8

Information for these chapters was based on conversations with Claude Garreck, Frédéric Mailliez, Lady Elsa Bowker, Thierry Meresse, Mark Butt, Josy Duclos, Rémi Gaston-Dreyfus, Béatrice Humbert, Peter Allen, Bernard Lefort, Jeanne Lecorcher, Miriam Lefort, Pierre Suu, Steve Stylandoudis, Vincent Martin, Ezra Zilkha. Published sources included Christopher Walker, "Arabs Are Convinced Car Crash Was a Murder Plot," the *Times* (London), September 4, 1997; Toby Rose, "Fayed's Nurse Never Existed," *The Evening Standard,* October 6, 1997; Richard Kay and Geoffrey Levy, "Let the Flag Fly at Half Mast," September 4, 1997; Alan Hamilton, Andrew Pierce, and Philip Webster, "Royal Family Is Deeply Touched by Public Support," the *Times* (London), September 4, 1997; Piers Morgan, "We Were Followed," *The Mirror,* March 2, 1998; Thomas Sancton and Scott Macleod, *Death of a Princess: The Investigation* (New York: St. Martin's Press, 1998); David Harrison et al., "Fayed Struggles to Clear Family Name," *The Observer,* September 14, 1997; Anthony Holden, "Why Royals Must Express Remorse," *The Express*, September 3, 1997; Craig R. Whitney and Youssef M. Ibrahim, "To Those Who Knew Diana's Driver, His Actions Are an Unsettling Puzzle," *The New York Times*, September 21, 1997; Nick Cohen, "Fayed's Footman," *The Observer Review*, September 14, 1997; Marianne Macdonald, "A Rift Death Can't Heal," *The Observer*, September 14, 1997; Jerome Dupuis, "Diana: The Unpublished Report of Witnesses at the Ritz," *L'Express*, March 12, 1998; "The Two Vital Questions," *The People*, November 9, 1997; Stephane Bern, "Diana's Mysterious Ring," *Madame Figaro*, April 17, 1998; "It Was No Accident," *The Mirror*, February 12, 1998; John Simpson, "Goodbye England's Rose: A Nation Says Farewell," *Sunday Telegraph*, September 7, 1997; and Polly Toynbee, "Forever at Peace," *Radio Times*, September 13–19, 1997.

BIBLIOGRAPHY

Allison, Ronald, and Sarah Riddell, eds. *The Royal Encyclopedia,* London: Macmillan, 1991.

Barry, Stephen P. *Royal Service: My Twelve Years as Valet to Prince Charles.* New York: Macmillan, 1983.

Boca, Geoffrey. *Elizabeth and Philip.* New York: Henry Holt and Company, 1953.

Brander, Michael. *The Making of the Highlands.* London: Constable & Company, 1953.

Bryan, J. III, and Charles J. V. Murphy. *The Windsor Story.* New York: William Morrow, 1979.

Campbell, Lady Colin. *Diana in Private.* London: Smith Gryphon, 1993.

Cannadine, David. *The Decline and Fall of the British Aristocracy.* New Haven: Yale Unversity Press, 1990.

Cannon, John, and Ralph Griffiths. *The Oxford Illustrated History of the British Monarchy.* Oxford and New York: Oxford University Press, 1992.

Cathcart, Helen. *The Queen Herself.* London: W. H. Allen, 1983.

——. *The Queen and Prince Philip: Forty Years of Happiness.* London: Hodder & Stoughton, 1987.

Clarke, Mary. *Diana Once Upon a Time.* London: Sidgwick & Jackson, 1994.

Davies, Nicholas. *Diana: The Lonely Princess.* New York: Birch Lane, 1996.

——. *Queen Elizabeth II.* New York: Carol Publishing Group, 1996.

Delderfield, Eric R. *Kings and Queens of England and Great Britain.* London: David & Charles, 1990.

Dempster, Nigel, and Peter Evans. *Behind Palace Doors.* New York: Putnam, 1993.

Dimbleby, Jonathan. *The Prince of Wales: A Biography.* New York: William Morrow, 1994.

Ferguson, Ronald. *The Galloping Major: My Life and Singular Times.* London: Macmillan, 1994.

Fisher, Graham, and Heather Fisher. *Elizabeth: Queen & Mother.* New York: Hawthorn Books, 1964.

Foreman, J. B., ed. *Scotland's Splendour.* Glasgow: William Collins Sons & Co. Ltd., 1961.

Fox, Mary Virginia. *Princess Diana.* Hillside, N. J.: Enslow, 1986.

Graham, Caroline. *Camilla—The King's Mistress.* London: Blake, 1994.

Graham, Tim. *Diana: HRH The Princess of Wales.* New York: Summit, 1988.

————. *The Royal Year 1993*. London: Michael O'Mara, 1993.

Hoey, Brian. *All the King's Men*. London: Harper-Collins, 1992.

Holden, Anthony. *Charles*. London: Weidenfiled & Nicholson, 1988.

————. *The Tarnished Crown*. New York: Random House, 1993.

Hough, Richard. *Born Royal: The Lives and Loves of the Young Windsors*. New York: Bantam, 1988.

Hutchins, Chris, and Peter Thompson. *Sarah's Story: The Duchess Who Defied the Royal House of Windsor*. London: Smith Gryphon, 1992.

Junor, Penny. *Charles*. New York: St. Martin's Press, 1987.

Lacey, Robert. *Majesty*. New York: Harcourt Brace Jovanovitch, 1977.

————. *Queen Mother*. Boston: Little, Brown, 1986.

Lathan, Caroline, and Jeannie Sakol. *The Royals*. New York: Congdon & Weed, 1987.

Maclean, Veronica. *Crowned Heads*. London: Hodder & Stoughton, 1993.

Martin, Ralph G. *Charles & Diana*. New York: Putnam, 1985.

Montgomery-Massingberd, Hugh. *Burke's Guide to the British Monarchy*. London: Burke's Peerage, 1977.

Morton, Andrew. *Diana: Her True Story*. New York: Simon & Schuster, 1997.

———. *Inside Buckingham Palace*. London: Michael O'Mara, 1991.

Pasternak, Anna. *Princess in Love*. London: Bloomsbury, 1994.

Pimlott, Ben. *The Queen: A Biography of Elizabeth II*. New York: John Wiley & Sons, Inc., 1996.

Sancton, Thomas, and Scott Macleod. *Death of a Princess: The Investigation*. New York: St. Martin's Press, 1998.

Sarah, The Duchess of York, with Jeff Coplon. *My Story*. New York: Simon & Schuster, 1996.

Spoto, Donald. *The Decline and Fall of the House of Windsor*. New York: Simon & Schuster, 1995.

———. *Diana: The Last Year*. New York: Harmony Books, 1997.

Thornton, Michael. *Royal Feud*. London: Michael Joseph, 1985.

Van Geirt, Jean-Pierre. *Diana, Enquête sur une tragédie*. Paris: Editions Ramsay, 1997.

Whitaker, James. *Diana v. Charles*. London: Signet, 1993.

INDEX